Scribe Publications
A Lighter Footprint

Angela Crocombe was born in Sydney in 1971. She has lived in Singapore, America, and the UK. She holds degrees in economics, political theory, and publishing, all of which are entirely unrelated to this book. She has also studied creative writing at RMIT. Angela has published eight educational books for children, as well as numerous magazine articles. Since 1995, she has worked in publishing. She lives in Melbourne, doesn't own a car, and is a vegequarian. For further information about the author and to provide feedback on this book, please go to the website **www.lighterfootprint.com.au**

A LIGHTER FOOT PRINT

A PRACTICAL GUIDE TO MINIMISING YOUR IMPACT ON THE PLANET

ANGELA CROCOMBE

SCRIBE
Melbourne

Scribe Publications Pty Ltd
PO Box 523
Carlton North, Victoria, Australia, 3054
Email: info@scribepub.com.au

First published by Scribe 2007

Copyright © 2007 by Angela Crocombe

All rights reserved. Without limiting the rights under
copyright reserved above, no part of this publication may
be reproduced, stored in or introduced into a retrieval
system, or transmitted, in any form or by any means
(electronic, mechanical, photocopying, recording or
otherwise) without the prior written permission of
the publisher of this book.

This book is carbon neutral

The publisher gratefully acknowledges the support of
the federal Department of the Environment and Water
Resources, and Sustainability Victoria for permission to
reproduce information available on their websites. For
more information see:

www.environment.gov.au
www.greenhouse.gov.au
www.sustainability.vic.gov.au

Book design by Design by Committee
Printed and bound in Australia by Griffin Press

National Library of Australia
Cataloguing-in-Publication data

Crocombe, Angela, 1971- .
A lighter footprint.

ISBN 9781921215599.

1. Climatic changes - Australia. 2. Australia -
Environmental conditions. I. Title.

551.60994

www.scribepublications.com.au

Contents

Preface

1 Introduction
11 Why me?
12 Why you?
14 What are greenhouse gases?
14 Kyoto and other hot air
15 The future
16 This book
17 A lighter footprint
18 An Ecological Footprint Quiz

2 Carbon Offset Schemes
22 Common offsetting methods
24 Different calculations
24 Companies offering carbon offsets
27 Offsetting only part of the picture

3 Transport
30 Cars
36 Public transport
37 Walk or bicycle
38 Air travel

4 Energy
43 Electricity
46 Gas
47 Renewable energy
51 What about nuclear?
52 Lighting
55 Heating
61 Cooling

5 Water
66 Average water usage
66 Embodied water
67 Water footprint
67 Be water wise
69 In the bathroom
72 In the kitchen
74 In the laundry
75 Outdoors
79 Re-using greywater
80 Installing water-saving systems

6 Food
86 Food miles
86 Ghost acres
87 Buy locally and seasonally
88 Farmers' markets
88 Water filters
90 Organic and biodynamic produce
92 Grow your own
92 Free-range eggs
94 Cruelty-free meat and poultry
96 Finding organic meats
96 Dairy products
97 Seafood
99 Processed food
99 Artificial colourings and preservatives
99 Fairtrade products
101 Genetically modified food
102 Eating out
102 The Slow Food movement
104 Become a vegetarian
104 Better yet, go vegan

7 Recycling
110 Refuse, reduce, re-use, recycle
110 Kerbside recycling
111 What can be recycled kerbside?
114 Where does my recycling go?
114 Compost
117 Litter
118 Plastic bags
119 Mobile phones
119 Cork
120 Polystyrene
120 Computers
121 Printer cartridges
122 Home entertainment
122 White goods
123 Cars
124 Chemicals, gases, paint tins and car batteries
124 Cooking oil
124 Other household items

8 Appliances and Household Goods
127 The energy rating label
128 Energy Allstars
129 Choice magazine

Contents

129 Refrigerators and freezers
131 Dishwashers
132 Clothes washers
134 Clothes dryers
135 Energy Stars and standby power
136 Home entertainment
137 Home office equipment
139 Wooden furniture
141 Rugs
142 Household cleaning
143 Fabrics and soft furnishings

9 Building and Renovating
148 Use of the sun
149 Climate
149 Choosing a good site
150 Room zoning
151 Flooring and walls
151 Windows
152 Skylights
153 Insulation
153 Lighting
154 Water
156 Hot water
160 Energy
161 Building materials
163 Waste minimisation
163 Indoor air quality
165 Timber
166 Garden design
168 Get expert advice

10 Ethical Investment
171 Triple bottom line
171 Ethical investment versus SRI
171 Fund performance
172 Screening methods
172 Investment options
173 Superannuation
174 Uranium mining – yes or no?
174 Ethical fund managers
175 UN principles for responsible investment
175 The Equator principles

11 Personal Care
179 Skin
181 Hair
182 Cosmetics
182 The Big Baddie list
186 Toothpaste
187 Natural skin protectors
188 Cotton balls
188 Sanitary products
189 Animal testing
190 Choose cruelty-free
191 Nappies
193 Clothes and shoes

12 In the Office
198 Individual changes
200 Overall changes to company policy
201 Know your paper
202 Communal facilities
202 Purchase energy star office equipment
204 Green power the office
205 Recycling at the office
205 Keep staff involved
206 Encourage sustainable transport to the office
209 Is that business trip necessary?
209 Assess your building's greenhouse performance

13 Travel and Events
211 Responsible travel
215 Holding an event

14 Be an Activist
224 Educate yourself
224 Use the media
225 Write to politicians
225 Volunteer
225 Plant trees
226 Go in peace

229 Resource List
235 Notes
Index

Preface

I believe that global warming is the biggest issue facing humanity today – it represents a far greater threat than terrorism, fundamentalism, or nuclear war. I am not alone in this belief. Scientists and many policymakers agree that the global population must reduce greenhouse gas emissions by at least 60 per cent by 2050. The United Kingdom, France, the European Union, and the US state of California have already agreed to this target and it is imperative that the rest of the world joins them as soon as possible.

Human-induced drastic climate change represents the tipping point in our relationship with the planet. It's a problem that has been building for many hundreds, if not thousands, of years and it won't disappear tomorrow. Even if we stopped producing greenhouse gas emissions today, the planet's temperature would continue to warm for several decades. Unless extreme action is taken, increasing population and consumption levels will endanger the survival of every living organism on the planet.

Those of us in the industrialised world have a greater obligation than most to achieve the goal of a drastic reduction in emissions. It is our countries that have generated the most greenhouse gas emissions since the Industrial Revolution, it is our ecological footprints that are the highest in the world, and it is our lifestyles that people in developing countries are trying to emulate.

Humanity does have the capacity to create a more sustainable future. We already have much of the knowledge and technology required to halt global warming. We just need the will to fully implement it.

Each and every one of us needs to play our part by reducing our ecological footprint. Everything we do and every item we own – the food we eat, the car we drive, the house we live in, and the consumer goods we acquire – has been made by drawing from nature's limited resources. We urgently need to realise that our individual actions have a significant, collective impact on the global environment. Every day, each choice we make will also impact the 6.6 billion other people who live on our planet.

By changing our own ingrained habits and replacing them with more sustainable behaviours we can reduce that impact, save money, and positively influence those around us. This is well within everyone's capacity and is utterly worth doing. We must seek to drastically reduce the heavy tread of our human footprint upon the earth, otherwise, our children and our grandchildren will have very little hope of enjoying a habitable planet.

I hope that this book can be a stepping stone on your personal journey to a sustainable future. We have no time to waste. I encourage you to begin walking with a lighter footprint today.

1 INTRODUCTION

The world is hotting up. The 10 warmest years on record have been since 1995. Scientists are telling us we're reaching a tipping point that may plunge us into global disaster due to small increases in average temperatures. Any debate regarding the existence of climate change is over, but is global warming enough to change the world as we know it?

In fact, small changes in the average overall temperature of the planet are already wreaking devastation on the polar ice caps, sea levels around coastal communities, and on volatile weather patterns. The amount of the earth's surface afflicted by drought has more than doubled since the 1970s. In Australia, the planet's driest inhabited continent, these changes are having a severe impact on our water resources and, in some cases, our livelihoods.

Sobering predictions from the latest report by the United Nations Intergovernmental Panel on Climate Change (IPCC), drawn from hundreds of esteemed scientists, say that the global increase in temperature since the mid-20th century is 'very likely' to have occurred as a result of human activity. These changes to the planet have been caused by greenhouse gases emitted from fossil fuels used since the industrial revolution, along with our ongoing destruction of the world's forests. Unless we reduce our emissions of greenhouse gases, the climate will change even more dramatically during this century.

The IPCC also said that things are going to get much worse for Australia. By 2020, within 800 kilometres of the coast, temperatures will increase between 0.1 and 1.3 degrees. By 2050, it could warm up to 3.4 degrees and this will significantly affect our environment. There will be more droughts, more bushfires, more cyclones, and less water to go around. By 2050, 97 per cent of the Great Barrier Reef will be bleached every year and climate change is 'virtually certain' to have serious consequences for our coastlines including erosion, sea-level rises, and damage to infrastructure.[1]

Now is the time for all of us to educate ourselves about this significant threat to the ability of the planet to sustain human life. Climate change is real and it's not just a problem for generations to come – the impact is already being felt by all of us and is set to exponentially increase unless we do something. If the causes of global warming are man-made, then humans must also be responsible for the cure.

Why Me?

I wrote this book because I felt that I could no longer remain on the couch paralysed with inaction over global warming; I had to do something, as small as it may be, about this seemingly overwhelming problem. I am not a scientist, a policy maker, or an authority on the subject. I am just an ordinary person who enjoys the numerous benefits of vibrant city life and looks forward to occasional weekend escapes to the country. But over the past 15 years, I have become increasingly concerned by dire warnings, debate, and controversy over the issues. They may come in different guises, but they all have in common the problem of humanity's heavy footprint on the planet.

Not so long ago, in my increasing sense of frustration and helplessness, I took a test that is readily available in

THIS BOOK IS CARBON NEUTRAL
The book you are holding is a carbon-neutral product. That means that all greenhouse gases emitted in the production, printing, and distribution of the book have been neutralised by purchasing carbon offsets that will decrease the equivalent amount of carbon dioxide emitted into the atmosphere. To find out how this is done, read **Chapter 2: Carbon Offset Schemes.**

various forms on the Internet — the ecological footprint quiz. This simple survey measures how many resources you consume as an individual, household, or nation, and then compares it to the limited amount of resources available on our planet. The first time I took the test, the result was that it would take 13.8 global hectares to support my life, and 7.7 planets to accommodate all humans if everyone lived my lifestyle. At the time, I

considered myself fairly environmentally aware already — I recycled, I caught public transport, and I tried not to use plastic bags. But there it was, staring me in the face and slapping me out of my ignorant assumption that I was doing enough. I was consuming a hell of a lot of resources for one person; far more than this planet can sustain. My lifestyle, as well as that of millions of other people in the Western world, was unsustainable the way it was.

Calculating my ecological footprint was the beginning of a long journey researching the voluminous literature on the subject — in books, articles, journals, and websites. The more I delved, the more overwhelmed I became by the magnitude of the problem. However, I also found, in all sorts of places, many intelligent people putting their energies to solutions for governments, business, and individuals to respond to this crisis.

Why You?

If I was consuming such a large amount of resources, it also meant my friends, family, and everyone else I knew was consuming far more than our planet can handle. In fact, Australians on average have one of the highest ecological footprints in the world, right up there with the United States and the United Arab Emirates. Despite our small population, we are punching well above our weight in using up the planet's limited resources. So I decided to collect my research, the tips I discovered, and the lessons I learnt, and share them with other people in the hope that they will see that reducing their footprint is both a desirable and an attainable goal.

1 INTRODUCTION

A Lighter Footprint is here to give you the information and resources you need to combat climate change. It doesn't mean you have to deny yourself any of the pleasures or the benefits of living in the 21st century. It will show you ways to use the resources we have in a smarter, more efficient way that will actually help you to save money.

In some ways, reducing your footprint is much easier than most people think. For example, most evidence suggests that we need to achieve at least a 70 per cent reduction in carbon dioxide (CO2) emissions by 2050. But you can do a whole lot better far more quickly. By following just a few suggestions in this book, you can reduce your own emissions and your family's emissions by well over 70 per cent in a few months, or possibly even a few days. So, even if our government refuses to take serious action, you as an individual can make a significant contribution all on your own.

Imagine if everyone reduced their emissions and showed the politicians how easy it is. The reduction in greenhouse gases would be phenomenal, and the immediate redirection of our money from coal-based industries to renewable energy suppliers and eco-friendly corporations would send the government and big business a clear signal that consumers will no longer support unclean energy sources.

Your ecological footprint

The ecological footprint quiz estimates how much productive land and water you need to support the resources you consume and the waste you throw away in daily life. The World Wildlife Fund's Living Planet Report, published in 2006, calculated the ecological footprint for Australia to be **6.6 global hectares per person**, the **fifth-largest** footprint in the world. The global footprint now exceeds the earth's capacity by around **25 per cent**.

Once you know your own ecological footprint, you can compare it to the biological capacity of the earth, estimated by the Earthday Network to be less than 1.8 hectares for each of the 6.6 billion people on the planet. Many people in poor countries are using less than that amount, but most people in Western countries are consuming far more. If we all lived the lifestyle of the average Australian, we would need **3.7 planets** to sustain life.

I have included a simple eco-footprint quiz in this book, so that you can get a preview of what counts towards your footprint and how many resources you consume, before learning ways to dramatically reduce it. You can also do a footprint quiz on the Internet at **www.earthday.net** or, for a more detailed Australian quiz, go to **www.isa.org.usyd.edu.au**

What are greenhouse gases?

To understand why climate change has such a negative impact on the planet, it's important to recognise the important role that carbon dioxide and other greenhouse gases play in maintaining the temperature. For the last 10 000 years, the average temperature of the earth has been 14 degrees Centigrade, which has been highly suitable for human civilisation. But since 1950, average temperatures have been increasing and the overall temperature of the earth is shifting.

Carbon dioxide plays a critical role in maintaining the balance necessary for all life. It makes up only three parts per 10 000 in the earth's atmosphere but it is hugely important in regulating temperature. It is one of the greenhouse gases, along with methane, that traps heat from the sun during the day and keeps the planet warm at night. However, the greater the levels of greenhouse gases, the more heat from the planet becomes trapped in the atmosphere and can't be released. Before too long, it's as if the planet gets a fever, which is where we are at right now.

Carbon dioxide is a waste product of burning fossil fuels such as coal, oil, and gas. We use fossil fuels in almost every aspect of our lives – for heat, transport, and lighting. Our lives are almost entirely dependent on them. As a result of our burning fuels at such a rapid rate to keep the lights of our economies burning, carbon dioxide in the atmosphere is increasing in a vicious cycle. Unless we break our dangerous habits, the earth's temperature will be irrevocably changed and the planet will become inhospitable to human, plant, and animal life, quite possibly within our lifetimes and almost certainly within our children's lifetimes.

Kyoto and other hot air

In 1997, the United Nations Kyoto Protocol set a goal of an overall global reduction in greenhouse gas emissions of 5.2 per cent of the emission levels of 1990. The actual level of emissions varies depending on the country, and under the protocol some countries can even increase their emissions. Kyoto has been criticised for many reasons, including the fact that it exempts many developing countries from this reduction because their greenhouse gas emissions are still small (but rapidly increasing) in comparison to Western countries. Indeed, it is argued that the industrial progress of developed countries over the last 150 years has caused today's climate change. The United Nations and many other leading scientists continue to say that the goals of Kyoto are not nearly enough to limit climate change, but at least it's a beginning. Other governments – notably the United States and Australia, who both refused to sign the agreement – say that the Kyoto Protocol is a waste of time.

Prime Minister John Howard has stated on numerous occasions that the goal of reducing climate change at the expense of economic growth is absolutely unacceptable. The alternative that Australia put forward, known as the Asia-Pacific Partnership plan and representing six countries that are responsible for around 50 per cent of the world's emissions, has been widely criticised for making no mandatory caps on emissions whatsoever.

Highly esteemed scientist, James Lovelock, said in his book *The Revenge of Gaia* that 'it is much too late for sustainable development; what we need is sustainable retreat'.[2] Tim Flannery, Australian of the Year in 2007, has stated that if we carry on with business as usual, three out of every five species will be extinct by the dawn of the next century. Most experts on the situation, be they scientific or economic, acknowledge that business as usual is no longer a viable option. We must act now or suffer the consequences.

The future

There is no doubt that governments, international bodies, and scientists will continue to argue about what policies are needed to combat climate change for a long time to come. But that does not excuse us with individual inaction. As James Lovelock says, 'The time of irreversible adverse change may be so close that it would be unwise to rely on international agreement to save civilisation from the consequences of global heating.'[3] When we watch on TV the impact of natural disasters that have killed tens of thousands and wreaked havoc around the world, it seems as if the politicians have their heads stuck in the sand. Individuals, grassroots organisations, and even large corporations are realising they need to act against this global crisis and are finding ways to reduce their footprint on the planet. You can too.

This book

In this book you will find the basic facts that you need to know, without scientific jargon, along with the methods for reducing your ecological footprint. I cover the major aspects of our lives that emit greenhouse gases, including our transport, electricity and gas usage, our food choices, recycling, and much more. I have also included many resources and organisations that can help you to learn more.

This is a practical handbook for everyone to use, regardless of your knowledge of climate change. You can flip through and find a couple of simple ways of reducing your impact today — such as catching public transport to work, or taking your own bags to the supermarket — through to information on changing your electricity to renewable energy sources, installing solar heating and water in your home, or building a compost heap. You can start by taking the simple ecological footprint quiz, which looks at the areas of your life that have a major impact on climate change. Then read through the sections dedicated to these aspects of our lives. After incorporating the suggested changes, you can take the quiz again to see the reduction in your footprint.

In no way is this book exhaustive, but it comprehensively covers the main aspects of our lives that have a direct impact on our ecological footprint and our release of greenhouse gases. It puts all the information in one place to save you time and energy so that you can focus on the most important aspect — quickly making the changes needed to reduce your footprint.

Some activities, such as switching to Green Power, switching your car to a hybrid, and offsetting all your travel emissions, have the potential to dramatically reduce your footprint. Incorporating them into your life will make a big difference. There are also hundreds of suggestions that make a smaller, but still important, emissions reduction within your life.

Many of the changes you make will also result in financial savings – a fantastic side benefit to walking with a lighter footprint. You will see boxes with snippets about what other people are doing, highlighted summaries, and top tips that provide simple, immediate ways to live more sustainably in your daily life. The final chapter highlights the major changes that, if incorporated into your life, can reduce your footprint by over 70 per cent.

A lighter footprint

My ecological footprint is currently at 2.7 global hectares, which is now far below the Australian average, but if everyone lived like me, we would still need 1.5 planets. So I'm still working on it ...

I believe the goal for all of us should be to reduce our footprint to the extent that we would need only one planet if everyone lived the same as we do. We will then be walking with a truly light step. And the more people we can convince to do the same, the greater will be our positive impact.

I hope you will find this information as useful and empowering as I have. There is no time to waste. It is absolutely imperative that we drastically reduce our impact as soon as possible, so that future generations can also appreciate the natural beauty and the privileged lifestyle that we currently take for granted on this remarkable planet.

An ecological footprint quiz

1. How many rooms do you have in your home? (include the bathroom, kitchen and laundry)
- **A** 1-5
- **B** 6-10
- **C** 11-15
- **D** 16+

2. How many people live in your home?
- **A** 5+
- **B** 3-5
- **C** 2
- **D** 1

3. How many whitegoods are in your home? (include fridges, freezers, dishwashers, washing machines, and dryers)
- **A** 0-3
- **B** 4-6
- **C** 7-10
- **D** 11+

4. How many household electronic items do you have? (include TVs, DVD/video players, home entertainment systems, stereos, computers, printers, and phone/fax machines)
- **A** 0-3
- **B** 4-6
- **C** 7-10
- **D** 11+

5. What is your average quarterly electricity bill?
- **A** $0-100
- **B** $101-200
- **C** $201-300
- **D** $301+

6. What is your average quarterly gas bill?
- **A** $0-50
- **B** $51-100
- **C** $101-150
- **D** $151+

7. What is your average quarterly water bill?
- **A** $0-150
- **B** $151-250
- **C** $251-350
- **D** $351+

8. What percentage of your grey water is recycled?
- **A** 51+ per cent
- **B** 26-50 per cent
- **C** 25 per cent or less
- **D** none

9. What percentage of your energy usage is accredited Green Power?
- **A** 100 per cent
- **B** 66-99 per cent
- **C** 33-65 per cent
- **D** less than 33 per cent

10. How often do you eat meat products per week? (beef, lamb, pork, chicken, fish)
- **A** never
- **B** less than 3 times per week
- **C** nearly every day
- **D** every day and sometimes twice a day

11. How often do you eat dairy products per week?
- **A** never
- **B** less than 3 times per week
- **C** nearly every day
- **D** every day and sometimes twice a day

12. How often do you eat processed and highly packaged food per week? (include takeaway, junk food, food with a lot of packaging)
- **A** never
- **B** less than three times per week
- **C** nearly every day
- **D** every day and sometimes twice a day

13. How often do you eat fresh fruit and vegetables per week?
- **A** every day and sometimes twice a day
- **B** nearly every day
- **C** less than three times per week
- **D** never

14. How much waste does your household produce per week? (assume a 55-litre bin)
- **A** less than half a bin
- **B** one-third to half a bin
- **C** half to one bin
- **D** more than one bin

1 INTRODUCTION

15. How much recycling does your household produce per week? (include paper, glass, and plastic, and assume a 55-litre bin)

- **A** half to one bin
- **B** one-third to half a bin
- **C** less than one-third of a bin
- **D** none

16. How much composted waste does your household produce per week?

- **A** 76-100 per cent of vegetable matter
- **B** 51-75 per cent
- **C** 26-50 per cent
- **D** 0-25 per cent

17. How many kilometres do you travel by car per week?

- **A** 0-25 km **B** 26-50 km **C** 51-75 km
- **D** 75+ km

18. How many journeys do you make by public transport, bicycle, or walking per week?

- **A** 13+ **B** 9-12 **C** 4-8 **D** 0-3

19. How many hours do you spend flying each year?

- **A** 0-2 **B** 3-8 **C** 9-12 **D** 13+

Ratings

Thirteen or more A's Congratulations! Your eco-footprint is between two and three global hectares. You are walking with a far lighter footprint than the vast majority of Australians. If everyone lived like you, we would only need one-and-half planets to survive. Unfortunately, that's still half a planet more than we actually have. Read on to discover more adjustments to your lifestyle so you can become carbon neutral.

Thirteen or more B's You are considered to be an average Australian with regards to your eco-footprint and consumption of resources. You are using between six and eight global hectares, which means that if everyone lived like you we would need nearly four planets to sustain humanity. Unfortunately, average is nowhere near good enough when you consider we have only one planet to share between us. More progress is needed and this book will provide you with plenty of practical solutions to reduce your footprint further.

Thirteen or more C's Your eco-footprint is around 10 global hectares, which means you are wasting far too many resources and your footprint is heavier than the majority of Australians. If everyone lived like you, we would need nearly six planets for humanity to survive. But with a few changes to major aspects of your lifestyle you can make a significant improvement to your footprint. This book is here to show you how.

Thirteen or more D's You should be categorised as a major environmental disaster zone! Your eco-footprint is over 20 global hectares. If everyone lived like you, we would need at least 13 planets to sustain human life – 12 planets more than the one we actually have! You need to read this book to learn how your impact on the planet can be drastically improved, not to mention improving your health and your appreciation of natural resources.

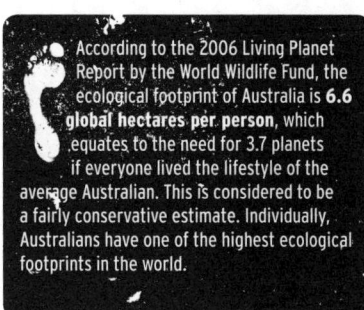

According to the 2006 Living Planet Report by the World Wildlife Fund, the ecological footprint of Australia is **6.6 global hectares per person**, which equates to the need for 3.7 planets if everyone lived the lifestyle of the average Australian. This is considered to be a fairly conservative estimate. Individually, Australians have one of the highest ecological footprints in the world.

2
CARBON OFFSET SCHEMES

2 CARBON OFFSET SCHEMES

Offsetting is the latest buzz word in business and everyday life for minimising our impact on the planet. There are currently well over 30 organisations around the world selling products that enable you to offset the emissions from your electricity, car, and airline flights. You calculate your emissions with a website-based calculator, and then pay a fee to 'offset', or neutralise, the amount of carbon dioxide produced by your activities. Planting trees, investing in renewable energy, replacing energy-efficient light bulbs in households, or something else, may make the offset.

These offset schemes raise an important question regarding responsibility — is it justifiable to blow out a huge expense on the planetary credit card, such as purchasing a petrol-guzzling, excessively greenhouse gas-emitting vehicle like the Bentley Arnage, and then to compensate for the emissions by buying offsets to cover it? Definitely not. The Bentley Arnage has a fuel efficiency of 19.5 litres per 100 kilometres – a whopping 4.5 times worse than the Toyota Prius. The government's Green Vehicle Guide gives Bentley's sedan a rating of zero out of 10 for its greenhouse gas emissions, where 10 is the most desirable.[4] Driving this highly inefficient car around creates huge emissions, and we shouldn't see offsetting as a way of justifying this purchase and removing the need to make a real reduction.

Real-time emissions from driving the Bentley will be reduced only by a complex, ongoing plan of storing carbon, which may take up to 30 years to consume the amount of carbon dioxide emitted in one year. Moreover, the offset scheme chosen may prevent further emissions from being released but do nothing to get rid of the emissions that have already entered the atmosphere. Offsetting is still a young and imperfect trading scheme. We need to incorporate it as part of a comprehensive plan to reduce our eco-footprint, not use it as our sole contribution to reducing climate change.

WHAT IS A CARBON CREDIT?
A carbon credit is equivalent to **one tonne of carbon dioxide** that is prevented from entering the atmosphere. In the Australian marketplace a carbon credit is currently valued at between **$16** and **$26**.

Common offsetting methods

There are a number of different ways to offset carbon and remove or sequester carbon dioxide from the environment. Here are three that are used by many offsetting companies:

Tree planting

Trees must have been planted on cleared land since 1990, thereby sequestering additional carbon in the environment beyond the level that prevailed in 1990. As the trees grow they will eventually soak up the equivalent amount of carbon dioxide in the environment to account for your usage. The sequestering process is usually measured over a 30-year period, so the benefit does not occur immediately. Trees are usually planted on land that has been cleared by forestry or farming. In some schemes the trees may be logged, although they must then be replaced as the carbon credit is usually guaranteed to remain for at least 100 years.

Light bulbs and showerheads

Some schemes focus on changing household behaviour by giving away free energy-efficient light bulbs and AAA-rating showerheads. (The showerheads save both water and the energy used to heat the water.) Not only does this have an immediate impact on greenhouse gas emissions, but the argument is that this method also changes behaviour over the long term. The reduction in actual emissions from this action must again be taken into account over a period of time, although not as long as tree planting.

Renewable energy

Some schemes invest in renewable energies such as wind or solar which, rather than removing greenhouse gases, prevent them from entering the atmosphere in the first place. The argument is that the more money invested in renewables, the cheaper they become and the less emphasis is placed on coal in the energy mix.
So this is again a preventive method that reduces the future emissions that enter the atmosphere.

Which scheme to choose?

Many organisations offer carbon offsetting for a price, and they all go about it in a slightly different way. So how do you know which one is best? Unfortunately, there is no simple answer. It's up to you to decide which scheme makes the most sense to you. The carbon market is still a voluntary market in Australia, so there are few guidelines as yet. We desperately need industry regulations from the government and a standard, independent auditing process so that consumers can easily compare and contrast these schemes. We don't have that yet, although there are standards provided under the Kyoto Gold Standard, the NSW Greenhouse Gas Abatement Scheme and the federal Greenhouse Friendly Scheme.

However, there are questions to ask that can help you to sort through the options.

Does it directly cut pollution in the atmosphere?

Any scheme should make a quantifiable difference in greenhouse gas emissions by reducing carbon dioxide in the atmosphere. Some schemes prevent an equivalent amount of carbon dioxide from being released; others reduce the carbon dioxide that is already in the atmosphere.

Is it externally accredited and independently audited?

There are differing standards on carbon offsetting, and you need to know which standard the company is using. If its scheme is not externally accredited and it is using its own standards, then be wary. Who is auditing its work to determine that it is really doing what it says?

Does it create ancillary benefits such as behaviour change or system change and would it have happened otherwise?

There is no point paying for carbon offsets when a company would have been required to do so anyway. Does the carbon offset go beyond the basic statutory requirements (such as the government requirement for electricity providers to source 10 per cent of energy from renewables), and does it create a continuing change in behaviour, such as maintaining a commitment to renewable energy?

Different calculations

Carbon offsetting companies do not all sell the same product at the same standards, and the calculators they use to calculate your emissions vary widely. For example, I went to a number of Australian organisations and attempted to calculate the emissions and money payable to offset a return flight from Sydney to Melbourne. Origin Energy said that my seat on the flight would be responsible for 0.52 tonnes of emissions and to offset it with renewable energy would cost me $8.27. Climate Friendly said I would emit 0.45 tonnes and it would cost me $9.51 to offset. Climate Positive said I would emit approximately 0.5 tonnes and it would cost me $14 to offset, but it would offset the entire amount through renewable energy and then plant two square metres of native trees to make my overall impact a positive one. Easy Being Green said it would generate only 0.4 tonnes of emissions and it would cost me $8.

There is still a lot of discrepancy due to different assumptions being made in calculations, and in the price that a tonne of carbon is valued at by different companies. It's hard to know if a higher price is also going to give you a greater benefit.

Companies offering carbon offsets

While there are many international carbon offset schemes, I have chosen to focus on companies that are doing their offsetting within Australia (in alphabetical order).

Australian Carbon Traders: It offset the 2006 Commonwealth Games and uses tree planting to offset emissions. Landholders, primarily Australian farmers, agree to plant and manage sites long-term. It primarily works with businesses, but you can purchase a $30 tree shirt that will fund the planting of enough trees to sequester one tonne of carbon dioxide.

Carbon Planet: It will offset your emissions with tree planting by Forestry NSW in accordance with the NSW

2 CARBON OFFSET SCHEMES

Greenhouse Gas Abatement Scheme. It conducts comprehensive greenhouse gas emission audits that take into account all aspects of your household or business, a particular activity, or even your whole life for its entire length.

Climate Friendly: It focuses on electricity, car, and airline emissions and is supported by Westpac, Tim Flannery, and the Australian Conservation Foundation. It purchases offsets in renewable energy programs that either comply with the Kyoto Gold Standard or satisfy Green Power requirements.

Climate Positive: For every tonne of carbon dioxide you produce, it offsets one tonne with renewable energy and plants enough trees to offset another 0.3 tonne. In this way, it argues, it makes you not just carbon-neutral but carbon-positive. Its renewable energy is bought as Renewable Energy Certificates (RECs), which are certified by the government and represent one megawatt hour of renewable energy. You can offset travel, diet, and household emissions.

Origin Energy: An initiative of the Origin electricity and gas company, it offsets car, plane, electricity, or gas emissions. It uses a combination of offset programs, including tree planting, diverting waste from landfill, giving away light bulbs, and renewable energy programs. It is independently verified by auditors but is not currently accredited.

Easy Being Green: It provides energy-saving and water-saving packs (light bulbs and showerheads) to households free of charge, and it tries to change behaviour at the same time as reducing emissions. Currently accredited under the NSW Greenhouse Gas Abatement Scheme and the Greenhouse Friendly program, it covers car, flights, energy use, and waste disposal.

Elementree/Beyond Carbon: It is committed to tree planting by native revegetation specialists to offset emissions. It does not measure and verify the carbon stored in its forests on an ongoing basis, but uses the calculations assumed by the Australian Greenhouse

---

CARBON OFFSET ACCREDITATION SCHEMES

■ **Kyoto Gold Standard** - international standard

■ **Greenhouse Friendly** - federal government scheme that accredits projects

■ **NSW Greenhouse Gas Reduction Scheme** - creates NSW Greenhouse Gas Abatement Certificates

■ **Mandatory Renewable Energy Target** - creates Renewable Energy Certificates

Office. It can calculate car, airline, and household energy emissions.

Greenfleet: This non-profit, government-supported program plants trees to offset car emissions. It aims to become compliant with the Kyoto Gold Standard but isn't yet. It calculates that a $40 payment per year will allow it to plant 17 native trees of various species that will consume 4.3 tonnes over time, which it takes as the average emissions from the average Australian car per year.

Offsetting is only part of the picture

Even if every one of us offset our plane, car, and electricity emissions, it would still only reduce Australia's carbon footprint by 16 per cent. Where is the rest of it coming from?

In every aspect of our lives we directly or indirectly generate greenhouse gas emissions, and we also need to take into consideration all our other purchases that are not directly quantifiable. Our furniture, our appliances, our clothing, the food we eat, and the drinks we consume, all add to our carbon footprint. Whether we buy our food from a local greengrocer who sources from regional farmers, or go to the supermarket and buy dates from Iran, avocadoes from New Zealand, and tuna from Thailand – it all makes a difference.

Offsetting should be part of a comprehensive plan to minimise the many different ways that we create a footprint on the planet. Through the chapters that focus on the major emission-generating aspects of our lives, we can learn to minimise our footprint in all of these areas rather than just emitting and paying later. Not only is it far more responsible not to pollute in the first place than to simply pollute and offset, but offsetting can only cover part of your emissions.

Minimising our footprint is relevant in every aspect of our lives. We need to adopt in our daily life practices that are more sustainable, that minimise greenhouse gases, and that have a minimal impact on the planet's, and our own, health. That is where this book comes in.

CARBON TRADING

In Europe, trading in carbon offsets is becoming part of the economy. Companies that are big carbon polluters are taxed on their emissions, and they must offset those large carbon emissions somehow. **If they are not able to reduce their emissions, they can offset them by purchasing carbon credits from other companies that are making a positive contribution to the environment.** Carbon trading is becoming a multi-million dollar industry in Europe, but Australia is not yet involved on a major level.

3 TRANSPORT

3 TRANSPORT

We all need to get around conveniently and efficiently, whether to get to and from work, to enjoy our leisure time, or to do the weekly chores. However, our transport emissions represent a large portion of our total emissions, and how we choose to travel, both within our daily routines and on our holidays, is having a huge impact on the global environment. The Australian transport sector was responsible for 80 million tonnes of greenhouse gas emissions in 2004, which amounted to 14 per cent of Australia's total emissions.[5] The transport sector is growing quickly in regard to emissions levels, and so it is an area that we need to scrutinise closely to improve the way we get around, not only as individuals, but also as a nation.

In this chapter I will look at how you can minimise your footprint by being smarter with your use of cars, airlines, and public transport. Many suggestions are easy to do and some involve big, one-off purchases, but by incorporating at least some of them you will make a reduction in your personal footprint and you may even discover a new-found love for riding a bicycle, or the joys of a leisurely stroll ...

Cars

Over 960 000 new cars were sold in Australia in 2006,[6] and if you add them to the well over 10 million cars already on the road, we have one car for every two people in the country. Cars are one of the biggest polluters in Australia in terms of burning fossil fuels and generating greenhouse gas emissions, both in their manufacture and in their day-to-day driving. Despite huge technological advances in other areas of our lives, cars have changed very little in the last 100 years, and there have been scant gains in fuel efficiency over the last 40 years. We use only a fraction of the energy embodied within fuel in order to move our cars. Most of it is lost through inherent inefficiencies in the engine and running accessories such as air conditioning, or idling in traffic.

Most of us take our cars for granted as an absolute necessity for modern living, particularly in rural areas where there are vast distances to traverse. With the growth in suburbia, our major cities spread over huge expanses. Unfortunately, our dependence on the car for the majority of our transport needs is largely to blame for pushing Australia's footprint per person so high, and for drastically increasing our greenhouse gas emissions. For the average Australian householder, nearly six tonnes of greenhouse gas and $8000 a year will be spent on transport, which represents 34 per cent of your total greenhouse gas emissions.[7] Cut out your dependence on the car and you have just taken a huge chunk out of your emissions.

Now, I'm not suggesting that you sell your car and start riding a bicycle everywhere (although that would be fantastic). Just being more aware, trying to use your car less, and making your journeys more efficient can make a difference. As we saw in the last chapter, carbon offsetting companies can also help you counter the emissions created by your car's pollution by buying trees on your behalf; and when purchasing a new or used car, there are resources that will help you to choose the most fuel-efficient, environmentally friendly car for your money.

When buying a new car, keep in mind that despite the trend towards four-wheel-drive vehicles for inner-city living, cars with bigger engines consume far more fuel, which increases not only your fuel bills but also your greenhouse gas emissions. So think twice about whether you really need that four-wheel-drive or if you just want to show off to the neighbours. Perhaps they will be more impressed if you can prove you are taking into account the impact of your car on the planet, not just its visual appeal.

Environmentally friendly cars

There are few totally green options available at the moment, but cars are getting cleaner, and as the problem of emissions from motor vehicles becomes more prominent we should see car manufacturers producing more low-emission cars. Here are some of the options that are available now or in the near future.

Hybrid

Hybrid cars, as their name suggests, combine electric and petrol power. An electric motor supplements the petrol engine, resulting in much greater fuel efficiency. The electric motor draws power from a battery that is recharged by a generator in the engine every time you brake, so there is no need to plug the car into an electricity source to keep the battery charged. Hybrids automatically turn off the petrol engine when stopped at traffic lights to minimise petrol use, and when you accelerate the engine switches back to petrol. The hybrid still emits carbon dioxide, but it is often less than half the emissions of a conventional model. The main hybrid cars currently available in Australia are the Toyota Prius, the Honda Civic Hybrid, and the Lexus GS450H and four-wheel drive RX400. Hybrid cars are more expensive than their petrol-only equivalents but they are cheaper to run and are better for the environment.

GREENEST CAR ON THE ROAD

The greenest car in Australia, according to **Green Vehicle Guide**, is the **Toyota Prius**, which has a fuel consumption of **4.4 litres per 100 kilometres** and emits only **106 grams** of carbon dioxide per kilometre. In comparison, one of the most popular cars on the market, the **Holden Commodore,** has a fuel consumption of **11 litres per 100 kilometres** and emits **260 grams** of carbon dioxide per kilometre. When purchasing a new car, by choosing a **hybrid** instead of a petrol guzzler, you can more than halve your transport emissions.

Diesel

Diesel vehicles have about the same environmental impact as petrol, but their emissions can be as much as 40 per cent less. Diesel is made from mineral oils from oil wells. Diesel cars have been common in Europe for many years, and big manufacturers have now released high-performance diesel models in Australia. However, traditional diesel must still be considered a short-term option as it is a non-renewable resource and still emits carbon dioxide. In the past, diesel engines also emitted much higher levels of particles than petrol engines. These have been linked to respiratory problems and lung cancer. However, new-generation diesel engines are far cleaner with less particle emissions, so diesel is considered to be a better environmental choice than petrol.

Biodiesel

Biodiesel is a fuel produced from renewable plant or animal sources and potentially includes recycled products. Biodiesel can be manufactured specifically for use in vehicles or it can even be 'home made' from used vegetable or animal oils. It can be used as an alternative to diesel, where its greenhouse gas emissions are very low, or mixed with diesel to reduce the reliance upon non-renewable diesel. It also reduces carbon monoxide emissions by 70 per cent, is non-toxic and biodegradable. Biodiesel is now becoming much more readily available at petrol stations throughout Australia and can greatly improve the outlook for the diesel car.

LPG or autogas

Vehicles running on LPG (liquid petroleum gas) typically emit 15 per cent less greenhouse gas and one-fifth of the toxic gases of petrol-fuelled cars. LPG is much cheaper than petrol, but it is less efficient as an energy source. It can cost a few thousand dollars to switch your car over to LPG, and it may not be possible in remote areas due to the need for LPG pumps. However, the federal government pays a grant of $2000 to any individual who converts a new or used vehicle to LPG, and $1000 when you purchase a new vehicle fitted with an LPG unit. For further information on the LPG Vehicle Scheme you can contact AusIndustry through its website at **www.ausindustry.gov.au**

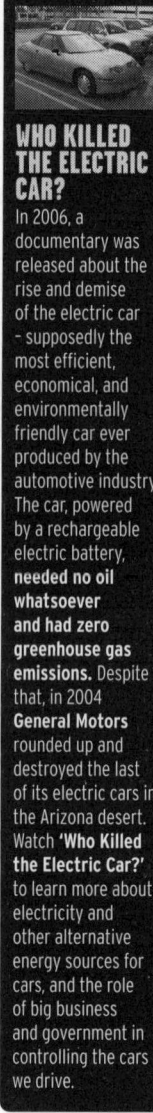

WHO KILLED THE ELECTRIC CAR?

In 2006, a documentary was released about the rise and demise of the electric car – supposedly the most efficient, economical, and environmentally friendly car ever produced by the automotive industry. The car, powered by a rechargeable electric battery, **needed no oil whatsoever and had zero greenhouse gas emissions.** Despite that, in 2004 **General Motors** rounded up and destroyed the last of its electric cars in the Arizona desert. Watch **'Who Killed the Electric Car?'** to learn more about electricity and other alternative energy sources for cars, and the role of big business and government in controlling the cars we drive.

Ethanol

President Bush talked about the future of ethanol to power cars in his 'State of the Union' address in 2006, and that may have been the first many of us had heard about it. Ethanol, or ethyl alcohol, is made from grains, usually from corn or sugarcane. Mixtures that have 10 per cent ethanol can be used in many new conventional vehicles without damage to the engine and are available at some service stations. But the most common ethanol fuel – E85, which is 85 per cent ethanol and 15 per cent petrol – can be used only in vehicles that are designed for ethanol.

Ethanol is 100 per cent renewable and non-carcinogenic. It still emits greenhouse gas, although up to 30 per cent less than petrol vehicles. There is concern that ethanol production diverts valuable land to grow grain crops as fuel rather than as food, which has the greatest impact on the poor. Although there are no ethanol cars currently in Australia, our first completely ethanol-powered vehicle may well be the Saab BioPower, which was demonstrated here in January 2007. The NSW government has also put forward legislation for standard feul to contain two per cent ethanol from 2007 onwards.

Hydrogen

One idea for the future is hydrogen fuel cells, which use hydrogen to create electricity to power a car. The only emission from hydrogen cars is small amounts of water. However, hydrogen is currently produced using non-renewable fuel sources and requires expensive infrastructure. It may become viable in the future, if appropriate technology can be implemented.

Offset your car emissions

Greenfleet is a non-profit organisation that is working on ways to reduce the impact of cars on the environment. For only $40 per year, which is also tax deductible, it will plant 17 native trees on your behalf, which it has calculated will absorb the greenhouse gas emissions that your car produces in one year (based on Greenfleet's assumed average of 4.3 tonnes of carbon dioxide per

OFFSETTING THE GRAND PRIX
The Australian Grand Prix, held in Melbourne, could be considered a disaster zone in terms of greenhouse gas emissions. But in 2006, **Greenfleet** worked with the organisers of the Grand Prix and planted **747 trees** in the Murray-Darling region to offset the estimated **200 tonnes of carbon dioxide** emitted into the atmosphere from the four-day event.

> **GREEN CAR LOANS**
> If you purchase a car with one of its car loans, **Go Green Car Loans** offsets **100 per cent of the vehicle's greenhouse gas emissions** during the life of the loan with Greenfleet. It has competitive rates, and also provides useful information about purchasing a new or used car. You can find them at www.mecu.com.au

car). Alternatively, calculate your own greenhouse gas emissions based on your particular car's fuel consumption and distance travelled. Since 1997, Greenfleet has planted nearly 3 million trees that will soak up extra carbon dioxide in the environment as they grow. Go to **www.greenfleet.com.au** to calculate your current car's yearly emissions, and to have them offset for a small fee.

Research before you buy

The fuel efficiency of a car can vary by up to 30 per cent depending on the brand and features of a particular model. The Australian government has a website at **www.greenvehicleguide.gov.au** where you can compare different models for factors such as fuel efficiency, air pollution rating, level of greenhouse emissions and overall efficiency of the vehicle. The guide gives each model a star rating; the more stars, the lower the environmental impact. The maximum rating of five stars is bestowed upon only four cars: **Toyota Prius, Mercedes-Benz A150, Fiat Punto and the Citroen C3**. You can also rate the fuel consumption of an old model, which is a handy feature if you are purchasing second-hand.

Share a car instead

Car sharing is a growing international trend that has recently expanded to Australia. With the high costs of buying and maintaining a car and the need to reduce greenhouse gas emissions, it makes a lot of sense. A number of city councils and savvy businesses now offer car share options for those who need to use a car only occasionally.

The shared cars have allocated parking spots in inner-city areas, and registered users can quickly book online or by phone, swipe themselves into the car and drive off. When they're done they park the car in the same spot and leave. The cars can be rented by the hour or by the day, and the fee includes petrol, comprehensive insurance, cleaning, and maintenance. It's cheap and hassle-free for individuals as well as small businesses that need a car occasionally but don't want the overheads of owning or leasing one. They are currently only in Sydney and

Melbourne, but look out for them in other cities in the next year or two. Here are the current players:

☐ **Go Get** was Australia's first car sharing service. It started in Sydney in 2003 and has expanded to inner-city Melbourne. Its cars are economical Toyotas, with small cars for inner-city driving and larger cars for weekend getaways: **www.goget.com.au**

☐ **Flexicar** started in Melbourne but is also now in Sydney and launching in Brisbane in late 2007. Flexicar uses Smart cars for most of its fleet, which are fuel-efficient, low-emission cars. Most important, all the emissions from driving the cars are offset by Climate Friendly: **www.flexicar.com.au**

☐ **Charter Drive** is based in Sydney's central business district and inner-city suburbs: **www.charterdrive.com.au**

Give car pooling a go

Over 80 per cent of journeys to work are made alone in a car. Car pooling can be an option for people who need to drive to work or drop the kids off at school daily, and could easily share transport with someone else. Although sharing the car with a stranger can seem daunting, you may find you make a new friend and enjoy the daily commute a lot more. The benefits for the environment and travel costs are clear. You can save thousands of dollars per year; get at least one car, if not more, off the road; and at least halve your greenhouse gas emissions. And if you travel on freeways you can use the transit lane for a faster journey.

One of the easiest ways to initiate car pooling is to put up a notice at work to ask if anyone else from your area is also interested. Talk to your employer, as they can benefit from the reduced need for car spaces if their staff are car pooling, and so may support your initiative.

You can also register your request on a number of car pooling sites that cater for lifts throughout Australia. Most of these offer security systems that keep your details private until you have found a partner that suits your requirements. Some of them are free, but other sites

DID YOU KNOW?
All new cars sold in Australia must now display a fuel consumption label, which provides information not only on fuel consumption but also on carbon dioxide emissions.

ask for a small fee. Here are just a few of the car pooling sites available:

☐ **E-carpool:** A not-for-profit organisation that uses maps and postcodes to link potential car poolers for daily commutes or one-off journeys: **www.e-carpool.com.au**

☐ **Sharemycar:** Advertises itself as Australia's leading free car pool service: **www.sharemycar.com.au**

☐ **Carpool-It:** One of the more sophisticated sites on the net, with a good search engine to match prospective car poolers. It costs approximately $10 per year: **www.carpool-it.com**

☐ **NeedARide:** For longer trips all around Australia you can either offer your available seats or request a lift to your desired location at **www.needaride.com.au** This site is perfect for backpackers and travellers who are keen to take a more sociable holiday and share the burden of travelling.

DID YOU KNOW?
Each kilometre of car travel avoided saves up to half a kilogram of greenhouse gas and 20 cents in operating costs.[10]

Public transport

Although public transport systems in Australia generally need better infrastructure and more support from government, buses, trains, and light rail systems are still a great way to get around, particularly in the major cities. They are also a mode of mass transport that is far more beneficial to the environment than cars or aeroplanes, and can be a lot quicker during peak times. Public transport, unlike the car, also gives you the freedom to read a book, do some work, close your eyes and drift off, or even socialise. I have had many stimulating conversations with people, swapped books and ideas, and even met my current partner on the train home from work, so I think it's a wonderful way not only to get around, but to meet people.

In terms of emissions, bus and light rail emit similar amounts of greenhouse gases over their lifetime, whereas trains produce more greenhouse gases due to the large amount of resources needed for the construction of rail lines.[8] But any form of public transport is far preferable to your car from an environmental perspective, particularly

if you are the only person in the car. It also takes the stress out of finding a parking space or, far worse, a parking ticket on the windscreen!

Catch a taxi

Most people don't think of taxis as public transport, but taxis are there for everyone to use and can be very handy for short trips when the bus or train just isn't going to cut it. Ninety-two per cent of the 16 000 taxis on the road are powered by autogas, so their total emissions are much smaller than your average car. And when you're done with the taxi, someone else can hop in and keep going, so they are a great form of community transport.

Walk or bicycle

A study in Sydney in 2002 found that 42 per cent of trips taken by car were for distances of under five kilometres.[9] That distance is easily covered by riding a bike, which in fact is usually a lot quicker, because you can sail right through any traffic congestion you may encounter and park your bike directly in front of where you want to go. Riding a bike is also a great way to get your exercise while doing your daily errands, so you don't need to worry about going to the gym. The greenhouse gas emissions from either walking or biking are, of course, zero, so this is the best form of transportation to help reduce climate change. You can also save thousands of dollars per year by ditching the car and using your bike instead.

Air travel

Australians are possibly the most-travelled people on the planet. Wherever you go, be it a tiny village in Africa, an island in the South Pacific, or a city right next to a war zone, chances are that another Australian will already be there to share a beer and swap travel tips with. Unfortunately, our love of exploring the planet contributes significantly to global warming. Airline travel represents the greatest release of greenhouse gas emissions in a short time that we as individuals can possibly make. Greenhouse gas emissions from the airline industry currently represent only two per cent of total emissions; however, this is tipped to rise dramatically over the next 50 years as the trend towards cheap flights and international mobility increases. The World Tourism Organization found that international tourist arrivals in 2005 achieved an all-time record exceeding 800 million. Fifty per cent of those arrivals were for holidays. Air transport is growing much faster than any other form of transport and it is predicted that we will reach nearly 1.6 billion international journeys by 2020."

There is also the problem of airline fuel. Aeroplanes use kerosene, which is petroleum-based and a non-renewable resource. While research and money are going into developing biofuels and various other power sources to run aeroplanes, there are intrinsic limits to what can be used at extreme altitudes and any alternatives are still decades away from becoming a commercial reality.

To make things worse, aeroplanes not only emit carbon dioxide, they also release water vapour and nitrogen oxides that have a warming effect of up to 2.7 times that of carbon dioxide alone. Emissions at high altitudes are contributing to climate change at nearly three times the rate of emissions closer to the ground.

Personally, this is one of the most challenging areas of the eco-footprint for me, because I grew up travelling. Before I was 10 years old I had already been to more countries than most kids my age knew existed. As an adult, I still like to travel overseas at least once a year and I love to explore other cultures and ways of living. When I first calculated my eco-footprint, the two trips I had taken to Europe that year – one for business and one for pleasure – practically doubled the size of my footprint and made me feel very guilty indeed. Since then I have learnt to cut down my flying time and offset my emissions when I do fly, in order to lessen my impact.

Minimising your footprint doesn't mean giving up on exploring the world, but it does mean doing it in a different, often more leisurely, manner and, ideally, enjoying more holidays within Australia rather than choosing to go overseas. It also means spending a little bit extra to offset the aeroplane emissions of your flights and being a responsible traveller when you get where you're going. **Chapter 13: Travel and Events** has more information.

Take the most direct route

Take-off and landing are the most fuel-intensive aspects of airline travel, so the more stopovers your flight has, the more fuel it will burn up. Therefore, pay a little more and try to get the most direct flight available, not the one that goes to London via Timbuktu!

Business travel

Business travel represents 16 per cent of all airline travel,[12] but how many of those trips are really necessary? We now have the technology to make conference calls by phone or video and link businesses all over the world. Instead of giving a presentation at a conference in person, it is now possible to use video conferencing and reduce 99 per cent of the energy you would use by flying. This not only saves the company a lot of money, it also saves on emissions. So next time your boss asks you to go on a business trip, why not suggest the benefits of doing business by phone or video instead?

Offset your airline emissions

Some travel companies recommend that after making your travel plans, you offset your emissions with a carbon offsetting company called ClimateCare (see Chapter 2: Carbon Offset Schemes). They even provide the calculators and links on their websites to do so. Intrepid Travel announced at the beginning of 2007 that all flights booked with it would include offsets in the price. Virgin Blue soon followed, offering passengers the opportunity to offset their flights when purchasing their tickets. Other travel companies are also looking at ways of minimising impacts.

Even if you're not booking your flights through a company that helps you offset, most of the carbon offsetting companies have calculators to help you offset the emissions of your flight through either planting trees or investing in renewable energy. By offsetting when you fly, whether for business or pleasure, as you kick back in your airline seat and watch the clouds go past, you will know that at least your seat in the aeroplane is carbon-neutral.

Top Tips for low-emission air travel

- Try to get the most direct flight to your destination available.
- Offset the carbon emissions from your flights once you have booked.
- Travel by plane less and spend more time on the ground when you get there.
- Minimise your emissions where possible by travelling short distances by train or bus instead.

4
ENERGY

We rarely pause to think about it, but without energy our lives would look very different indeed. Only when it's taken away do we realise how much we rely upon electricity and gas to prepare our meals, to keep cool in summer and warm in winter, to stay up after dark reading or watching TV, or even to have a shower. A blackout these days is a rare and highly inconvenient occurrence that has us scrambling about to find candles and wondering what to do with ourselves. Without the benefits of electricity and gas, the entire rhythm of our lives is interrupted and our everyday habits and routines quickly grind to a halt.

It's no wonder that energy usage in the average Australian household represents around 60 per cent of our individual greenhouse gas emissions.[13] Seventy-five per cent of our energy needs are currently supplied by coal-fired power stations,[14] utilising fossil fuel that is rapidly depleting and polluting the planet as it goes. Our power stations are not only using up finite coal stocks, but also sucking up our scarce water supplies at a rapid rate. For every megawatt a coal-fired power plant generates, it consumes two tonnes of water and spews out 1.5 tonnes of carbon dioxide.[15] Our energy usage is the front line of our battle against global warming.

Numerous renewable energy sources can replace our reliance on coal and make us viable in the long term. No one of them provides the total answer to our problems, due to their intermittent supply and other limitations, but if combined they can handle the majority of our electricity needs with a small amount of gas or clean coal as a backup. Energies such as solar, wind, geothermal, and possibly even nuclear now need to be considered as replacements for coal. The investment of money and research into these technologies will stimulate business and make Australia economically viable into the future, without the enormous reliance we currently place upon coal both locally and as an export. Some of these power sources also give us the opportunity to take control of our energy needs by building or renovating our houses to include solar panels, so that instead of contributing to greenhouse gas emissions each one of us can actively reduce our energy emissions to zero and become part of the solution to climate change.

Electricity

The average household in Australia emits well over 8 tonnes of greenhouse gas pollution each year just by running lights, appliances and heating.[16] But there are many simple ways to reduce this figure and decrease your reliance on electricity and gas by becoming far more efficient in the home. In addition, you can offset your usage and support the further development of renewable energy sources by switching your electricity to Green Power. This is easy to do and can eliminate your greenhouse gas emissions from using electricity. By being aware of how our energy choices impact on our emissions and by seeking to maximise efficiencies and go green wherever possible, we can go a long way towards neutralising our carbon emissions in this aspect of our lives.

 **Your electricity bill** shows your greenhouse gas emissions each quarter. By checking your bills before and after making changes to your behaviour or choosing Green Power, you can see the impact it is having on your emissions.

one with the highest level of accredited wind and solar that you can afford. If need be, get the entry-level Green Power package, which is cheaper, and switch to a higher percentage of accredited renewable energy later on.

Carbon offsetting

Even if you don't have a Green Power supplier in your area (currently the case only for some Northern Territory residents) or you don't want to change your current supply for any number of reasons, you can leave your electricity bill as it is and offset your emissions through a carbon offsetting company. There are many carbon offsetters that enable you to do this, as described in **Chapter 2: Carbon Offset Schemes**. Most have calculators on their websites, which can quickly help you figure out the cost to offset your emissions based on your most recent electricity bill, or on the state average if you don't have a bill to work from. They don't involve any contracts; you can make a one-off payment or arrange to make a regular deduction for each bill. However, be aware that it is better to get Green Power, which prevents any greenhouse emissions from going into the atmosphere in the first place, than to offset, which compensates for your emissions after they have occurred.

Gas

Natural gas and LPG (liquefied petroleum gas) are common in Australian households for cooking and heating. Gas is a good alternative to electricity because it is a far more efficient heat source that produces only one-third of the greenhouse emissions generated by electricity. Gas comes at a cheaper cost to both your wallet and the environment. It is still a fossil fuel and therefore non-renewable, so it is not the complete answer to our problems, but because of its much lower emissions it is definitely preferable to electricity whenever there is a choice between the two.

Natural gas is not yet available in all locations due to lack of infrastructure. If you live beyond the pipelines, you can purchase LPG in cylinders and use appliances adapted to take this form of gas. Unfortunately, the cylinders need to be transported over large distances, so LPG is not only double the price of natural gas but its transport also contributes extra greenhouse gas emissions.

Green Power your gas

Some suppliers offer a Green Power option for your natural gas. They aren't able to provide gas from renewable sources, but the Green Power scheme will at least offset the emissions generated from the gas you are using by investing in tree planting or supporting renewable energy projects. Origin Energy supplies green gas in New South Wales, Victoria, and South Australia and more suppliers will no doubt provide this option soon.

Renewable energy

Renewable energy can be powered from a variety of sources – solar, wind, bioenergy, wave, hydro, geothermal – and fed back into the electricity grid to supply our homes. Let's take a look at each of these.

Solar

Solar energy is Australia's largest renewable energy resource and particularly appropriate in our sunburnt country. It produces no greenhouse gases and has an almost limitless supply. Photovoltaic solar cells convert energy from sunlight into electricity in the form of direct current (DC), which is then converted into alternating current (AC), like that obtained from the electricity grid. A large array of photovoltaic cells can be set up to channel electricity into the grid, or a couple of panels can be mounted on the roof of your home. Solar thermal energy is different from solar photovoltaic cells in that it uses heat to create steam, which then turns turbines similar to a conventional power station. Although photovoltaic cells are more suitable for a small scale, solar thermal has great potential to drive conventional power stations. Several large-scale solar projects are currently under way in Australia. Some houses use their own solar panels on the roof to provide all their electrical needs and can even sell electricity back to the grid when they have an excess of solar power.

> ### Solar cities
> The Australian government has put forward $75 million to work with industry, business, and local communities to stimulate the awareness and practical application of solar energy in a number of Australian cities. Blacktown, Adelaide, Townsville and Alice Springs are the first four cities to receive the solar city funding. They have each been given 3000 photovoltaic panels to install on private and public housing, 2400 solar hot water systems, 13 500 smart meters – which provide real-time information on energy use – and over 70 000 energy-efficiency packs for households and businesses in the city. These cities are able to provide a positive example of the benefits of renewable energy, and the government estimates eventual annual savings of $9 million off the electricity bills for these cities.

Wind

Wind energy is actually a form of solar energy, as wind represents the sun's energy reaching the lower atmosphere, and comes from the movement of air caused by thermal gradients and the earth's rotation. A wind farm must have a strong and steady wind, usually at an average speed of over 6.5 metres per second or 23 km/hr. Wind energy uses no greenhouse gases and the supply is almost limitless. Once the set-up costs are covered, there are no ongoing expenses except for maintenance of the turbines. Wind energy is intermittent as it relies upon wind patterns, but widely dispersed turbines that can take advantage of where the wind is blowing can generally solve this problem.

Wind farms sometimes come under attack for being noisy, but the latest technology is significantly less noisy and you can hold a conversation at the base of a turbine without needing to raise your voice. There has also been some concern regarding the impact on bird life, but in reality extremely few bird deaths result from wind farms. Areas are always carefully assessed to ensure there will be no risk to rare or threatened birds before a wind farm can be built. When you think about it, cities are not conducive to bird life and nor are coal power plants, so that argument is not particularly convincing.

Australia's present total installed wind capacity is small, but it is already producing 817 megawatts, which is enough to power 460 000 homes.[17] Many more wind farms are under development or in planning stages. At the moment, wind power is removing 2 and a half million tonnes of greenhouse gases from the atmosphere every year, which is the equivalent of taking 575 000 cars off the road.[18] Imagine how much more it can do if we ramp up our investment in this clean, readily available energy source.

Bioenergy

Bioenergy is generated from organically based matter, or biomass. Various materials can produce bioenergy, including waste from the agricultural industry such as animal manure, solids, and gases produced from landfill sites, forestry and food industry residues, and agricultural or energy crops. Biomass can be either dry, such as straw or forest residue, or wet, such as refuse from animal farms and sewage. Because these crops can be harvested and replenished they are considered renewable, and although they still produce emissions, they produce significantly less than fossil fuels do.

Gas from landfill sites and sewage treatment plants is currently used to generate small amounts of electricity in some states. Landfills and rubbish tips can provide energy because organic matter produces methane gas as it breaks down. Capturing and burning the methane generates energy, while also preventing methane from escaping into the atmosphere. Methane produces over 20 times as much pollution as carbon dioxide. However, much larger amounts of landfill gases are needed to produce electricity, compared with other sources including fossil fuels, so they aren't currently very efficient. Some industrial sites such as paper mills and piggeries use their waste streams to produce bioenergy that can be used within their plant, reducing expenses and improving efficiency.

Hydroelectricity

The power of a fast-flowing stream, or a dam, can generate hydroelectricity. Most of the hydro in Australia is coming from existing sources that are now fully utilised. Once the initial cost of the plant is covered, there are only

> **WHAT IS CLEAN COAL?**
> When discussion about future energy sources comes up, politicians often talk about 'clean coal' as a big part of Australia's future energy supplies. The clean coal process will strip carbon dioxide emissions from coal, either before or after it is burnt, and then inject them back into the ground rather than releasing them into the atmosphere. It will not eliminate greenhouse gas emissions, but it may reduce them by 30 per cent. Clean coal is still at the research stage: a workable process is 15 to 20 years away, and it will cost millions of dollars to build new clean coal power plants.

minimal ongoing costs as the water can be stored as a power source and hydro produces no greenhouse gases. However, constructing a dam or diverting water from a river can greatly disturb the local aquatic and land-based ecosystems for a long period of time. Dams reduce the flow in river systems, and hydro generators have caused numerous ongoing problems such as the damage done by the Snowy Hydro Scheme to the Snowy and Murray Rivers. There may be opportunities for placing some mini-hydro generators on existing water-supply infrastructure, but we must be careful not to further damage our precious water supplies.

Wave and tidal

The power of the oceans can be harnessed to generate electricity utilising the strength of waves or tides. The energy of a wave depends on how large it is and how fast it is travelling, and it can be captured by turbines either on shore or floating on the sea close to the shore. Tidal energy is captured through the use of tidal turbines or tidal barrage systems, which can trap large areas of water and need large tidal currents. Pilot plants of this energy source are currently under development within Australia.

Geothermal

Geothermal energy is extracted from the natural heat that is found in the earth closer to the core, usually at depths of three to five kilometres. There are two sources of geothermal energy: hot dry rock, which uses the direct heat of granite rocks as an energy source; and hydrothermal, which pumps water through the hot rocks to produce hot water and steam. This is a new technology that needs more research, but it has great potential. A number of projects are currently under development to tap geothermal energy in central and eastern areas of Australia. Useable heat has already been discovered in a body of granite in South Australia that is estimated to contain enough heat to supply all of Australia's energy needs for 75 years.[19]

What about nuclear?

Nuclear power is sometimes suggested as a potential major energy source in Australia. Nuclear power plants are low in greenhouse gas emissions during operation, but the building of a nuclear power plant creates significant emissions and uses an enormous amount of energy. Uranium mining also takes a huge toll on the natural environment, while much of Australia's uranium mining occurs in environmentally significant areas such as Kakadu. The cost of nuclear is also far higher than the cost of investing in renewables. A nuclear power plant could not become fully operational for at least 15 years and possibly much longer, due to the strict process of permits required and the many years needed for construction.

There are also major issues regarding safe disposal of radioactive waste from nuclear power plants. The waste lasts tens to hundreds of thousands of years and there is currently no safe method to dispose of it. Many people are strongly opposed to nuclear power, no doubt due to these issues as well as the numerous accidents that have occurred at nuclear power plants, the worst of which was the Chernobyl disaster in 1986. Despite the government's insistence on the benefits of a nuclear future, most environmental organisations and ordinary people throughout the world are adamant that nuclear is not the answer for our future power needs.

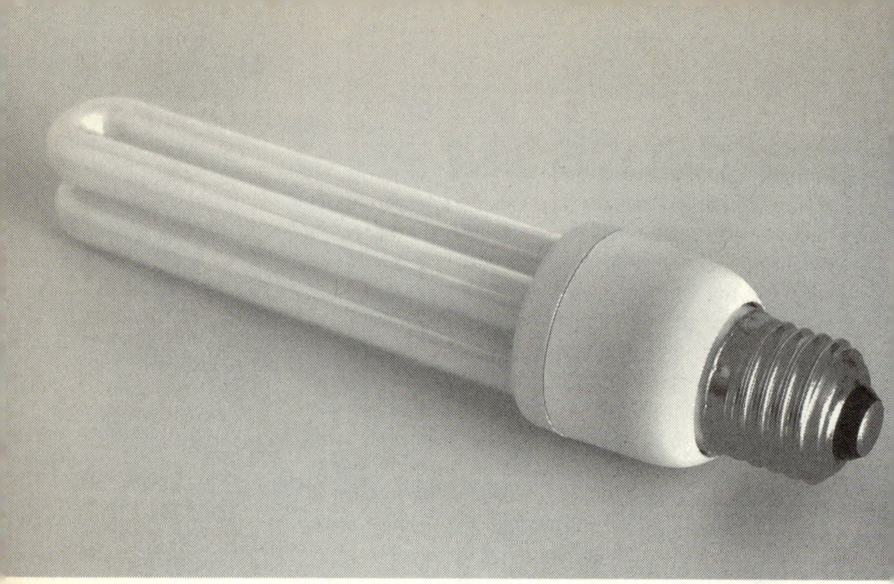

Lighting

The lights you use, both inside and outside the home, provide opportunities to save a great deal of electricity and money by making simple changes to consumption. Approximately five per cent of our household energy usage is on lights, and most Australian homes generate around three-quarters of a tonne of greenhouse gas emissions and spend up to $100 a year on their lighting.[20] This figure can easily be halved with a few adjustments to the type of lighting you use and how often you use it.

Light bulbs

Several different types of globes can be used for lighting the home, one of which, the compact fluorescent lamp, is significantly superior to the others.

Incandescent

The most commonly used type of light, incandescent bulbs come in wattages ranging from 25 to 100. They last only 1000 hours before needing to be replaced, and they are very inefficient, using only six per cent of their energy as light. The rest of their energy is wasted as heat emanating from the bulb. Don't be fooled by long-life incandescent bulbs either. They may last longer but they are no more efficient during use.

DID YOU KNOW?
In early 2007 the federal government announced a plan to phase out incandescent light bulbs by 2009, encouraging consumers to replace them all with compact fluorescents as soon as possible.

Halogen

Halogen lights are commonly known as downlights. They are twice as efficient as incandescent globes and generally last up to 3000 hours. Halogen lights provide focused pools of light and are suitable for lighting small areas or specific targets such as a bench top or wall feature. Low-voltage halogens are only slightly more efficient than normal bulbs of the same wattage and still produce a great deal of heat. Because of the focused light of the bulbs you may need more halogen bulbs to do the same job as other types of bulb. Another negative aspect of halogens is that they need a transformer, which is usually placed in the ceiling, so any insulation needs to be removed from around the transformer to prevent a fire hazard. This reduces the efficiency of insulation, which is important for helping to keep rooms cool in summer and warm in winter. The net result is you may need to pay more on your electricity bill due to the poor insulation around the halogen.

Fluorescent

These are the most energy-efficient form of lighting inside the house. Fluorescent lamps use only a quarter of the energy that a standard incandescent bulb needs and can last up to 10 000 hours before they need to be replaced. They cost more than incandescent bulbs but usually pay for themselves within 12 months.

There are two types of fluorescents: compact fluorescent lights (CFLs), which are designed to fit in conventional light sockets with either bayonet or screw fittings; and tubular lamps, which are the traditional straight or circular tubes. Compact fluorescent lights are ideal for most areas of the house, although in rooms where lights are turned on and off frequently, such as the bathroom, the life of the bulb will be reduced. The tubular lamps are best for security lighting or rooms that have lights on for a long time, such as the living room, as they take a while to power up; again, turning them on and off frequently will reduce their lifespan. The standard fluoro generally emits cool light, which may be harsh, but you can purchase 'warm white' bulbs that provide a warmer light similar to incandescent bulbs.

TOP TIP Switch all your indoor bulbs to compact fluorescent lights (CFLs) today. You can cut your lighting bill and your greenhouse gas emissions by nearly 75 per cent.

Solar

Solar lighting is perfect for outdoor applications. It has no greenhouse gas emissions and, once you buy the light, the power is completely free. Solar lights have a solar panel on top that generates electricity during the day and stores it in a battery for powering the light at night. They can provide up to eight hours of lighting if they get enough sunlight during the day. They are a great way of lighting outdoor areas easily, as there is no need to connect to the electricity supply. However, they do need to be in full sunlight during the day, are not as bright as mains lights, and are not able to work as motion detector lights. The price of solar lights starts at around $10.

Light fittings

Pendant fittings hang from the ceiling and provide the maximum light possible from a single globe, so they are recommended for general lighting in a room. Recessed lights or downlights provide a pool of light and are good for highlighting a specific area, but you need up to six to light a room to the same level as one pendant light. Lamps or fittings with multiple globes are an inefficient and expensive method of lighting as six 25-watt globes are required to produce an output equivalent to one 100-watt globe. Dark lampshades and dark-coloured walls also reduce illumination considerably and require higher-wattage globes to do the same job.

Comparative costs

The table shows the lifetime costs for using different globes to produce the same amount of light. You can see that although the compact fluorescent has a higher purchase price, the lifetime cost is less than one-third that of other light sources.

COMPARISON OF COSTS FOR VARIOUS TYPES OF LIGHTING
(assuming an electricity cost of 15 cents/kilowatt)

Type of bulb	Purchase $	Lifespan(hours)	Running costs over 6000 hours	Lifetime cost
11-watt compact fluorescent	$7	6000	$9.90	$16.90
60-watt incandescent	0.80 cents (6 bulbs for $4.80)	1000	$54	$58.80
50-watt halogen	$2 (3 bulbs for $6)	2000	$45	$51

Top Tips for lighting efficiency

- Switch the lights off every time you leave a room.
- Keep your light bulbs and lampshades clean so they work at maximum efficiency: dirty globes or shades can reduce light by up to 50 per cent.
- Make good use of natural light from north-facing windows during the day.
- Use the lowest-wattage light to adequately illuminate an area.
- Use compact fluorescent light bulbs as much as possible.
- Don't leave outdoor lights on all night – use a motion sensor or a timer.
- Make sure that any sensor lights you have are turned off during the day or when not required so your movements don't turn them on unnecessarily.
- Use solar-powered lights in the garden.
- Don't have several lights activated by the one switch: it is inefficient and doesn't allow you to accurately control the lighting level you need.
- Use lamps to supplement general room lighting for specific tasks.
- Avoid using downlights in rooms that have insulation: they will cause heat loss through the removal of insulation.
- Downlights are best used in small areas that need specific pools of light.
- Avoid using multiple-globe light fittings as they are inefficient.
- A light-coloured room will appear lighter and reflect light better than a dark-coloured one.

Heating

In the southern states of Australia, most houses need some level of heating during winter. What type of heating will be the most efficient and minimise your greenhouse gas emissions? There are so many different heaters on the market it can be confusing to sort through the options. This is a quick guide to the various types of heating, as well as their impact on your greenhouse gas emissions.

Radiant and convective heating

Generally speaking, there are two types of heat:

Radiant heat is emitted from a hot surface – such as the glowing red surface of a bar radiator – and primarily heats objects or people close to the heater, rather than the entire room.

Convection heat consists of currents of hot air, such as those created by a fan heater or ducted heat.

Many heat sources, including wood heaters and some gas heaters, combine both types of heat, moving hot air and producing heat directly at their source.

Space heating versus central heating

Central heating systems are large heaters; they are generally expensive to install but they can heat most of your home at one time. To get the most efficiency, a central heater should be zoned so that you can turn off the heating in empty rooms and have it on only in the rooms you are currently using. Space heaters are smaller and designed to heat a single room or zone of your home, rather than the whole place.

The type of heating that suits your needs depends on the area you wish to heat, how many people use the space, how often people are in the space, your budget, and energy-efficiency requirements. If you need to heat only one or two rooms for short periods of time, space heating is generally more economical to run. If the whole house needs to be heated for long periods of time, a central heating system is more expensive initially, but cheaper to run in the long term. You should purchase the most energy-efficient heater you can afford, both to help the environment and to save money in the long term.

Heater size

Heaters are generally sized according to the amount of heat needed to maintain a comfortable indoor temperature, generally 18-21 degrees Celsius, on a cold winter day. Of course, it's preferable to put on another layer of clothing rather than turning the heat up, because

---

BEST HEATING OPTIONS BY ROOM

Single room: one or more efficient gas space heaters.

Bathroom: if required use a radiant heater such as a strip heater or infrared lamp, mounted at least 1.4 metres above the floor and away from water areas.

Living areas for long periods, sleeping areas for short periods: high-efficiency gas space heaters for living zones and electric space heaters with thermostats for sleeping areas, or a zoned central heating system.[22]

Living and sleeping areas for long periods: a zoned central heating system.

the lower you keep the heat, the lower your emissions and your heating bill. The energy required to heat your home can also vary greatly depending on the level of insulation you have. An energy-efficient home may need only 60 watts of heating per square metre of floor area, but an uninsulated home with a lot of draughts may need up to 130 watts per square metre for comfort.[23] To find out exactly what size heating system you need, discuss it with your supplier, or put the dimensions of your room into the heating calculator provided by the Australian Consumers' Association at **www.aca.com.au/cp/energy/quizheatingcalc.cfm**

Electric heaters

There are many different types of electric heaters, from small, radiant portable ones through to fan heaters, oil-filled column heaters, and electric wall panels. Electric heaters are quite expensive to run and emit up to six times the greenhouse gases of an efficient gas central heating system. Therefore they should be avoided where possible. If you already have an electric heater or don't have gas supply to your home, be sure to follow the Top Tips to maximise the heating efficiency of your electric heater. Ideally, switch to a gas heater that is far more efficient.

Gas heaters

Using natural gas or LPG for your heating produces around one-third as much carbon dioxide as reverse-cycle air conditioning or electric heating. Natural gas is also much cheaper to run than most other options, apart from solar heating which is the ideal. Keep in mind that adequate ventilation is needed with gas heaters to maintain air quality, and make sure when you purchase a gas heater that it has a good external flue to keep the air clear. Without an external flue or frequent opening of windows, a gas heater can compromise air quality within the house and allow the growth of mould.

> When purchasing a new gas heater make sure to get one with an Energy Star rating of 4 to 6 stars.

All new gas heaters are rated for energy efficiency by the Australian Gas Association and most also carry energy star ratings (see **Chapter 8: Appliances and Household Goods**). The more stars on the label, the more energy-efficient it will be, the lower your greenhouse gas emissions, and the more money you will save. You can purchase a gas space heater or gas central heating and there are many different models. Gas central heating can be a very energy-efficient heating choice and includes: ducted air heating that works like ducted air conditioning; hydronic heating, where water is heated in a central boiler and then circulated to panels in each room; and in-slab heating, where a concrete floor slab is heated internally by gas-heated water pipes. In-slab heating is efficient only if it is gas-heated, as electric in-slab heating has the highest greenhouse gas emissions of any heating system.

In general, we have become very reliant upon heaters, both indoors and outdoors, and we need to be more conscious of dressing appropriately for the climate rather than expecting artificial heating to do the work. By dressing for the weather conditions we drastically reduce the need to turn heaters on, thereby preventing greenhouse gas emissions altogether.

Wood heaters

Wood fires are beautiful to look at but they are not the most efficient source of heating, particularly if you have

an open fire as opposed to a slow combustion fire. Ninety percent of the radiant heat from an open fire is lost through the chimney, and pot-belly stoves are only marginally better. However, efficiency can be improved by using a metal fireplace insert that allows room air to be circulated and heated or a fan that helps to distribute the warm air.

The best type of firewood heater is a slow combustion stove with an airtight firebox and an air inlet that regulates the amount of air supplied to the combustion chamber, as well as a fan to distribute the heat. They are up to 70 per cent efficient and must comply with Australian standards regarding their flue gas emissions. You can get slow combustion wood heaters in a variety of sizes, with large convection models that use a fan to distribute heat up to 130 square metres.

Heating: Electricity versus natural gas

Electricity

POSITIVES

- You can offset your emissions through Green Power.
- Electric heaters don't produce polluting gases in the home.

NEGATIVES

- Portable electric heaters can be costly to run.
- Electricity produces much higher greenhouse gas emissions than natural gas.

Natural Gas

POSITIVES

- Gas is much cheaper than electricity to run.
- Gas produces far fewer greenhouse gases than electricity.
- Gas heaters carry a star label that advises you of their energy efficiency.

NEGATIVES

- Natural gas isn't available everywhere, and LPG has transport costs.
- Gas produces toxic combustion gases within the home, so you need to ensure your gas heater has a flue or manage the gases by opening windows frequently.

As far as greenhouse gas emissions are concerned, the overall environmental impact of burning wood can vary depending on its origins. Firewood should always be very dry, as you will waste energy burning green wood. The burning of wood releases the carbon stored within, producing approximately 1.5 kilograms of carbon dioxide per kilogram of wood.[24] If the wood you are using is sustainably forested and is being replaced by new trees, the trees will absorb carbon dioxide from the environment for their growth and so will eventually offset the emissions from burning. Therefore, when you are buying firewood always choose wood from sustainable forests. Smoke from wood fires contributes to air pollution, and you need to factor in the carbon dioxide produced in cutting the wood and transporting it from its original location, which add to the greenhouse gas emissions.

Solar heating

Solar heating uses solar panels that generate warm air and then transfer it through ducts and diffusers into your room. It can complement gas or other forms of heating in a room, but is generally not enough to heat a room consistently on its own, as it is dependent on sunshine. The panels need to be placed on an unshaded north-facing roof or wall; if you have storage capacity, the hot air can be stored and used when needed. Commercial units available in Australia cost approximately $2500 plus installation costs.[25]

TOP TIPS for heating efficiency

- Minimise heat loss by sealing all gaps between doors, laying rugs on bare floors and closing up unused fireplaces and unused pet doors. Air leaks can account for up to 25 per cent of heat loss and create draughts that will chill you even further.

- Draught-proof your windows with insulation strips, pelmets, and thick curtains that sit close to window frames.

- Zone your home and keep all doors closed between different zones so that you are heating only the area required, not the entire house.

- Ensure that the ceiling space above heated areas is insulated.

- Don't vary the thermostat temperature too often – it will overwork your heater and increase heating costs.

- Clean your air conditioners and heaters regularly so that they are at maximum efficiency and not working harder because of dust build-up.

- Rather than turning up the heater, why not put on warmer clothing? Every one-degree increase in temperature will lead to a 10 per cent increase in both heating bills and emissions.

- Reduce the temperature at night before you go to sleep. Most people sleep better with cooler air in their bedrooms.

- Open up curtains to north-facing windows on sunny winter days to allow in the heat from nature.

- The better draught-proofed your house is, the more important it is to have adequate ventilation, so open up windows for a short time every day to prevent mould and pollutants building up, particularly if you are using gas heating.

- A ceiling fan is an efficient way to move the hot air that builds up at ceiling level down to the floor to keep you warm.

- A timer on your heater can automatically turn the heat on or off at pre-selected times to warm a room before you wake up and to turn it off when you're not home.

- At the end of the cool months make sure to shut down your gas heater completely, as otherwise the pilot light will still be consuming gas.

Cooling

The principles explained for heating also apply to cooling your house. Attention to matters such as insulation, sealing gaps and having thick curtains closed around the windows to prevent air loss are as important in summer as they are in winter. Several options are available for cooling your house, and your choice will depend on the size of the area you want to cool, the height of the ceilings, and the regularity and duration of cooling needed. Of course, the best method of controlling the temperature of your home is energy-efficient house design that maximises shade in summer and makes the most of winter sunshine. However, that won't be possible unless you are building a new home or doing major renovations, so read on for the best option for your current situation. You can read more about creating an energy-efficient house in **Chapter 9: Building and Renovating.**

Fans

Fans – whether small portable units, ceiling fans, or whole house fans – are the most economical cooling option to purchase and run. They provide a cooling effect by moving the air around a room or a person. Fans cost an average of only two cents per hour to run,[26] which is an absolute bargain!

Portable fans

These are available in a variety of different models and are most suitable for cooling one or two people in a small area. Look for one with an oscillating function, so that it changes direction, and a speed control. They cost up to $200 and are very handy as you can move them to whatever room you want to spend your time in, including the bedroom at night.

Ceiling fans

These are great for bedrooms or other rooms of the house where you may be sitting or lying down for a long time. Some ceiling fans have a reversing function, which is useful in winter to bring down hot air that builds up at ceiling level. Look for one with speed controls and curved blades for better movement.

Whole-house fans

These are installed in a roof space with a ceiling shutter immediately below; they work by moving air to create cooling cross-ventilation in rooms, while expelling hot air via the roof. They create an updraft and draw in fresh air through windows, so are best placed in areas with a lot of movement such as hallways, stairwells or other high-traffic areas. These are an energy-efficient alternative or addition to air conditioning and can decrease your cooling costs by up to 60 per cent.

Air conditioners

Although popular, these are one of the least energy-efficient options for cooling your house and also have high purchase and running costs. The different types of air conditioners include:

Portable split systems, or fixed (fascia) units: one-room units that are usually connected to a power outlet

Split systems: fixed units with separate indoor and outdoor sections that are connected by piping

Ducted systems: installed into the roof or floor and can cool and heat the entire house

Reverse-cycle air conditioning: an electric heating system that also provides cooling.

The reverse-cycle air conditioners are the best deal: they can transfer three or more units of heat for every unit of electricity used, so they provide the most economical form of air conditioning. Most air conditioners are labelled with an energy rating sticker that provides information on the efficiency level and greenhouse gas emissions, so when purchasing a new system choose the most energy-efficient one (see **Chapter 8: Appliances and Household Goods**).

Sizing your air conditioner

It is important to choose an air conditioner that has an output to suit your cooling and heating requirements. An oversized one will turn itself on and off more frequently, which is less efficient and overworks the system; an

---

AIR CONDITIONER CHECKLIST

When purchasing an air conditioner look for:

- programmable timer and thermostat controls
- economy settings
- multi-speed fans
- movement sensors, which reduce power when the room is unoccupied
- zoning capacity on whole house systems
- sleep modes that automatically lower the thermostat
- adjustable and rotating louvres so you can adjust air flow
- a reverse cycle that is very efficient.

undersized one will have to work far too hard to meet your needs. As a general guide, you need 125 watts (0.125 kilowatts) per square metre of floor area in living areas, and 80 watts (0.08 kilowatts) per square metre in bedrooms.[27] The output in kilowatts (kW) is listed on the energy rating label. However, if you have high ceilings or poor insulation this may vary, so check with your supplier to make sure you are getting the unit to suit your needs. With larger systems, particularly ducted systems with outputs greater than 11 kilowatts, contact your electricity supplier to ensure you have sufficient power supply available before you commence installation.

> Whatever type of air conditioner you choose, make sure it has an energy rating of at least five stars.

Top Tips for maximising cooling efficiency

- All new air conditioners must display an energy rating, so go for the maximum number of stars possible to ensure greater efficiency over the running costs. On units of a similar size, you can save up to $220 a year by choosing a unit with six stars.

- Larger units have a COP (co-efficient of performance) rather than an energy rating, which measures the amount of heat or coolness the unit can produce for each unit of electricity. The higher the COP, the lower the running cost for units of equivalent size. Look for a COP of at least two.

- Ensure that the outside component of your air conditioner is placed in a shady spot to reduce its workload and maximise efficiency.

- Ensure you purchase the correct size air conditioner for your needs; an undersized or oversized unit will not be efficient and may well end up costing more to run.

- Close all windows, doors, and gaps to maximise cooling efficiency.

- Ducted heating and cooling systems should always be zoned into two or more areas so that sleeping and living areas can be cooled separately. This will reduce your running costs by up to 50 per cent.

- Check your thermostat setting. Adjusting the thermostat by one degree can save 10 per cent on your energy bill. Find a temperature that you can live with and try not to over-cool or over-heat your home.

- When you are expecting a hot day, turn the air conditioner on early rather than waiting until the air is really hot. That way, the air conditioner doesn't have to work so hard.

- A programmable thermostat is a good feature to have. It will help in setting the most appropriate temperatures and will automatically turn the system on and off at different times of the day.

- An economy cycle will gradually increase, or decrease, the output temperature of the air conditioner for a few hours after it has been turned on, thereby maximising efficiency.

- Keep windows shut during the day to keep the heat out, then open them in the evening once it starts to cool down.

- Deciduous trees or vines outside north-facing windows will shade the house from the sun in summer and allow sun through in winter when they lose their leaves.

5
WATER

5 WATER

Water, or more accurately the lack of it, is front-page news in Australia. Many areas of the country are permanently drought-ridden, with losses to crops and livestock often making life hell for farmers. In 2007, reservoirs fell to an all-time low, most states instituted permanent restrictions, and the issue became a political hot potato. Australia is one of the driest places on this earth but, despite all this, our water usage per person is still one of the highest in the world.

The majority of the world's water resources are captured in our oceans and are unsuitable for human use. Only three per cent of the world's water is fresh, and less than one per cent of this fresh water is actually accessible to humans.[28] Australia is extremely low on water resources in comparison to other countries and has always suffered from extreme weather conditions, particularly droughts. With global warming we can expect those extremes to be exacerbated with further periods of drought, greater issues of erosion, salinity, and desertification of our soil, interspersed with torrential floods that will potentially cause huge damage. The impact of global warming on our freshwater supply, creating a water shortage of global magnitude, is already shaping up to be one of the biggest survival issues of the 21st century.

As a nation, we are beginning to realise that the way we've used water in the past is not sustainable. When you're not allowed to water the garden or the lawn with mains water at any time, it's a clear signal that our water habits need to drastically change or we risk running out of water altogether. The government has targeted our biggest industrial water users and is forcing them to reduce their consumption. Household users are responsible for 12 per cent of Australia's total water use, so we need to play our part in reducing water usage as well.

Every drop of water is precious, and even in the big cities, where we are not confronted with the realities of our water shortage on a daily basis, there's no excuse to throw it away. Water has also drastically increased in price over the last few years, and as supplies become even more restricted, we can only expect that water

prices will continue to escalate. With simple methods of minimising our consumption and recycling as much as possible, we can reduce our usage and our water bills. By doing this, we can reduce the need to dam further rivers, avoid costly water treatment at sewage plants, and also significantly reduce our greenhouse gas emissions.

Average water usage

The average Australian household consumes between 150 000 and 300 000 litres of fresh water per year. When you factor in all the food we eat and the water that goes into the products we buy, it is estimated we are each responsible for using about one million litres of water per year. That represents enough water to fill Sydney Harbour 48 times over.

Your daily use can vary between 130 and 200 litres, depending on where you live, but the interesting point is that only 10 litres of that total is used for basic survival needs, such as drinking and food preparation. The rest of our water usage is discretionary and variable, depending on how efficient we are with it. We can all reduce our water consumption at little or no cost to ourselves, by utilising water-saving measures such as low-flow showerheads, fixing leaks, and using a bucket in the shower to trap water. These small changes, when combined, can make a huge difference to our water usage.

Embodied water

When considering an individual's water usage, we look at the amount of water that we take from the tap, but we should also take into consideration the embodied water in products that we use in the household. This is the amount of water used in growing, processing, and transporting the products we consume. For example, it is estimated that it takes 1000 litres of fresh water to produce one litre of milk, 3000 litres of water to produce one kilo of rice, or a staggering 16 000 litres of fresh water to produce one kilo of beef.[29] When you consider the embodied water in many foods and household products that we take for granted, our water usage becomes quite extraordinary.

Water footprint

Much as you can calculate your own eco-footprint, you can also calculate your water usage. UNESCO-IHE Institute for Water Education and the University of Twente in Netherlands have developed a water footprint that calculates the total volume of fresh water used to produce goods and services consumed by an individual, business, or nation. This organisation has calculated the national footprint for each country and includes the goods and services consumed, even if they have been produced outside the country. According to their calculations, Australia's footprint is 1393 megalitres (1393 million litres) per person per year. That is an absolutely enormous figure and far beyond what we individually consume from the tap. In fact, 18 per cent of that amount is consumed outside Australia and represents the embodied water in the products we import as a country. Our water footprint on average is also higher than most countries because Australians are generally big meat-eaters, and beef in particular consumes large amounts of water. In general a vegetarian has a much smaller water footprint than a meat-eater, because much less water is needed for crops than for livestock. To calculate your own water footprint, take a look at **www.waterfootprint.org**

Be water wise

In each area of the house there are numerous ways to become more water wise and adapt your household usage for the better. In the following section, I will look separately at the bathroom, laundry, kitchen, and outdoor areas. But first, there are a few general tips that are relevant to all areas of the house.

AAA water efficiency

Many appliances and plumbing fixtures have a water efficiency rating, provided by the Water Services Association of Australia. Although this scheme was officially phased out in 2006 in favour of the WELS Scheme (see overleaf), references are common to the AAA showerhead and some products are still sold with this rating.

DID YOU KNOW?
Australia is the driest inhabited continent on the planet, with over 70 per cent of our land consisting of desert or semi-desert, and yet we are one of the biggest consumers per person of water on the planet.

The A-rating scheme covered washing machines and dishwashers as well as toilets, taps, and showerheads. The most efficient showerheads, taps, and toilets were rated at AAA, and some dishwashers and washing machines received a AAAA rating. If you find a product labelled with this rating scheme, go for at least AAA. Otherwise, look to the water rating label below.

Water rating label

> Look for the water rating logo

The National Water Efficiency Labelling and Standards (WELS) Scheme helps you to make informed decisions about the most water-efficient products on the market through a ratings system from one to six, with six being the most efficient. It is now mandatory to label all showers, taps, toilets, urinals, clothes washers, and dishwashers with a rating from WELS, which is similar in appearance to the energy rating label that is described in **Chapter 8: Appliances and Household Goods**.

> Choose new products with a high water rating and low water consumption to save big on your water usage.

Go for a minimum of a three-star rating, with more stars wherever possible. However, keep in mind that the water usage can vary widely between products with the same star rating, so it is worth comparing water consumption per minute and over a period of 10 years, as there are substantial water savings to be made with some products. You can search for the most water efficient products and look at their water consumption before purchasing at **www.waterrating.gov.au**

> Installing aerators will cut your total water usage in the sink by half forever at a cost of only a few dollars now.

Install aerators on your taps

Costing only a few dollars at the hardware store, tap aerators or flow-control valves can save water usage from running taps in the bathroom and kitchen by half.

They reduce flow without reducing water pressure and are fantastic for washing your hands, rinsing vegetables, or washing anything else in the sink. You can also adjust the flow back to full strength when you need more water. Aerators are easy to install by just unscrewing the tap and replacing. Even I managed it, and I am far from handy around the house.

Fix any leaks

Many of us have a dripping tap that is annoying but never seems to get fixed. If you actually put a bucket under the leak for a few days, you would realise how much the water adds up. A slowly dripping tap can waste up to 20 000 litres of water per year. Many leaks can be easily fixed – by replacing the washer if it's in a tap, or by tightening the connection if it's to a washing machine. Make sure that you don't have a slow leak in the toilet as well, as a leak can barely be visible but still make a substantial impact on your water usage.

To check whether you have any leaks, turn off all water sources in the house and then look at your water meter. If the meter is still moving, you have a leak somewhere. Now you just have to find it! Look under your sinks to see if there are any drips; check the washing machine connections; double check all your taps; assess the toilet by putting some food dye in the cistern – the storage section that holds the flushing water – and see if it leaks through to the toilet bowl. If you feel uncomfortable about fixing the leaks yourself, it's definitely worth getting a plumber to fix them and save plenty of water and money in the long term.

In the bathroom

About 40 per cent of water use in the average home is in the bathroom, with the toilet and shower each consuming approximately 20 per cent of your water. This is an area where small changes can make big differences to your consumption. The main changes in the bathroom are to cut down wasteful water usage with simple strategies, and install efficient water heating where possible (water heating is discussed in **Chapter 9: Building and Renovating**). Even more savings can be made by re-using grey water from the shower area and redirecting it with buckets, or a more sophisticated grey water system, to your toilet or your garden.

Flushing the toilet

An old-style single-flush toilet can consume around 11 litres every time you flush it. That's a lot of water going down the pipes! Modern dual-flush systems are far more economical, using approximately six litres for a full flush and only three for a half flush. Consider purchasing a dual-flush toilet when renovating or upgrading your bathroom. If you can't afford an entire new unit, you can replace just the cistern with a dual-flush one.

If this isn't possible – perhaps if you're renting – install your own water-saving device by filling a few water bottles and putting them in the cistern. This has the effect of reducing the amount of flushable water in the cistern. Depending on how many bottles you put in, it can save up to six litres on each flush, reducing your total water usage in the toilet by more than half. You can also buy toilet dams or install a flush regulator, which allows you to flush only for as long as you hold down the button. Check your local hardware store for these and plenty more toilet water-saving devices that are very economical to purchase.

If you're up to the challenge, don't flush unless you really have to, as you save at least three litres of water every time you let the yellow stuff mellow in the bowl. You can also empty your bucketed extra water from the shower into the toilet instead of pressing the flush button to minimise water usage.

You can save up to 35 000 litres of water per year within your household just by utilising these tips on economical flushing.

Water-efficient showerheads

Most standard showerheads use around 20 litres of water every minute, whereas a water-efficient showerhead uses

only seven to nine litres per minute. A water-efficient showerhead costs no more than an inefficient equivalent. You can buy a cheap, three-star showerhead for less than $20, and with an average seven-minute shower you will save over 30 000 litres of water per year. As delightful as showers are, it's also important not to linger. By reducing your showers to five – or even three – minutes, the savings are even more impressive.

Some ways to reduce shower time include shaving your face using water from the sink, and your legs using a bucket. By turning off the shower while you are lathering your hair, you can also significantly cut down on shower time. Many people shower twice a day, which is great for smelling good but seems a little indulgent with our ongoing water crisis. If you must shower twice a day, then reduce your shower time to a quick dip, under three minutes, so that your total time using the shower is still minimal. The purchase of a simple egg-timer for the shower costs only a few dollars, but it encourages the whole family to minimise their shower time. You can also install mixer taps in the shower; these prevent wastage as you try to get the water to the right temperature, as the mixers combine the water within the pipes.

Your local water supplier or the local council may provide discounts or free offers on water-saving showerheads, so visit their websites. Alternatively, the non-profit Save Water website will easily provide you with information relevant to your postcode, and link you through to your local water supplier at **www.savewater.com.au**

SHOWER BUCKET

Keep a bucket in the shower to capture the cold water that comes through before it heats up, and use this extra water in the toilet, washing the car, or on your garden. You will be amazed at how many litres you can save and recycle with a simple bucket system. Just empty it before it gets too full so you don't have any spillage in the house or suffer from the dreadful 'bucket back' that is afflicting the nation!

In the bath

There is no need to fill the bathtub; use only as much water as needed. Children (and pets) require significantly less water than an adult in the tub. Check the temperature of the water as it runs in; if you make it too hot you will have to add extra cold water. And when you've finished with your bath, don't just pull the plug – re-use the water. People in many parts of the world are used to sharing bathwater (no kidding – it's really not that bad) or, like the bucketed water from the shower, it can be used to flush the toilet, on the garden, or to wash the car.

Top Tips for being water wise in the bathroom

- Turn the tap off while brushing your teeth. Instead, just wet your brush briefly and use a glass of water for rinsing. This can save around 4000 litres of water per year.

- Switch to a water-saving showerhead and halve your water usage in the shower immediately.

- Install a timer in your shower and spend only five minutes in there. You can save up to 20 litres for each minute less you shower.

- Put a bucket in the bathroom to capture the shower water wasted while the water is warming up. Use this excess water on the garden.

- Turn the tap off when shaving or washing your face and put a plug in the bowl instead. This is just as effective as running water and uses much less.

- Fill the bath to only half or three-quarters. You can save up to 100 litres each bath time.

- Utilise the single flush on a dual-flush toilet or insert a few filled water bottles to reduce the water usage from an older toilet.

- Before you flush, remember the old saying, 'If it's yellow, let it mellow; if it's brown, flush it down'.

In the kitchen

About 10 per cent of our water usage is in the kitchen, and it's also one of the most commonly used social spaces within the home. This provides a great opportunity not only to save water, but also to share your water-saving tips with family members. In this area, being water-wise is all about having an efficient dishwasher and minimising water waste in the sink.

The dishwasher

When purchasing a new dishwasher, choose one that has a high water rating as well as a high energy rating. Both of these labels should be displayed on the dishwasher in the shop. When using your dishwasher, only turn it on when you have a full load and use the rinse-and-hold setting to rinse all your dishes in the meantime, rather than running a tap to clean them. Some dishwashers also have a water-saving, or economy, setting and it's preferable to choose that setting when running the machine. Some of the newer model dishwashers use only 18 litres of water, which is only a little more than if you washed by hand. For more information on purchasing an energy-efficient dishwasher, see **Chapter 8: Appliances and Household Goods**.

The kitchen sink

A great deal of water gets wasted in the kitchen sink when we run the taps to wash our hands, clean vegetables, or rinse plates without considering the amount of water going down the plughole. To avoid this, put a plug in the sink when rinsing; even better, buy a cheap plastic tub that fits into the sink and can be used for rinsing. The water can be re-used within a short period of time and then tipped on the garden. But don't leave the water sitting for too long, as within 24 hours it can become stagnant and unsuitable for secondary uses.

Don't waste precious water rinsing the plates before putting them in the dishwasher. Scrape the vegetable scraps into a small bin that can be tipped into the compost rather than rinsing them down the sink. Always use a sink strainer, as scraps that go down the drain end up clogging up waterways, causing all sorts of problems. In-sink disposal units are not such a great idea as they can consume up to 30 litres of water per day and also get food scraps mixed up in the waterways. Far better to recycle your kitchen scraps immediately by using a compost heap, worm farm, or Bokashi bucket to get rid of them (see **Chapter 7: Recycling**).

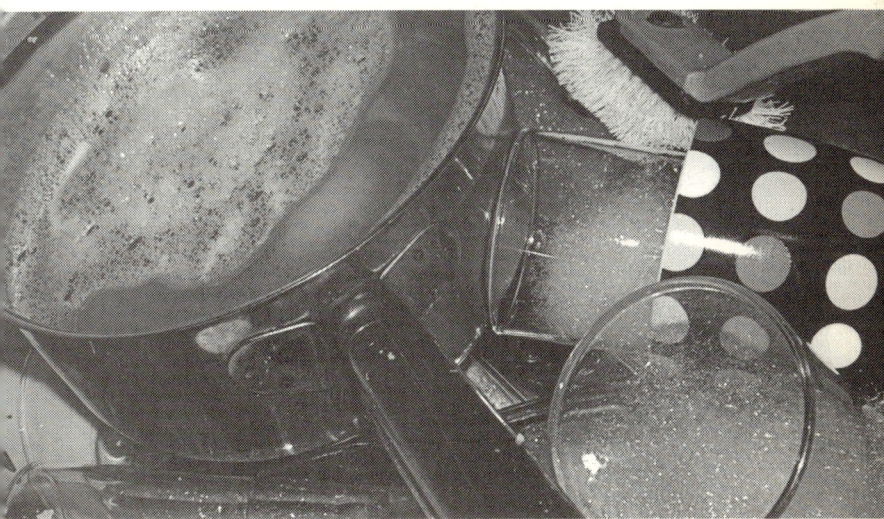

Top Tips for being water wise in the kitchen

- When washing your dishes by hand, half fill your second sink with rinsing water. If you don't have a second sink, stack the washed dishes in a dish rack and rinse them with a kettle of hot water at the end.
- Use only a small amount of dishwashing liquid, and make sure it's biodegradable, so there is less to rinse off at the end.
- When heating your kettle, put in only as much water as needed immediately, which saves on water and electricity.
- Install flow-controlled aerators on your kitchen taps, which can reduce usage by up to 50 per cent.
- Don't use running water to defrost frozen food. Ideally, place food in the fridge to defrost overnight, or put it in a bowl in a sink of warm water, which can then be used for rinsing dishes or general kitchen use.
- Use a half-full sink, or bowl of water, to rinse your fruit and vegetables rather than running a tap continuously to wash them. If you normally rinse under a tap for 3–5 minutes you can save about 40 litres of water. The bowl of water can then be re-used on the garden.
- When boiling water on the stove, always keep the lid on the saucepan. It will save electricity and water.
- Re-use your cooking water (once it's cooled down) for other kitchen uses or on the garden.
- Make sure your water thermostat is not set too high and your pipes are insulated, so water comes through at the correct temperature and can be used immediately.
- You can save water by hand washing, particularly for small loads. An average dishwasher uses up to 35 litres of water, whereas washing by hand will use only 15 litres and much less if you are economical.
- Turning on a tap for a drink and waiting until the water cools during summer can waste up to six litres of water. Instead, fill a bottle with water and keep it in the fridge for when you need it.

In the laundry

Up to 20 per cent of total water usage in the home is in the laundry, and there are plenty of opportunities to cut down on water usage, as well as on detergents and electricity, in this area.

The washing machine

Purchasing an energy-efficient washing machine that uses minimal amounts of water and electricity to do a good job can make the biggest reduction of water usage in the laundry. Again, use the ratings system to point you to the most efficient ones and keep in mind that front-loading machines are generally more water-efficient than top-loading machines. However, there are some efficient top-loaders on the market, and an efficient machine can save you over 50 litres every time you do a wash. For more information on purchasing an energy-efficient washing machine see **Chapter 8: Appliances and Household Goods.**

Top Tips for being water wise in the laundry

- Adjust the water level to suit the size of the load and preferably wait until you have a full load to do a wash. This can save you a huge amount of water and also save on electricity costs.

- If you have only a few items that need washing but need them immediately, it's far more efficient to wash them by hand in a bucket or laundry trough.

- Old washing machines can use up to a bathtub full of water per load, so look at updating your machine if it is more than 10 years old. The efficient models on the market use around 60 litres per load.

- Use the minimal amount of detergent when washing and make sure it's biodegradable, so that if you are re-using the water there will not be chemical run-off.

- When doing a few loads at a time, use the suds-saver option if your machine has one; this will also save on water and detergent.

- Capture the water from your washing machine's rinse cycle with a bucket and use this on the garden, avoiding vegetables that you want to eat raw.

Outdoors

A large portion of our household water usage is outdoors, and much of this can be reduced with smart water-saving techniques and recycling water from indoors to be used outside. There are many easy things to do that will not cost a cent but will save a great deal of money in the long term, as well as drastically reduce your water consumption.

Washing the car

Washing the family car in the driveway and mucking around spraying the kids with the hose used to be an iconic Australian activity. But times have changed and many states have now banned washing the car with a hose, for good reason. You can waste enormous amounts of water using the hose on the car, and it's often impossible to collect the runoff from the driveway. It is far more economical to use a commercial car wash, which has machinery specifically built for washing and which recycles 100 per cent of the water it uses.

There are even some car wash services that use no water at all. Try to go to the car wash when you are out and about already, so you do not burn fuel getting there and back. If a commercial wash isn't practical, re-use a couple of buckets from household use on the car to give it a good wash and recycle your water at the same time.

Pervious pavements

One way to help retain rainwater is to use what is known as pervious pavement for areas such as driveways, car parks, and paths. These allow water to percolate through to the water table below and be available for plants and trees to draw up, rather than simply running off, or remaining stagnant on the ground when it rains. Examples of pervious pavement include gravel and porous asphalt. Also available are eco-pavers that allow water to infiltrate the spaces between the pavers; these were used with great success at Homebush in the villages built for the Olympic Games.

Pools

The backyard pool is another Aussie icon that we are loath to give up and there is currently one pool for every 12 homes. It keeps us cool in the hot months of summer and with global warming, it's likely we're going to be looking for relief in our pools even more than before. But pools are water guzzlers and it's actually far better for the environment to make use of your local public pool than to build a new one at home. In many states you need a permit to build a new pool and there are strong restrictions regarding refilling your pool. If you have a pool or spa already, minimise evaporation by installing a cover for the pool and spa when they're not in use, and ask the kids to minimise their dive bombs and excessive splashing to help out the environment.

The lawn

You may be surprised to know that a lawn is a relatively new addition to our everyday lives. It is actually a luxury associated with increased affluence and leisure time that has been a common feature of the average suburban home only since the 1950s. The lawn comes under harsh criticism for its lack of biodiversity, the large amounts of water needed to maintain it, and the need for both herbicides and regular mowing with machinery that increase smog, use up fossil fuels, and cause noise pollution. All in all, the lawn may be an idea whose time has passed. Why not give up on mowing the lawn and plant some native bushes and grasses that need far less maintenance instead? Think of all the extra time you'll have!

If you are still committed to the lawn, then keep in mind that it is often the most over-watered part of the garden. A lawn needs only 10 millimetres of water, yet most receive far more water than is needed. If water restrictions in your state don't ban watering the lawn, next time you do water place a container on the ground and stop when it is approximately 10 millimetres full. Time how long this takes so you will know the maximum amount of time you need the sprinkler or hose on next time.

The garden

The garden is another area where small changes make a big difference. Many of our gardens contain plants that are inappropriate to our climate and require far more water than is viable. We also tend to water far more than is necessary.

Ideally, the garden should be designed to keep plants with similar water needs together. Rainwater can often be channelled from the gutters and directly to the areas of high water use, which will reduce the need for watering. High water use areas include lawns, fruit trees, vegetable patches, exotic shrubs like azaleas and camellias, and many bulbs. High water use plants often prefer some shelter from wind and don't like too much sunlight.

Watering should be done first thing in the morning or at night, to reduce the loss of water through evaporation. The most efficient method of automatic irrigation is by drippers, which deliver water directly to the roots of your plants. Hand-held hoses are often more efficient than automatic irrigation systems, which make it easy to accidentally over-water by leaving them on too long. A hand-held hose should always be used with a trigger nozzle to reduce water wastage.

In some states, gardens cannot be watered at all. Recycled buckets of water saved from the kitchen, laundry, and shower can be vital in keeping your favourite plants alive.

To keep your soil nutrient-rich and porous, don't apply chemical fertilisers. Instead, use compost from your compost heap and/or liquid drained from a worm farm or Bokashi unit, which makes excellent fertiliser when mixed with water. You can also purchase worm waste from a commercial operation as a natural source of nutrients.

Mulching is also a good way to improve water efficiency by reducing run-off, limiting weed growth, and improving soil conditions. Types of mulch include grass clippings, compost, leaves, torn-up newspapers, bark, woodchips or stones. Some councils even provide free mulch to their residents.

Most native plants need much less water than non-natives and are already adapted to Australian conditions. They also provide habitat for native animals. Look for native plants that tend to grow well in your area, as they will vary throughout the country. Exotic plants from South Africa, California, and other hot countries are also good at coping with minimal amounts of water.

DID YOU KNOW?
Through overuse and extensive farming, the flow of the Snowy River was reduced to such a critical level – about one per cent of its original flow – that drastic measures were needed to restore the flow of the water, and it will never fully recover.

Top Tips for being water wise outdoors

- Use a broom or brush to clean outdoor driveways and pavement areas, instead of hosing.

- If you wash your car or boat at home, try to do so on lawn or bare ground so that the water runs off into the soil, and use a bucket instead of a hose.

- Re-use water from your shower or bath to water the plants or wash the car.

- Don't use garden blowers to clean your outdoor area. They use up fossil fuel, create noise pollution, and only shift the problem to a new area instead of actually cleaning it up.

- Don't make major changes to your garden in summer as the ground is very hard and new plants are more likely to die. Wait until after autumn rains when conditions are more suitable for plant growth.

- The best time to water the garden is early in the morning or at night where you will not lose precious water to evaporation.

- Mulch around your plants to save water and prevent evaporation, as well as the growth of weeds.

- Water the roots of plants, not the leaves, as water will evaporate easily from leaves.

- Less frequent, deep watering is best, as it trains the root systems to be hardy.

Re-using grey water

Grey water is the name given to water that is discharged from showers, washing machines, and dishwashers. Grey water can be re-used in other areas throughout your home for huge water savings. Grey water does not include the water that is flushed through your toilet – for obvious reasons – or from dishwashing, as the cleaning agents and fats in dishwashing water may be unsafe.

By re-using grey water, either to flush the toilet or recycling onto the garden, you can reduce your water consumption by many tens of thousands of litres per year. Grey water recycling can be a simple system of buckets in the shower and kitchen or on the final rinse stage of the laundry cycle, or a more elaborate set-up that requires council approval.

Grey water can contain bacteria that may include disease-carrying organisms. Extreme care needs to be taken to ensure that there is no possibility of grey water being confused with drinking water or of people coming into direct contact with grey water. It also contains organic matter, detergents, soaps, and salts, which can damage the environment. That's why it's vital to use biodegradable, non-phosphorous detergents in your washing machine and on your body, as many of them contain harsh chemicals that can damage the environment if not recycled properly. Plants may be affected in the long term by these chemicals if they aren't treated carefully, not to mention the impact on children or pets that may accidentally come into contact with the grey water.

A more sophisticated method of recycling grey water requires an approved plumbing design and treatment system, which you can easily incorporate into your home when renovating or constructing a new home. This is discussed in **Chapter 9: Building and Renovating.**

Installing water-saving systems

There are many other ways of reducing your mains water consumption when renovating or building a house that may cost a few thousand dollars upfront, but which can make a huge difference to your yearly water costs and greenhouse gas emissions. The installation of many of these systems attracts a government rebate and they will pay for themselves in reduced water charges after a few years of use. For more information on large purchases such as solar water heating systems, rainwater tanks, and installing extensive grey-water and black-water recycling systems, refer to **Chapter 9: Building and Renovating**.

Top Tips for recycling bucketed grey water

- Keep a bucket in the shower to capture the water flow when it is warming up and use it to flush the toilet or on the garden.

- Use a bucket in the kitchen sink to capture vegetable rinse water, but don't re-use dirty dishwashing water.

- Capture the rinse-cycle water from the washing machine by diverting it into a bucket.

- All bucketed grey water that has not been treated through a grey water system should be re-used within 24 hours.

- Don't put grey water on edible plants or fruit.

- Keep grey water away from areas frequented by children and pets.

- Don't use the grey water from nappy washing or from very soiled clothing.

- Don't use grey water if a member of the house has an infectious disease.

- Don't over-water. Excess grey water can clog the soil and create areas of potential slime

6
FOOD

My mother often reminds me that when she was growing up in Belfast during World War II, nobody was concerned about what they ate. Nobody counted calories or checked product labels, nor did they worry about losing weight. Their major concern was having enough food to survive. My grandmother cooked simple meals for the family of eight children, plus parents and grandparents, using whatever seasonal produce was available, which often wasn't much. Meat was scarce, a few squares of chocolate were an occasional treat, and if they nagged enough the kids might occasionally be given a fresh lobster by the local fisherman when he brought his catch in.

Eating has now become a great deal more complicated. Conspicuous consumption is always on the menu, with supermarkets and takeaway joints open 24 hours a day. We're always in a hurry and pressed for time, so we often grab fast food instead of making a meal ourselves.

When buying groceries, it's difficult to choose among the cornucopia of products on the shelves and we end up taking junk foods that are familiar because of excessive advertising and product placement.

To be aware of the food chain and be more disciplined about what goes into our mouths is important if we aim to minimise our negative impact on the planet. A whole host of factors and often a long journey have contributed to getting food from its original state and onto our plate. If we don't pay attention to this process, we are in danger of not only increasing the human-induced level of greenhouse gases, but also condoning bad farming practices, and even jeopardising our health.

You're going to hear a lot more about ethical eating as people wise up to what's on their supermarket shelves. Ethical eating involves becoming aware of a whole swathe of different issues including factory farming, genetically modified crops, organic food, free-range eggs, vegetarianism and, of particular importance in the context of global warming, 'food miles'. Often foods have travelled enormous distances to get to our supermarket, and sometimes the cheapest product is the one that has travelled the furthest and used the greatest amount of fossil fuels. It's cheaper because the farmer who produces the original product has been paid a ridiculously low price for it and many of the external costs have not been factored in. If a product was truly priced it would include the cost of all the side effects of producing it – the usage of fossil fuels, pollution, environmental degradation, community impact and, in the case of animal products, outright cruelty.

Ethical eating is a complicated issue that requires awareness of numerous different factors while also recognising there are no hard and fast rules, and that it's virtually impossible to know that everything you eat has been ethically produced. It would drive you insane ensuring that every single piece of food that went into your mouth has satisfied these stringent requirements, unless of course you are fortunate enough to live on a self-sufficient property where everything you eat has been grown either by yourself or by local producers whose farming practices you have closely scrutinised.

The power in the concept of ethical eating is that it encourages us to ask questions and demand more information about where, how, and by whom our food is produced. Questions to ask are: Where has this product come from? What kind of regulations regarding sustainable farming practices have been abided by? Has it been processed in that place or travelled elsewhere to be processed? How did it then travel to our supermarket shelves? How much packaging does it have and is that packaging recyclable?

Maybe you would make a different decision in relation to purchasing a particular food item if you knew the answers to just some of these questions. Knowledge reduces the baffling array of products thrust in our faces to a more intelligible perspective and helps place the ethics of the company selling the product on display. It allows us to recognise that the factors contributing to this product and its price are influenced by international and national economics, politics and regulations. For example, many companies source their raw products from countries that have far looser restrictions regarding sustainable farming practices than Australia; they then ship the product here to be processed or packaged, which allows them to say that the product has been made in Australia.

One in three children in Australia now have at least one allergy, ranging from mild to life-threatening,[30] and surely this must in some way be related to the increasingly toxic lifestyle of the 21st century. The vast array of seemingly harmless chemicals present in our food and our daily lives may not be a problem individually, but when combined, day after day, from numerous food, household and environmental sources, they become dangerous to our health and the health of the planet. While most of us can't avoid the effects of pollution or the stresses of city living, we can control what we put in our own and our children's bodies, thereby minimising the amount of chemicals our already over-stressed systems are forced to process.

To buy sustainably farmed produce is often more expensive, because it is a true cost that takes into consideration the external factors. Organic and local farming is not as intensive as factory farming, which is controlled by large corporations and benefits from economies of scale. Organic farms don't produce as much food, but nor do they do anywhere near as much environmental damage. While there is no doubt that you will pay more for organic produce, the benefits to your health over the long term are generally agreed to be substantial – there are as yet no objective studies on the long-term effects of chemicals in our foods – and the minimisation of harm to the environment over the long term is, without question, highly beneficial. If you can't get organic produce, the fresh fruit and vegetables that are in season in your area are usually cheap and tasty, so they are also a good option. Most importantly, when purchasing either organic or local fruit and vegetables you reduce the greenhouse gas emissions generated to provide you with your food.

We can no longer be like my mother's generation, where there was no need to concern ourselves with what we ate or where it came from, because the vast majority of food available then was fresh, local produce. Now, if we close our eyes to the realities of feeding a planet of billions of people and the multinational profit-driven organisations that seek to take charge of making that happen, then we are naïve at best and more likely in denial. We owe it to the planet and ourselves to become more aware of what we put in our mouths.

This chapter will cover some of the issues to consider in navigating the minefield that is eating today, as well as provide you with resources to obtain further information. At the end of the chapter is a list of top tips that helps to simplify the complexities and will be of benefit in the supermarket.

Remember that the vast majority of us cannot possibly eat ethically all the time. But the more we choose foods with an awareness of where they have come from, the more we create a demand for farming that will not come at such a great external cost, and the better our bodies will feel about the food we use as fuel.

Food miles

'Food miles' relates to the distance that a piece of food has travelled to arrive on your plate, and how it has travelled – whether by boat, truck, rail, or air. Often the distances and the countries of origin will surprise you. Most canned tomatoes in the supermarket today come from Italy, and our canned asparagus is from Peru. Almost all canned tuna has come from Thailand, and mussels have travelled all the way from China.

The ability to consume a wide variety of foods from all over the world may be fantastic for satisfying our demanding palates and our dinner party menus, but the increasing distance that food travels adds substantially to global warming, lowers food quality, and hurts local farmers.

Australia imports only about 10 per cent of its fresh fruit and vegetables, and due to our varied climate we can grow most fruit and vegetables year round. However, the vastness of our continent also means that food is transported great distances to service different regions. According to the *Sunday Age*, more than 167.3 million tonnes of food is transported around the country every year at a distance of 2.5 billion kilometres. Eighty-five per cent of this travelling is done by road, and makes a huge contribution to greenhouse gas emissions.[31] So an increase in the price of petrol has the potential to make a big difference to the price of your fruit and vegetables. Not only is this bad news for the environment and global warming, but it also imposes harsh conditions on the fruits and vegetables that get to your table. For example, tomatoes are often picked green, and farmers now favour robust varieties that have sacrificed taste, because they are better able to sustain the long journeys without bursting. They may arrive at your home intact, but they sure don't taste as tomatoes used to taste.

Ghost acres

Part of the problem with food miles is the phenomenon of 'ghost acres' – vast tracts of land devoted to growing food (usually soy or corn) for factory-farmed animals. It is estimated there are already 44 million ghost acres in

Thailand, and huge areas of Brazilian rainforest have also been cleared to grow food for grain-fed, factory-farmed animals. The true cost of exploiting these countries and their land, along with the cost of shipping these grains to the country breeding the animals, is never calculated in the price that the customer pays. Tim Lang of the Centre for Food Policy states, 'In Brazil alone, the equivalent of 5.6 million acres of land is used to grow soya beans for animals in Europe. These "ghost acres" belie the so-called efficiency of hi-tech agriculture.'[32] As the cost of land in developed countries increases, it seems likely that multinational corporations will use more and more 'ghost acres'.

Buy locally and seasonally

To combat the negative impact of 'food miles' and 'ghost acres', it makes sense to buy products that have been produced locally and, in the case of fruit and vegetables, are in season. Most city dwellers have no local farmers, but they can still be conscious of buying produce that has been created in their own state or at least in Australia, where excessive resources have not been used to create or transport the product. In the supermarket we now have fruits and vegetables that have travelled more than the average person, apples that have been in cold storage for months then coated with wax to give them a shiny glow, and tomatoes that have been grown hydroponically and sprayed with a cocktail of fertilisers. Whenever possible, it is best to avoid these in favour of seasonal, local produce. Local fruit and vegetables in season are cheaper, readily accessible and probably tastier, being close in proximity and time to where they were picked.

The concept of buying locally also aligns with the philosophy of 'think globally, act locally' by reinforcing the importance of supporting your local greengrocer and your local producers rather than giving your money to a national or multinational corporation. In regards to minimising your footprint, if you walk to the local store you use less fossil fuel than if you drive your car to a distant supermarket to get better savings. Of course, this is clearly not possible for many people who live in the country or too far away to walk to the nearest shops,

> **THE 100-MILE DIET**
>
> In 2004, two Canadians pledged to only eat food that had been grown within 100 miles (160 kilometres) of their home. They did it for an entire year, and by promoting their success have started a movement of 'locavores' who are committed to eating local produce, wherever they live. Not an easy assignment, but when you consider that the average meal in North America may have travelled 2500 kilometres to get to the table, it's an appealing concept. To find out more about the diet and get tips about eating local, go to **www.100milediet.org**

but it's still true that you minimise your emissions by shopping as close to home as possible.

However, as Peter Singer and Jim Mason point out in their book, *The Ethics of What We Eat*, buying locally may not always be the best option in our complicated world. Local vegetables may have been grown with artificial heat or light, thereby using a large amount of fossil fuel. Driving to numerous small, local farms may use more fuel than going to one supermarket and buying what is available there. Buying a food such as rice from a country that has the climate and water resources for it may be more environmentally sustainable than buying this same product grown in Australia, where scarce water resources are used to irrigate rice crops. Therefore, this is not a hard and fast rule, but in general it is best to support local farmers and growers if you live in a region where this is relevant, and to buy produce that is in season with the local weather conditions.

Farmers' markets

Farmers' markets are booming all over Australia. They provide a fabulous opportunity to purchase locally grown products from farms whose small size enables them to avoid the damaging, mass-production methods of large farms. At a farmers' market you will meet the people who have actually grown the produce and they will tell you what pesticides and fertilisers they use, when the produce is picked, and how fresh it is. Farmers' markets are now regularly held in all cities in Australia and many country towns. To find out where and when your local farmers' markets are held, contact your local council or visit the website of the Farmers' Markets Association at **www.farmersmarkets.org.au**

Water filters

Although our tap water is treated to remove contaminants, these methods don't remove all impurities and doesn't take into account the fact that you may have old pipes to your home. Therefore, it's worth buying some sort of water filter to remove any impurities and chemicals that may have found their way into your tap water. Many types are available, ranging from cheap jugs with filters that can be replaced every two months, to more expensive systems that are attached to your tap or water outlet. It's also far better for the environment to have a water filter at home and take a refillable water bottle with you when you go out, rather than constantly buying bottled water. Only a small percentage of water bottles are recycled; most of them end up in landfill.

Seasonal fruit and vegetable guide

These represent the peak season, when there is a cheap, plentiful supply; it may vary depending on where you live in Australia.

SUMMER
FRUITS: apricot, banana, blackberry, blueberry, boysenberry, cherry, currant, fig, gooseberry, grapes, loganberry, lychee, mango, nectarine, rockmelon, watermelon, nashi pear, nectarine, nuts (almond, hazelnut, macadamia, peanut, pecan, pistachio, walnut), Valencia orange, passionfruit, peach, pear (red sensation, Williams), plum, raspberry, strawberry, star fruit, tomato.

VEGETABLES: capsicum, celery, red onion, eggplant, garlic, ginger, okra, leek, squash, sweet corn, zucchini.

AUTUMN
FRUITS: apple (Fuji, Gala, Golden Delicious, Granny Smith, Jonathan, Pink Lady, Red Delicious), lime, honey murcot, mandarin, mango, honeydew melon, papaya, pear (Beurre Bosc, Corella, Packham, Red Sensation), persimmon, tomato.

VEGETABLES: celery, leek, mushroom (field, pine, Slippery Jack), olive, parsnip, red onion, swede, turnip, zucchini.

WINTER
FRUITS: apple (Fuji, Gala, Golden Delicious, Granny Smith, Pink Lady, Red Delicious), Ellendale and Imperial mandarin, navel orange, pear (Beurre Bosc, Corella, Packham), star fruit, tamarillo, tangelo.

VEGETABLES: artichoke, avocado, beetroot, broccoli, brussels sprout, cabbage, cauliflower, celery, fennel, garlic, kale, olive, parsnip, swede, turnip.

SPRING
FRUITS: apple (Fuji, Golden Delicious, Granny Smith, Lady Williams, Pink Lady, Red Delicious, Sundowner), pink grapefruit, blood orange, Valencia orange, papaya, pear (Beurre Bosc, Corella), strawberry, tamarillo, tangelo.

VEGETABLES: asparagus, broad bean, broccoli, fennel, leek, mushroom (morel), pea (green, snap, snow), sweet corn, zucchini.

YEAR ROUND
FRUITS: grapefruit, pineapple.

VEGETABLES: Asian greens, green bean, carrot, lemon, lettuce, mushroom (button, cup, flat, oyster, shiitake), onion, potato, pumpkin, rhubarb, silver beet, spinach, sweet potato.

Organic and biodynamic produce

DID YOU KNOW?
In 2004 *New Scientist* reported that 'Organic farming increases biodiversity at every level of the food chain – all the way from lowly bacteria to mammals. This is the conclusion of the largest review ever done of studies from around the world comparing organic and conventional agriculture.'[33]

The demand for organic produce has strengthened in the past few years and supermarkets now cater to our needs with small organic sections of fruit, vegetables, and other products. While most of us are not able to supply all our daily food needs with organic produce, the more organic food you can consume, the fewer chemicals you are ingesting, the greater the nutrients in the food you are eating, and the more you are helping the organic industry to grow. You are also minimising the greenhouse gas emissions generated to produce your food.

Organic fruit and vegetables are generally grown locally and in season because they cannot be transported very far and do not have the preservatives that conventional produce does. And yes, organic produce does cost more than conventional produce – sometimes only a few cents more, but at times up to double the price. However, it's worthwhile knowing that your food has not been doused with fertilisers, pesticides and other chemicals to preserve it, and that the land used to grow it has been farmed sustainably. But the very best reason for buying organic is that it tastes better! Surely it's worth paying extra for all those benefits?

Biodynamic farming was pioneered by Austrian philosopher Rudolf Steiner, and has stricter requirements than those for organic produce. It emphasises the importance of ecological harmony and environmental sustainability, and food is grown with particular composts, preparations, and natural activating substances. You can purchase some biodynamic products in the supermarket, and numerous biodynamic products are available in health food stores.

Supermarkets now offer many packaged goods, such as pasta, canned tomatoes, tea, and soy milk, which are organic. Many of these have been produced overseas and their food miles may well undo in many minds the goodness that can be derived from purchasing organic. We all need to make up our own minds as to which is more important to us, organic or local, and whether the pesticides potentially sprayed on the food are worse than the greenhouse gases emitted in transporting them to us. There are no easy answers, and as I said in the opening paragraphs, it is impossible to make a perfectly ethical decision regarding our food every time. An awareness of these issues and general adherence to these principles is more important overall.

Finally, you need to exercise caution when buying organic or biodynamic, because there is not one governing organic body. Many products are labelled 'natural' or 'chemical free' or sometimes even 'organic', when in fact they are not. However, there are some accreditation bodies that do have standards you can trust. The Australian Quarantine and Inspection Service (AQIS) is the government authority which verifies that a certification organisation has complied with the National Standard for Organic and Biodynamic Produce. Imported products have a variety of different certification methods, depending on where they came from. But when it comes to Australian produce, the logos assure you that the product and the land it came from is certified organic or biodynamic, and grown without chemicals and pesticides.

> Look for logos that certify produce as biodynamic or organic

> Buy organic fruit and vegetables and certified organic or biodynamic products wherever possible, particularly if they have been produced locally.

Grow your own

Instead of buying all your fruit, vegetables and herbs, why not grow some of your own organic produce? Nothing tastes as good as a vegetable or piece of fruit you have just picked. A simple veggie patch near the house can be a wonderful way to supplement your kitchen, relieve stress with some light gardening, and consume mulch from your compost heap. Even in a block of flats, it's easy to grow a few herbs in a box on the windowsill. They will taste a thousand times better than the overpriced hydroponic herbs you get from the supermarket. Not only will you save on the pesticides, herbicides, and transport emissions from a conventional supermarket, you will also save plenty of money as you eat from your garden. If you're feeling adventurous, you can even have a few chickens in a small backyard that will eat weeds, worms, and household scraps, while providing you with organic, free-range eggs. There are plenty of books on organic gardening that will give you the basics of growing your own. A good online resource is the Gardening Australia website at **www.abc.net.au/gardening**

> The best chicken eggs to purchase are free-range and certified organic, biodynamic or from a certified free-range farm.

Free-range eggs

I was staggered to discover that 85 per cent of Australian eggs are still farmed in battery cages where the chickens have no more than 550 centimetres (less than two sheets of A4 paper) per bird, and where de-beaking (cutting off the end of the bird's beak so it cannot peck) is performed on all chickens without anaesthetic.[34] The standard industry practice for producing eggs causes a great deal of unnecessary stress and pain to the chicken, and it follows that the eggs purchased from those chickens are not going to be the most healthy for you. In the United Kingdom since 2002, two major supermarket chains – Marks and Spencer and Waitrose – have sold only free-range eggs. Australian supermarkets are not there yet, but the more consumers that demand free-range the more likely it is that they will also cut out the battery cage eggs.

Even RSPCA-endorsed, barn-laid eggs have had serious ethical concerns raised about them by various animal liberation groups. The RSPCA has signed an agreement with Pace Farms, the biggest egg producer in Australia, to endorse their barn-laid eggs, purportedly produced under ethical conditions, and the RSPCA in turn receives two cents from every egg purchase. The media release from Coles and the RSPCA says that these birds have 'room to stretch their wings' but with a code of practice of seven birds per square metre they certainly don't have room to stretch them far.[35] There is no requirement against de-beaking and while there must be ventilation and daylight in the barn, the birds are not free to go outside. They are confined to a large barn with thousands of other chickens and a few windows to allow in daylight for the entirety of their short lives.

The majority of Pace Farms' chickens are housed in their large-scale factory farming system, where they are living under far worse conditions than the more fortunate RSPCA-endorsed chickens. In addition to concerns regarding the treatment of the barn chickens, it does not

> To find out what happens to meat before it gets to our table, read *The Ethics of What We Eat* by Peter Singer and Jim Moran, which will open your eyes to the business of slaughtering animals on a mass scale.

seem ethical to support a company that produces any eggs under factory farming conditions, whether they are endorsed by the RSPCA or not.

Eggs are advertised on many carton labels as being from grain-fed or vegetarian-fed chickens. Unfortunately, the grain that many of these chickens are fed may be genetically engineered (GE) soy, which is currently being trialled in Australia and grown in many other parts of the world. Under current Australian labelling laws, meat, dairy, and egg products do not need to be labelled when the animal they have come from has been fed on genetically engineered crops.

By far the best option to choose is organic, free-range eggs from chickens that are allowed to roam and eat worms, bugs, seeds, and other things they would normally scavenge. As free-range production is primarily self regulatory – which means the producer may not have to prove the actual living conditions of their chickens – it is best to choose eggs that have been accredited by the Free Range Farmers Association or by FREPA (Free Range Eggs and Poultry Australia), or are certified organic or biodynamic. Those farms will have had been inspected to ensure that the chickens receive non-GE feed and live in surroundings that allow them space, the ability to peck, and room to truly stretch their wings. There are many free-range farms but few have bothered to go through the stringent requirements of bird care required by the accreditation process, so choose wherever possible those that have been externally audited and become accredited organic. There will be a logo on the egg carton confirming they are accredited.

> Buy organic or biodynamic meats where possible and reduce your meat consumption overall to offset the increased cost of meat in your diet.

Cruelty-free meat and poultry

Beef and lamb have been farmed on Australian land for the past 200 years and have been an important foundation of our economy. However, there have been huge consequences for the land as a result of unsustainable farming practices, with soil erosion, desertification, and nutrient loss big issues for today's farmers. Many of the cattle and sheep farmed in Australia for eating have a relatively peaceful existence before they are sent to the slaughterhouse; however, it is there that many of them are fed grain intensively to bulk up their weight and are kept in confined spaces so they don't burn calories. Most animals are required by law to be stunned before slaughter, but sometimes this is not successful and they experience a great deal of suffering before they die.

A feedlot is the most intensive form of cattle farming, where cattle are kept in confined spaces and fed large amounts of high-protein grain to bulk them up for market. According to the Meat and Livestock Association of Australia (MLA), there are around 600 accredited feedlots in Australia, which can process numbers of almost 860 000 cattle at any one time.[36] MLA proudly states that supermarkets currently draw 40-50 per cent of their meat supplies from feedlots, and a large percentage of restaurants also source their meat from feedlot cattle. This is projected to increase over the next five years.[37] Thus in all likelihood the meat you purchase at the supermarket has come from cattle raised in intensive feedlots and fed large amounts of high-protein feed, which is unnatural for stomachs used to processing grass, in order to fatten them up. Most Australian cattle are fed for 70 days in feedlots, although animals for export markets are kept in the feedlots for 150 days to make the meat marbled and fatty, which is popular in Japan and Korea.[38]

Veal is one of the worst meats you could possibly eat from an ethical perspective. Young male veal calves are removed from their mothers on their first day of life, placed in a narrow crate where they cannot walk, deprived of any kind of bedding and kept deliberately anemic so their flesh is white, which attracts higher prices.[39] Nobody who aspires to being an ethical eater can possibly convince himself that eating veal is a justifiable practice. In fact, it's a particularly cruel and intensively farmed meat.

Piggeries have also received a bad report card and a great deal of negative publicity in Australia. Pigs in factory farming conditions are kept in stalls so small that they can barely move. Breeding sows have it even worse, cramped in tiny stalls with all their babies piled in on top of them and no room to move or turn around. As soon as the

DID YOU KNOW?

One calorie of animal protein requires more than 10 times as much fossil fuel input, thereby releasing more than 10 times as much carbon dioxide into the environment, as one calorie of plant protein.

NAVIGATING THE SUPERMARKET

■ Steer towards the organic section first for your fruits, vegetables and packaged goods. Most large supermarkets now have their own organic 'house' brand.

■ If the fruit and vegetables you want are not available as organics, choose those that are in season and locally produced.

■ Avoid the aisles with highly processed junk foods and drinks. Out of sight is out of mind.

■ Choose the organic meat options, rather than conventionally produced.

■ Read the ingredients – avoid excessively chemical ingredients, look for GE-free soy products, and avoid products with sugar added.

piglets are weaned, the sow is made pregnant again and most have around eight litters over a four-year period. In order to avoid supporting this highly intensive method of pork production you can now purchase free-range pork and bacon, which is a far more ethical option.

What about chicken meat, the ubiquitous, cheap source of protein on every menu? Most chickens have been raised in factory farms just as terrible as the egg producers, if not the same farms, and often they are pumped full of growth hormones and food additives to increase their bulk. Being such a small animal, the accumulation of all these chemicals within their meat is even greater. There are also concerns from environmental groups that Australian chickens are being fed GE soy and corn shipped in from overseas because it is significantly cheaper than Australian feed. Whether this is true or not, there is no doubt that the best chicken meat to eat is from free-range, organic farms.

Finding organic meats

Catering to consumer demand, supermarkets have begun stocking free-range and organic chicken and other meats. The cost can range from just a dollar or two more per kilo to two or three times the price. It's worth it. Farmers' markets are also a good option for obtaining organic meats or at least produce from small-scale farms where the animals are raised under better conditions. Most health food stores stock, or can order in, organically and biodynamically bred chicken, beef, pork, and lamb, ensuring that the animals have led lives with no chemical additions, no GE feed, and minimum suffering on their way to your table. It is far preferable to reduce your meat consumption and eat only meat that you know has been organically produced than to continue to eat meat produced under standard industry conditions.

Dairy products

Unfortunately, the dairy industry has similar problems to intensive animal farming for meat. The animals may live in very cramped conditions and be given antibiotics to prevent infections or make them produce more milk, and the cows are made pregnant every year so as to increase milk production. As soon as the calf is born, it is taken away from the mother and fed formula milk, and the cow's milk is used to feed us. Most male dairy calves have only a short, painful life as a vealer to look forward to. Wherever possible, it is better to buy your milk, cheese and yoghurt from certified organic or biodynamic dairy farmers, or from small farms where you know the cows live relatively peaceful lives.

Seafood

A staggering 71 per cent of the seafood Australians consume does not come from local waters.[40] It is frozen and imported, and may come from countries with less strict guidelines about harvesting the fish, including allowing the use of dragnets. In 2005, the global fishing fleet was 2.5 times larger than could be sustained by what the oceans produce,[41] 52 per cent of global fish stocks are fully exploited, and 24 per cent are overexploited or recovering from extreme exploitation.[42] Some deep-sea fish, such as the orange roughy and the Chilean sea bass (also known as the Patagonian toothfish), which can live up to 150 years, are already so over-fished globally that their stocks may never recover. Yet they are readily available from your local fishmonger.

Many fishing methods capture huge numbers of other sea creatures as 'by-catch'. Sharks, dolphins, and endangered sea turtles are thrown overboard once sorted, usually dying or dead. Another concern is bottom trawling, where nets weighted with pieces of iron are dragged along the sea floor, capturing everything in their path, often destroying coral formations and making the area uninhabitable for the many sea creatures that live there.

Although Australia has some sustainable fishing regulations in place, a large percentage of the fish we eat in cans or fresh has been caught in countries, such as Thailand, that have fewer regulations about their fishing practices and where overfishing is harming their coastal communities.

In Australia, we also have a great deal of farmed fish. Aquaculture uses large netted cages similar in style to feedlots, only underwater. The effluent from these sea-

QUESTIONS TO ASK YOUR FISH MERCHANT

If the answer to any of these questions is **'yes'**, then choose a different fish.

1. Is the species long-lived (over 20 years), slow growing or a deep-sea species (found below 500 metres)? This makes them extremely vulnerable and less likely to recover from overfishing.

2. Is it a shark or ray? (They may be known as flake.) Sharks and rays are slow-growing, long-lived and produce few young. They are extremely vulnerable to overfishing, and several species are threatened with extinction.

3. Is the species imported? Only choose imported seafood if it comes from environmentally accredited fisheries.

(Information courtesy of Australian Marine Conservation Society) cages pollutes coastal waterways and escaped fish may threaten local eco-systems. Large quantities of wild fish are caught in order to make fish meal, which is then fed to the caged fish. The quantity of fish-feed used is far greater than the amount of human food they provide. Farmed salmon are also given far more antibiotics than any other meat source, which is really not an appetising thought.

DID YOU KNOW?
It takes up to 12 kilograms of wild fish to produce one kilogram of farmed tuna, and up to four kilograms of wild fish to produce one kilogram of sea-caged Atlantic salmon.

The Australian Marine Conservation Society has produced a Sustainable Seafood Guide as well as a pocket guide to reduce the confusion that can occur when trying to buy sustainable seafood. You can order one by calling **1800 066 299** or going to **www.amcs.org.au**

The Marine Stewardship Council (MSC) is an independent, non-profit organisation that currently provides the only international recognised standard of environmental practices for wild capture fisheries. Its blue product label ensures that seafood has come from a well-managed fishery that practises sustainable fishing with minimal harm to other sea creatures and the marine ecosystem. By March 2007, only 22 fisheries had been certified to the MSC standard, but the produce from these fisheries amounts to over 600 products worldwide. In Australia, some products by John West, Talley's, Sealord and Bird's Eye carry the blue product endorsement from the MSC and are a far more sustainable choice when it comes to seafood for your dollar. For more information on ethical fishing practices and products with the blue eco-label go to **www.msc.org**

>Look for the MSC logo on your canned seafood.

OVER-FISHED SPECIES TO AVOID
- **Blue warehou** – also known as trevally, seam bream, snotty trevalla
- **Commercial scallop** – also known as Tasmanian scallop, southern scallop
- **Eastern gemfish** – also known as hake, king couta, silver kingfish
- **Orange Roughy** – also known as deep sea perch, sea perch
- **Redfish** – also known as nannygai, red schnapper
- **School shark** – also known as flake, snapper shark, tope
- **Silver trevally** – also known as silver bream, white trevally
- **Southern bluefin tuna** – also known as tuna
- **Deepwater sharks** – also known as also known as 'flake', white fillet
- **Oreos** – also known as deep sea dory, dory

(Information courtesy of Australian Marine Conservation Society)

Processed food

Many resources go into creating every piece of food we eat, but foods that are closest to nature have less processing and therefore use less resources. So it is best to buy grains, meat, and vegetables and do your own cooking wherever possible, rather than buying packaged or pre-cooked foods. It also seems to be the case that the more processed a food is, the more packaging it has, and so it is far more damaging for the environment, both in the amount of fossil fuel used to create the packaging and in the disposal of waste when the packaging is thrown away.

Artificial colourings and preservatives

Additives in our food and drinks introduce chemicals into the body and some of them, such as the artificial sweetener aspartame, have been linked to serious health concerns. Not only are they bad for our health, but they are also bad for the environment both in manufacture and when they come out of our bodies as waste and pollute the waterways. We are fortunate in Australia because it's a government requirement to label ingredients in food. Checking the ingredients list on a product before you buy is a really good habit to get into. You'd be surprised how many of the products you consider to be completely natural actually have added sweeteners, colours, and flavours to make them look good, last longer, and taste more appealing – not to mention more addictive. Avoid foods and drinks with lots of added sugar and salt, and particularly reject foods that have lots of synthetic additives including glutamates, such as monosodium glutamate, and sulphites. These ingredients do not provide any helpful nutrients to your body and could well do significant harm in the long run.

> Check the ingredients list on the packaged or canned goods you purchase. Reject artificial sweeteners or too many chemical names and numbers.

Fairtrade products

Fairtrade is a growing international movement to ensure that producers in poor countries receive adequate payment for their products, rather than being exploited by the vagaries of international markets and the buying power of multinationals. The Fairtrade label is licensed by Fairtrade Labelling Organizations International (FLO), based in Germany. It maintains a register of certified producer co-operatives and associations throughout the world and ensures that minimum standards are maintained at Fairtrade farms. The payment the farmers receive for their goods covers the cost of production as well as providing a living income, long-term contracts, and development support for their business. The price often differs substantially from the current market price, which is influenced by international market fluctuations, but it ensures that the farmers are able to survive on what they earn.

> Buy fairly traded products where available, particularly Fairtrade coffee, which is now available in major supermarkets and coffee shops.

In the past decade, the Fairtrade movement has really taken off, particularly in the United Kingdom. It started with Green & Black's chocolate, but has now spread to many more products. Coffee has become by far the most successful Fairtrade product. In December 2001, the international coffee price crashed to a 30-year low, and since then farmers have been forced to sell their coffee for a great deal less than it costs them to produce. According to Oxfam, of the total value of the coffee market, only 10 per cent went to coffee-producing countries in 2002. The rest went to a few large multinationals.[43] Most farmers working the land to produce coffee do not even have enough money to feed their family, while the three dollars we pay for a latte in Australia often only helps to boost the profits of multinational corporations.

Fairtrade products are available in Oxfam shops throughout Australia and New Zealand, and supermarkets such as Coles and Woolworths now sell Fairtrade coffee. A number of retailers and cafes throughout Australia stock Fairtrade products, and you can locate those near you by going to **www.oxfam.org.au/campaigns/mtf/fairtrade**

You can also find out more about the fair trade campaign at the Fair Trade Association of Australia and New Zealand: **www.fta.org.au**

Genetically modified food

Genetically engineered (GE) ingredients are sneaking into our foods as multinational corporations continue to look for ways to increase profits. Genetic engineering takes genes from one organism and inserts them into another to create a new hybrid organism that supposedly defeats the inherent weaknesses of the original. Genes from bacteria, viruses, plants, and animals are inserted into canola, corn, soybeans, and cotton to make these crops more productive and resistant to disease. They are being grown as a US$44 billion crop industry in five main countries – the United States, Canada, Brazil, China, and Argentina. These crops, which are known as 'genetically modified organisms' or 'GMOs', are processed into foods and sold all over the world. Little scientific research has been done on the long-term impact of these crops, not only on the environment but also upon humans, so they are in fact a giant experiment on humanity. In addition, GE products once released into the environment are very difficult to control; they may reproduce forever, thereby developing a life of their own far beyond their original use.

There have already been numerous problems with GE canola, which was recently trialled in Australia, where farmers near to the GE crops had their own crops contaminated.[44] There are currently no controls put in place by the government or compensation for farmers whose crops have been compromised, and this is a very worrying situation.[45]

How will you know if a product has genetically engineered ingredients?

GE ingredients are currently hidden in many foods coming from overseas, and it's also possible they are being shipped in and fed to Australian livestock that produce meat, eggs, and milk. Under current labelling laws, only foods in which GE proteins can be detected need to be labelled as GE, and there are many exemptions including all bakery, restaurant and takeaway food, highly refined foods such as oils and processed foods, and foods made of ingredients from animals fed GE food. That's a long

> **Look for labels that state the product does not have GE ingredients or is GMO-free, and support companies that publicly state they don't use GE ingredients.**

SEED SAVERS

Concerned with the loss of traditional fruit and vegetable varieties, the Seed Savers network are strong advocates for retaining traditional or 'heirloom' seeds and plants, thereby educating people and protecting cultural diversity in plants. The Australian website has a host of information on heirloom seeds: **www.seedsavers.net**

list of exemptions! The most common products with GE ingredients come from imported canola, corn, and soy products, as well as local and imported cottonseed. Processed foods that have been imported from the United States or China using these ingredients, or made in Australia from imported ingredients, are most at risk. The reality is that you can't always know if a food has GE ingredients, but many companies now promote the fact that their products are GE-free, so look for labelling to that effect. Greenpeace has also created a list of companies that don't use GE ingredients at **www.truefood.org.au**

> When eating out, ask your waiter about the origins and farming practices used on your food. If in doubt, eat the vegetarian option.

Eating out

Attempting to eat ethically while dining out can be difficult at best and almost impossible in certain towns. However, some restaurants do promote products on their menu that are organic and sustainably produced. Many restaurants also focus on sourcing as much fresh, locally produced food as they can because they know that it tastes better and people ask for it. Don't be afraid to question your waiter about the origin of the produce on the menu. He or she may not know and will have to refer back to the kitchen, which is great, because it makes the chef aware that people are concerned about the origins of their food. The more we ask for organic, free-range, and sustainably produced food, the more likely we are to obtain it. If in doubt, eat the vegetarian option on the menu, which is most likely to have originated close to home.

The Slow Food movement

In 1986 in Italy, a group of concerned local citizens protested against the opening of another McDonald's restaurant. This was the beginning of the Slow Food movement, which is now an international organisation with over 700 groups worldwide. Their aim is to protect the pleasure of eating well from being smothered by fast food culture. Slow Food groups promote gastronomic culture, develop taste education, and most important for the environment, they conserve agricultural biodiversity and protect traditional foods at the risk of extinction.

They have their own publishing company, Slow Food Editore, which publishes over 60 titles including the famous Slow food: the case for taste by Carlo Petrini, President of the Slow Food movement.

In 2003, the Slow Food Foundation for Biodiversity was created. This is a non-profit, independent organisation that is concerned with protection of seed diversity. They claim that 30 000 vegetable varieties have been lost in the last century, with 75 per cent of European food diversity and 93 per cent of American food diversity lost since 1900. Australia has a number of Slow Food groups, and the largest Slow Food festival has been running in Victoria since 2005 with a two-week program from late August. For more information visit **www.atasteofslow.com.au**

DID YOU KNOW?
It takes 1350 litres of water to produce one kilogram of wheat, but it takes 16 000 litres of water to produce one kilogram of beef!

Become a vegetarian

Do you want to really make a huge difference to your greenhouse gas emissions? Then become a vegetarian. Global meat consumption has increased fivefold in the past 50 years as more and more people can afford to eat meat. This is a huge industry that has an enormous negative impact on the planet.

Animal agriculture produces more than 100 million tonnes of methane per year, created by animals passing gas and producing manure. Methane is one of the major greenhouse gases having a negative impact on climate change; in fact it is responsible for nearly as much global warming as all other non-carbon-dioxide greenhouse gases put together. Some people say that it is even more potent than carbon dioxide in causing global warming.

The mass use of land for large-scale livestock farming also has other negative effects. In the United States, 80 per cent of all agricultural land is used to raise animals for food and to grow the grain that feeds them. This is an enormous overuse of resources as well as a cause of deforestation, land clearing, and soil erosion. Mass agriculture uses large amounts of fossil fuels in the machinery that works the land, and transportation over large distances of both animal feed and meat products also takes its toll on the environment and produces excessive greenhouse gas emissions. Chemical fertilisers and pesticides sprayed on crops used for animal feed further pollute the environment – and the crops themselves – with potent toxins. Livestock also use on average 50 per cent of our scarce water resources and generate major problems with the pollution produced by their manure. By going vegetarian, we can have a huge impact on reducing greenhouse gases in the environment.

Better yet, go vegan

Most vegetarians eat eggs, butter, milk, and other dairy products, a diet that is known as lacto-ovo vegetarian. But a vegan eats no animal-based products at all, and this is ultimately the best practice for the environment. It may not be an easy choice in today's world, but it is of maximum benefit to the reduction of climate change.

VEGETARIAN RESTAURANTS
There is always a vegetarian option on the menu – if there isn't, ask the kitchen to provide one. For a national list of vegetarian restaurants go to the Vegetarian Society website at **www.veg-soc.org/restaurants**

According to *New Scientist*, it's more beneficial to the environment to green your diet than your car. By switching to a hybrid car, you will save just over one tonne of greenhouse gas emissions in a year, but by becoming a vegan you can save 1.5 tonnes of emissions.[46] Imagine the impact if you did both.

Top Tips for ethical eating

- Eat less meat and animal-based products. It will make a huge difference to climate change.
- Use a water filter to remove impurities and chemicals from your tap water.
- Buy organic where you can, and buy your fruit and vegetables in season as much as possible.
- Buy only free-range eggs, preferably certified organic ones.
- Shop locally – get to know your local neighbourhood by walking rather than driving, support local retailers not multinationals, and support local producers.
- Check the ingredients list and reject any products that are excessively packaged or stuffed full of artificial colours, flavours, and sugars.
- Avoid genetically modified foods by checking that your soy-based products have no genetically engineered organisms. Also avoid factory-farmed animals, which may have been fed genetically modified foods.
- Make sure your coffee is Fairtrade.
- Use local farmers' markets to buy your fruit, vegetables, and meats where possible.
- Ask for organic options in restaurants, supermarkets, and other shops. The more we ask for them, the more likely retailers are to stock organic products.
- Buy canned fish that has been certified by the Marine Stewardship Council; look for their logo on the can.
- Ask if your seafood has come from overseas and if it is a long-lived or deep-sea species. If the answer is yes, then it's best avoided.

7 RECYCLING

7 RECYCLING

Let's face it – we live in a disposable society. Since I was a child it has become standard practice to wade through layers of cardboard, plastic, Styrofoam, and bubble wrap after you have bought something to get to the item you have actually purchased. It usually gets tossed all over the living room floor for your child or dog to play with, before being gathered up and taken outside to fill most of the garbage bin. We use the object for a year or two but then the new model comes out, our old one doesn't seem so fast any more or it breaks down, and we decide to upgrade. So, what do we do? We throw it out and buy the new model, complete with lots of packaging, and the cycle continues. When you think of how many things in our home that fit into this routine – mobile phones, appliances, computers, and stereos – it becomes quite scary how much we are throwing away.

Until a few decades ago, we had very little waste to throw out. Most things were repaired and recycled as a matter of course because most of us didn't have the money to buy new products, nor did manufacturers have the resources to make new containers for them all the time. Milk bottles, beer bottles, and soft drink bottles were sent back to the company, washed and then refilled. Clothes were handed down from older to younger child, friend, or neighbour. Most goods were made locally and because they were not shipped thousands of kilometres they didn't need elaborate packaging to protect them for the journey. Food scraps were given to the dog or the chooks, or thrown onto the compost heap. Paper and cardboard waste were used for kindling or put in the backyard incinerator, which dad would usually fire up once a week. And if something broke, we took the time to fix it ourselves or asked someone else to fix it for us, because we couldn't afford to just go out and buy another one. We expected things to last for a long time, not to be replaced every six months.

Times have changed. We now have the capitalist mentality of unending wealth and consumption. Advertising serves to instil the idea and reinforce the message that we want, we need – nay, we deserve – the latest gadget, timesaver or fashion accessory. Endless purchasing and consumption keep the economy going and inflation rising,

CLEAN UP AUSTRALIA DAY

After travelling the world and being appalled by global levels of rubbish and pollution, Sydney builder and solo yachtsman Ian Kiernan started Clean Up Australia Day in 1990. It has now become Australia's biggest annual environmental event. Kiernan took the idea to the United Nations in 1993, and Clean Up the World Day was born. Now more than 35 million people in 120 countries take part in cleaning up rubbish in their local area each year. For more information and to register, go to www.cleanup.org.au

which is what the politicians and economists tell us is vital for society. But this unending cycle comes at a high cost to the planet, as once we purchase the latest item, where does all the stuff we no longer want end up? Landfill. Few of us ever visit the landfill sites where the detritus of our lives ends up, where mountains of household rubbish, much of it still in working order, is piled up for the carrion, the scavengers, and the industrial machinery to work over. Landfill is where capitalism goes to die.

Australia is one of the highest producers of waste in the world and this can be linked to our high levels of household incomes and gross domestic product. The more money we have, the more we can afford to buy, and the more we can afford to throw out. Australians sent over 17 million tonnes of rubbish to landfill in 2002-03, and we generated over 1.5 tonnes of waste per person, only half of which was recycled.[47]

Recycling is the only way to prevent our rubbish from ending up in landfill. Recycling our glass, plastics, and paper is a concept that Australians have really taken to over the last 10 years, and most of us understand the importance of recycling. Almost all households do some recycling, but only a small proportion recycle everything that can be recycled. There is much more that we can do to significantly reduce the amount of our household waste going to landfill.

We can recycle all of our plastics, glass, cartons, metals, and paper. We can minimise our purchases of heavily packaged food and always take cloth bags with us to carry our groceries in. We can use a compost bin or a worm farm to get rid of our food scraps. We can think of alternate uses for packaging around the home. If we do these simple things, we will have very little to put in the garbage bin that goes straight to landfill each week.

As for those many consumer goods that we no longer need for one reason or another, they can continue to provide use and function to someone rather than being thrown away. When we no longer want a product it's easy to get into the habit of considering how it could be of use to someone else and making the effort to get it to them. Numerous charities gladly take clothing and household

7 RECYCLING

items that we no longer want but are still in reasonable working order. They will even come and collect if you have a big enough load. Then there are recycling places for all manner of items, including mobile phones, paint tins, batteries, oil, computers, and much more.

Finally, if the item you have is still working but you're a bit hard up and you really want something else, then why not swap it? There are a number of swap sites that work on the barter method and you can get something back that you want or need more than what you're giving away.

This chapter will help you to think more about what happens to the products you no longer need, and will give you some ideas for improving your recycling of household rubbish as well as many other household goods.

Refuse, reduce, re-use, recycle

The basic principles of recycling can be summarised by four simple words – refuse, reduce, re-use, and recycle. It's easy to remember and even easier to do. First, refuse plastic bags at the supermarket by bringing your own cloth bags. Reduce your need for new products and try to bring as little unnecessary packaging into your home as possible. It's cheaper and better for the environment to buy in bulk where you can and make the things you already have last longer rather than buying new ones. Try to buy as many recycled products and those in recycled packaging as you can, such as toilet paper, tissues, and office paper. Once you have finished with an item, look at ways of re-using it and the packaging. Glass jars can be used as storage jars, newspaper can be used to wrap presents, and plastic bottles can be used with a spike to drip water the garden. If you can't find a new use for the item, then recycle it by putting it in the recycling bin or handing it over to a recycler; if it's a household item you can donate it to charity, give it to a friend, or sell it on eBay. As long as someone is using the item, it eliminates the need for the materials and energy to be used in creating a new one.

BUT IT ALL GOES IN THE ONE TRUCK!

People become suspicious when they see the contents of their recycling bin going into the same truck as the rubbish. In fact, some trucks are divided on the inside to keep recyclables and landfill rubbish separate, and some contractors use the same truck at different times of the day. As long as you've done the right thing with your recycling, according to their contract collectors must recycle what they say they are going to, so rest assured your recyclables are not going to landfill.

Kerbside recycling

Over 90 per cent of Australians have access to some form of kerbside recycling provided by their council. Some people are cynical about what happens to the goods they put into the recycling bin, telling you that it just gets mixed in with the ordinary household rubbish, or that the amount of fuel used by the trucks overrides any benefits from recycling. But that is simply not true. Many studies have concluded that recycling makes a huge contribution to reducing waste. The National Packaging Covenant Council found back in 2001 that, after subtracting the costs, recycling gave an overall benefit worth $266 million per year to Australia.[46] The benefits are undoubtedly much greater today.

Recycling makes an important reduction of household rubbish and has a compound effect on our emissions.

Recycling sends less material to landfill sites, which cuts down on greenhouse gas emissions by reducing the methane generated by materials breaking down. It also significantly reduces the water and air pollution generated from waste. Recycling also has an important secondary effect by reducing greenhouse gases emissions and the use of fuel and water in the creation of new products, because much less energy is used in the production of recycled goods than if they must be created from scratch.

What can be recycled kerbside?

While there is some variation in what can be recycled, depending on the council area you live in, some general rules can confidently be followed. Its important to take note of these and help your neighbours with it too, because if there is contamination in the recycling bin, even from plastic bags left in the bin, the recycling company will not accept it. If you're in doubt about whether a product can be recycled, it's best to leave it out of the bin. If they don't accept the bin, most recyclers leave a sticker on it to let you know it was too contaminated to be emptied.

The following are the main categories that can be placed in your recycling bin:

Paper and cardboard

Include newspapers, magazines, writing paper, cards, egg cartons, advertising leaflets, envelopes with plastic windows. No waxed cardboard or waxed paper, thermal fax paper, paper that is contaminated with food, or used tissues.

Tips: Make sure to flatten your cardboard boxes. If paper needs to be separated from the rest of the recycling, tie it with string and put a brick on top so it doesn't blow away. Don't wrap your newspaper in plastic bags.

What it becomes: More newspapers, recycled paper, egg cartons, kitty litter, new cardboard.

Other uses: Write on both sides of writing paper.

DID YOU KNOW?
When you recycle one glass bottle, you save the amount of energy needed to light a 100-watt bulb for four hours.

THE FOUR RS
REFUSE unnecessary products, packaging and plastic bags.

REDUCE your need for packaged goods.

RE-USE goods you already have.

RECYCLE everything else.

Newspaper can be used to wrap presents, wipe up spills, or light fires. Shredded paper can be used as mulch. Schools and kindergartens may be able to use cardboard boxes of all sizes.

Glass

Include all glass jars, as well as clear, green, and amber bottles. No oven-proof glass (it has been chemically treated), wine or drinking glasses, broken windscreen or window glass, ceramics, china, light globes.

Tips: Remove all lids (most are steel and can also be recycled). Rinse off any food in a bucket or used dishwater. Try not to break bottles as it makes them difficult to sort.

What it becomes: Primarily new glass jars and bottles.

Other uses: Re-use glass jars as storage containers. Wine bottles make good water bottles or vases.

Plastic

Plastic containers have a recycling code number, often on the bottom. All councils recycle plastics with codes one to three, and some councils accept codes four to seven as well. To check which code numbers your council recycles, go to your local council website or www.recyclingnearyou.com.au Plastic bags cannot be recycled kerbside; take them to your local supermarket, which will have a recycling bin. Disposable nappies also cannot be recycled.

Tips: You can leave the lids on plastic containers, but rinse out any food remains.

What it becomes: new soft drink bottles, garbage and compost bins, irrigation and drainage pipe, detergent bottles and industrial textiles.

Other uses: Plastic bottles can be used with a spike as a slow-drip water system in the garden.

Drink cartons

Include Liquidpaperboard milk and juice cartons, brick-shaped cartons, including long-life milk and juice cartons. Don't put them in with paper if your recycling is separated. They should be put with the glass, tins and plastic.

Tips: Rinse the cartons in used dishwater or a bucket of grey water. Where possible, flatten them and fit them inside an open carton – you can fit up to six flattened milk cartons inside one.

What it becomes: Office paper (five sheets of paper can be made from one milk carton), cardboard, and fuel briquettes.

Other uses: Schools and kindergartens often use milk cartons for projects. They also make good seedling containers with a few holes punched in the bottom.

Aluminium, foil, and steel

Include aluminium soft drink and beer cans, food and pet food cans, jam jar lids, aluminium foil without food remains, bottle tops, aerosol cans. No aluminium cans with steel ends and foil chip bags.

Tips: Remove any plastic caps, rinse the cans and lids in a bucket of grey water or used dishwater. Place steel can lids inside cans and crush cans to maximise space.

What it becomes: New aluminium or steel cans, structural steel for buildings, car parts, and other new steel products.

Other uses: Re-use cans as vases, pencil holders, or biscuit cutters.

HAND ME A HANKIE

Although paper serviettes and tissues often can't be recycled because they are contaminated with food or human matter, practically every Australian household has plenty of both. The tissue has become a ubiquitous item both in the home and as litter left outdoors, but nobody wants to pick up a dirty, used tissue! Millions of tissues and paper napkins end up in landfill each year, which could be prevented by the far more environmentally sound option of using a handkerchief or cloth napkin. Bringing out a nice hankie to blow your nose in public is so much better for the environment and far more sophisticated!

DID YOU KNOW?
It takes the same energy to produce one aluminium can as it does to recycle the same can 20 times over.

Where does my recycling go?

It depends on which company is processing your recycling, but in general your recycling products go to a material recovery centre where they are placed on a conveyer belt and separated by machine or by hand into paper, plastics, metals etc. Each product then goes through a separate process of several steps to remove contaminants and separate the different types even further before they are packed for processing. They often need to travel to a processing plant before being turned into new products that use recycled material. One of our biggest recycling companies, Visy Recycling, processes more than 900 000 tonnes of paper and cardboard, 450 000 tonnes of glass, and more than 20 000 tonnes of plastic every year.[49] This material is kept out of landfill and saves both energy and materials in the manufacture of new products.

Compost

Approximately 40 per cent of our household garbage going to landfill is food waste.[50] When food and garden wastes break down without air, as in landfill sites, they produce the greenhouse gas methane, which is almost as potent as carbon dioxide. But there is a better way to get rid of your food scraps – composting. Composting simply breaks down organic materials by utilising the decomposition process of bacteria and fungi, mimicking the natural process of decay within a forest. It takes between a few weeks and a few months for composted material to break down and be ready to use on the garden.

By having a compost bin and recycling your food waste you can make a big difference to greenhouse gas emissions, and it's something we can all do, even if we live in an apartment block.

There are a number of products and a great deal of information out there on composting, so I won't go into detail. Outdoor compost is most common, but there are also options for indoor recycling of organic matter that are perfect for people living in apartments or without the opportunity to start a compost heap and I will briefly mention these.

> Every kilogram of food or garden waste that is composted instead of going to landfill saves one kilogram of greenhouse gases.

Bokashi bucket

Bokashi is a Japanese word that means 'fermented organic matter'. Several Australian retailers sell these 20-litre buckets that sit under your kitchen sink or in your laundry and break down food scraps. You can put everything in there, including cooked and uncooked meat, which most other composting methods cannot cope with. When you put scraps in, you throw in a handful of the Bokashi matter, which is just grains mixed with natural micro-organisms in a liquid culture. The Bokashi causes anaerobic fermentation without smells or flies, and it takes three to four weeks for your scraps to be turned into a nutrient-rich material that can then be buried in the garden. A liquid is also produced from the fermentation process which needs to be drained off regularly. It can be mixed with water and used as a nutrient on the garden or poured down the drain where it will help clean up the waterways by competing with harmful bacteria.

Most Bokashi manufacturers recommend having two buckets, so that when one is full it can continue to ferment for a couple of weeks while you use the other bucket, before being buried in the garden. However, you can also use just one bucket and allow the process of further fermentation to occur in the garden. If you don't have a garden, ask the neighbours if you can bury it in their garden or use it in pot plants and tubs. This fantastic method of getting rid of all your food scraps costs under $200 for a starter kit that includes two buckets and your first batch of Bokashi, which should last you three to four months. More information is available at **www.bokashi.com.au**

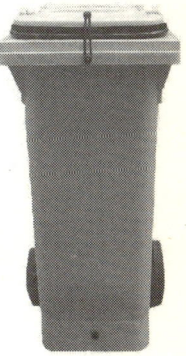

Worm farm

Worm farming, or vermiculture as it is known, is a great way of getting rid of food waste. The farms can be placed indoors or outdoors; they are odourless and don't attract flies or pests. Worms eat most kitchen scraps, including vacuum cleaner dust, torn newspapers and tea leaves, but no animal products. They can eat up to their own body weight in food every day, although you may need to break material down a little so it's easier for the worms to digest. Worm farms have a number of layers and the worms eat their way up the layers leaving rich worm manure behind, which is a fantastic fertiliser that can be easily removed by taking out the lower layers.

There are a number of worm farms on the market, most of which cost between $50 and $100. One brand, Can-O-Worms, won an Australian Design Award; it has minimal external packaging, and is available at K-Mart and Mitre 10 stores. A great source of information on worm farming, as well as some bizarre photos of people who love worms just a little too much, is a site called **www.thewormman.com**

Outdoor compost heap

An outdoor compost heap can be handy in houses or apartment blocks with gardens: not only does it provide a place to get rid of all the kitchen scraps, but it also gives fantastic mulch to improve the soil in the garden.

There are many compost bins on the market, ranging from a simple one for about $40 up to many hundreds of dollars, and it really depends on what you want from your compost bin as to what you want to pay. The more expensive ones boast that they can break down your material much quicker, which can be useful if you have a great deal of green waste. If you don't want to buy a bin and would prefer to do it yourself, you can make your own heap in the corner of the garden and cover it with a plastic sheet or hessian or old carpet to keep moisture and heat in.

The care and maintenance of an outdoor compost heap or bin is fairly easy; just ensure that there is plenty of layering and variety between wet and dry material in the bin. It also needs to be turned regularly to help aerate the compost and mix up the damp food waste and the drier garden waste. You may occasionally need to add water to your compost to keep it moist and speed up decomposition, but it shouldn't be too damp as this will block out air and cause it to smell. It should be well ventilated and out of direct sunlight, if possible, as this can dry it out. The temperature can get up to 70 degrees in a good compost heap, and all sorts of critters, including worms, millipedes, spiders and other bugs, will be

COMPOST AND WORM FARM INGREDIENTS

Include fruit and vegetable scraps, tea bags and tea leaves, coffee grounds, egg shells, vegetable cooking oils, bread, dead flowers, grass cuttings and other green waste, sawdust, wood ash, vacuum cleaner dust, and small amounts of paper.

Don't include meat, bones and dairy products, fish, animal fats, cakes or sweets (they attract mice), magazines, sawdust from treated timber, fresh animal manure, large woody branches, or persistent weeds like blackberry and couch grass.

attracted to it, which will help it break down even further.

You should always wear gloves when working with compost materials because numerous organisms and bacteria live in there. If you're ever in doubt as to whether something can be composted, there is a great UK website where you just type in the ingredient you want to compost and it tells you immediately if it should go in or stay out: **www.compostthis.co.uk**

Litter

While almost everyone agrees that litter is ugly and an unnecessary mess in society, 30 per cent of people litter in public places.[51] Most littering occurs at transport stops, smoking areas, and market sites. The more litter already exists in a place, the more people will decide that it's okay to litter.

Littering is a huge social cost in our society that we all end up paying for through our taxes, as local councils and state governments pay millions every year to clean it up.

Although a lot of litter is recyclable material, none of it will ever get recycled. Even worse, much litter ends up in stormwater drains and goes on to pollute waterways and destroy marine life. It's worth knowing that littering is actually a crime and people can be fined on the spot for littering, as well as taken to court where fines can be thousands of dollars. So if there's no bin, hold onto your litter until you get home so you can recycle it; pick up other people's litter where you can; and consider dobbing in someone who's being particularly irresponsible to the national Litter Report Line on **1800 352 555**.

Plastic bags

> Recycle plastic bags at the local supermarket and prevent them taking 400 years to break down in landfill.

Plastic bags are an unfortunate symbol of the wastefulness of our times. Most plastic bags will be used for an extremely short period from the supermarket to home and never used again. Approximately 6.9 billion plastic bags are consumed annually in Australia and 6 billion of these are supermarket checkout bags. At least 80 million plastic bags end up as litter in our environment and have a significant impact on marine life, killing up to 100 000 marine animals each year.[52] After the animal dies and its body decomposes, the plastic bag is again released into the environment to do more damage. Plastic bags can take up to 400 years to break down, and it's a chilling thought that if we continue the current pattern, plastic bags may well outlive human civilisation. What an ugly legacy for us to leave behind.

RECYCLING HOT SPOT

Planet Ark has created a website to answer recycling queries about where common household goods can be recycled throughout Australia at **recyclingnearyou.com.au** It often directs you to your local council, which is always a good resource for recycling information in your area.

Although all major supermarkets have bins to recycle plastic bags, less than three per cent of plastic bags are currently recycled. We drastically need to improve this figure, as well as stop using so many plastic bags in the first place. Some state governments are considering a levy on plastic bags and some stores, including Bunnings, Ikea and Aldi, have voluntarily introduced a levy. We can all do our bit by refusing plastic bags wherever possible, always keeping cloth bags in the car and handbag to carry any purchases, and recycling any plastic bags that we do end up using. Plastic bags are a major issue that we can all drastically improve with these simple strategies. Let's not allow plastic bags to become our legacy!

Mobile phones

Australians change their mobile phones on average every 18 months, so there are a lot of old phones out there. Sometimes they are handed on to a friend or family member but more often they sit around in a bottom drawer or get thrown out. The Australian Mobile Telecommunications Industry, which includes a number of manufacturers and all the major service providers, has banded together to form MobileMuster to recycle our old phones. The service is free to consumers and runs at a net cost to the industry. They separate the components into batteries, circuit boards, handsets, accessories, and packaging. The batteries are shipped to South Korea to be heated to extreme temperatures so that the various metals, including nickel, cadmium, and cobalt, can be extracted for re-use. The circuit boards are shipped to South Korea or North America to recover precious metals including silver, gold, and copper. Handsets are processed locally to become plastic fence posts and pallets. Accessories are also processed and recycled where possible.

By late 2006 MobileMuster had already saved over 400 tonnes from landfill, and the industry hopes to be recycling 150 tonnes per annum before 2008. There are numerous places you can hand in your old mobile, including ANZ banks and Optus stores. For a full list of nearby outlets go to **www.mobilemuster.com.au** and type in your postcode.

Cork

While currently in decline in favour of plastic corks, the traditional corks that have been used in wine bottles since the 17th century are a sustainable and recyclable product. Cork comes from the bark of the cork tree, which is grown in Portugal, northern Africa, and western Mediterranean countries. It takes 40 years for the bark of the tree to first become thick enough to be stripped of the cork. This doesn't damage the tree, which continues to make bark and is stripped every nine years for its approximate 200-year life. Every part of the bark is harvested for cork seals or flooring, and even the dust is recycled to generate electricity.

CIGARETTE BUTTS— OUR WORST OFFENDERS

There are approximately 7 billion cigarette butts littered in Australia each year, which could circle the earth nearly four and half times if laid end to end![53] Most people don't realise that cigarette butts take up to 15 years to break down and end up polluting waterways and topsoil. They have even been found in the stomachs of birds, turtles, and other marine life. Take responsibility for cigarette butts by picking them up, and encourage others to do the same. A used film canister makes a great portable butt container, or you can purchase small, portable ashtrays at most supermarkets; some local councils provide them free of charge.

Used corks can be turned into many objects, including place mats, coasters, and floor tiles. Some bottle shops have a recycling service and the Girl Guides also collect corks as a fundraising project throughout Australia. You can find your nearest collection point by going to **www.recyclingnearyou.com.au** and typing in 'cork' and your postcode.

Polystyrene

Polystyrene, sometimes known by the brand name Styrofoam, is not biodegradable, nor is it easily recyclable. However, it is cheap to produce from oil and is therefore popular with manufacturers. Approximately 33 000 tonnes of polystyrene is manufactured every year in Australia – a huge volume when you consider how little it weighs – and only a tiny percentage of this is recycled.[54]

Polystyrene packaging surrounds many new electronic goods, wine, and CD casings. It even makes plant pots and coat hangers. It is also used extensively in the food service industry in disposable cutlery, clear salad bar containers, meat and poultry trays, and cups. Almost all of these products end up in landfill. Yet many offices, cafes and shops still use polystyrene, particularly as cups for hot drinks. Some polystyrene products have a symbol on them with a triangle and a six in the middle. Although this looks remarkably similar to the recycling code, it is in fact a Plastic Identification Code and does not necessarily mean that the product can be recycled in your area.

Avoid polystyrene as much as possible in cafes by taking your own mug or refusing a polystyrene cup and explaining why you would prefer a paper cup. Reject products packaged in a lot of polystyrene where possible. For large amounts of polystyrene, such as the packaging surrounding new electronics or white goods, there is currently only one recycling facility in the capital cities (apart from Darwin and Hobart) where you can drop off polystyrene product; they are listed on the industry website at **www.repsa.org.au**

Computers

Most of us like to upgrade our computer every few years in order to get greater memory capacity, increased speed, and

> **HOW CAN I RECYCLE THIS?**
> If you are looking for creative ways to recycle common, and uncommon, household objects, an intriguing blog called **www.recyclethis.co.uk** offers advice and responses on how to recycle or creatively re-use all sorts of items, ranging from bags of plaster, to used tennis balls, to soap shards, to you name it ...

the latest features. We often don't know what to do with our old computers and they end up gathering dust in the garage for years and eventually go to landfill. But many chemicals and heavy metals such as lead, mercury, and cadmium are present in our computers, which leach into the soil and cause environmental problems in landfill.

There are a number of computer recyclers throughout Australia. Many of them actually refurbish your old computer and put new software on it, and then donate it to disadvantaged individuals and community groups. They may charge to pick up or to drop off your computer, particularly if it needs repairs. While it's good that they are helping the community, they may be re-using the best computer parts and not actually recycling those that are no good. Other companies actually recycle and resell computer parts and dispose of the associated waste in an environmentally sound way.

If your old computer no longer works, make sure to send it to a company that will recycle the component parts rather than just sending them to landfill. If it's still in working order then it may be best to donate to a refurbishing company that will ensure it goes to someone who really needs it. To look at the many businesses that will take used computers in your area go to **www.recyclingnearyou.com.au**

Printer cartridges

Printer cartridges are used regularly in homes and offices and are not recyclable by normal methods. While printer companies press consumers always to use brand-name replacements, a thriving industry offers cheaper equivalents and cartridge refills for a reduced price. The no-name equivalents do not help the environment, but refilling a cartridge instead of replacing it offers substantial environmental savings as well as small economic savings.

Some printer cartridges are not refillable, and most can be refilled only a limited number of times. Thus, when you can no longer use a cartridge yourself, it's a good idea to make sure the cartridge gets recycled. Planet Ark offers a cartridge recycling service for all inkjet, laser cartridges, toner bottles, drum kits, and PCUs for all brands of fax, photocopier, and printers. They boast that zero waste goes to landfill from their service, and they manufacture plastic rulers and other products from the cartridges. Drop-off points for old cartridges are at retail outlets for Australia Post, Officeworks, Harvey Norman, Dick Smith, and many other locations. For larger businesses they also offer a collection service. For more information, go to **www.closetheloop.com.au**

Home entertainment

Electronic goods contain precious metals, toxic heavy metals – such as the lead found in TV cathode ray tubes – plastics, glass and metal circuitry, which can all leach into the environment if sent to landfill. There are currently few options for effectively recycling old televisions, stereos, DVD, and VHS players. This is worrying, given the short lifespan and rapid turnover rate of these products. The Department of Environment and Water Resources says that 2.5 million major appliances are being discarded to landfill every year. A non-profit called Product Stewardship Australia has been formed to organise better disposal and recycling of TVs initially and to look at other electronics down the track, but as yet there is no national system for recycling TVs, stereos, and VHS/DVD players. Hopefully this will be remedied shortly and a recycling system put in place. In the meantime, if an item still works then donate it to charity so someone else can use it.

White goods

Major household items such as fridges, washing machines, dryers, and dishwashers contain significant amounts of metals that can be recycled. Of course, if it still works quite well then it would be better donated to a second-hand or charity store, but if it is broken then recycling the valuable metal components is the best option. Most councils have drop-off stations or regular pickups where you can safely deposit large items such as whitegoods for metal component recycling. Check with your local council for further details.

Cars

Motor vehicles impose a heavy cost on the environment in manufacture, use and eventual disposal. We can cut this by recycling car parts and products wherever possible.

Parts

Cars are one of our most expensive consumer purchases and when they break down, it can sometimes cost many thousands of dollars to get them repaired. Using recycled auto parts in car repairs can save you up to 50 per cent of the cost of a repair job, and it also saves the embodied energy and the greenhouse gas emissions involved in producing a new item.

The Auto Parts Recyclers Association of Australia is an industry body that determines safe practices for recycling old cars. This non-profit organisation services over 330 auto parts recyclers, and it provides an online parts locator to help businesses or individuals find the part they need second-hand at **www.apraa.com**

End-of-life vehicles

Also affectionately known as 'bombs', these are vehicles that have given up the ghost and need to be retired off the road. This is the case for more than 500 000 vehicles every year. Many of them are not recycled and they end up leaching toxic fluids and heavy metals into the environment and generating approximately 10 000 tonnes of waste.[55] Many companies will remove your old bomb free of charge and make sure that the parts are recycled. Look up the Yellow Pages for the nearest car recycler or check with your local council.

Used motor oil

We use oil in practically all motorised items, including cars, trucks, boats, lawnmowers, and chainsaws. Much of this needs to be changed regularly, and we often forget that it can also be recycled. Every year, industry and individuals generate at least 250 million litres of used oil in Australia.[56] If we don't recycle this oil, it can pollute the waterways and the soil. It only takes one litre of oil to contaminate one million litres of water, so it is an extremely bad idea to pour oil down the drain.

Second-hand oil can be cleaned and re-used for many products, including industrial burner fuel, hydraulic oil, and even new lubricating oil. When changing oil you should always do it in a well-ventilated place; wear gloves, use a spill tray to catch any drips, and put the oil into its original container or something similar. You should recycle your oil as soon as possible because it is a fire hazard and could potentially leak. Many local councils accept oil for recycling at their transfer stations, and some petrol stations will take used oil. The government has a website with further information and advice on where to recycle your oil at **www.oilrecycling.gov.au**

Chemicals, gases, paint tins, and car batteries

These are all quite toxic and should not be sent to landfill as they will leach into the soil and may end up in waterways. Most Australian councils have a program to help you recycle these items without damaging the environment. Gas cylinders can be swapped and refilled many times, and you can usually return these to refilling outlets. Car batteries are recycled by auto-parts recyclers. Check your local council website or the *Yellow Pages* for the nearest drop-off point.

Cooking oil

Cooking oil should not be poured down the sink as it will block drains and cause problems in the waterways. Small amounts of vegetable oil can be placed in your compost heap or stored in a jar or an old milk container and put in your garbage. For large amounts, check with your local council for recycling options in your area: some recyclers take cooking oil for recycling into biofuels, cosmetics, and stockfeed.

Other household items

Charity shops and opportunity shops in Australia are always crying out for household items that they can either pass on to the poor or resell in their shops. We all have a minefield of books, clothes, toys, manchester, and furniture in our houses that we don't really want, are still in good condition, but we can't be bothered

---

WHY NOT FREECYCLE?

Freecycle is a global community based on giving away stuff you no longer need. It started in Tucson, Arizona, as an attempt to prevent so much junk being thrown into landfill. There are now nearly 4000 groups throughout the world working on this basic concept of free exchange. There are well over 100 Freecycle groups throughout Australia, and to join your nearest one, or start one yourself, go to **www.freecycle.org/groups/australia**

doing anything with. It doesn't take long to go through the house and pull out what you don't need to send on to charity. Or, if you're hard up for cash you can have a garage sale, a market stall, or sell it on eBay.

Many charities have a truck that will collect large furniture such as couches and tables. Op shops can no longer take mattresses due to government regulations. Keep in mind that they don't want your old unusable rubbish either, and they spend millions each year disposing of junk that has been dumped at their stores overnight. So send them only items that they can actually use, and put it in a charity bin, deliver it during opening hours, or phone and ask them to pick it up. The following are some charities that have websites where you can find out what they will accept and book a pickup:
www.salvos.org.au, **www.vinnies.org.au**, **www.smithfamily.com.au**

Top Tips for recycling

- Remember the four Rs – refuse, reduce, re-use, recycle.
- Buy recycled products as much as possible, particularly toilet paper, tissues, and office paper.
- Know your local council's rules for kerbside recycling and encourage your neighbours to follow them too.
- Put a 'No Junk Mail' sign on your letterbox to discourage the littering of advertising materials.
- When out, bring home your litter if there's no bin or it's full, and encourage others to do the same.
- Don't drop cigarette butts. Carry a used film canister with you as a portable ashtray.
- Take cloth bags with you at all times to put your shopping in.
- Take plastic bags back to the supermarket for recycling.
- Get into composting with a compost bin, a Bokashi bucket, or a worm farm and reduce your household waste by up to 40 per cent.
- Before throwing something out, consider carefully how it can be recycled and make the effort to do so.
- Recycle used oils, chemicals, paints and other toxic products to prevent them going to landfill and leaching into the environment or polluting our waterways.
- Donate unwanted goods to charity or to a Freecycle network.
- By doing all the above you will make a significant contribution to maximising recycling, minimising excess usage of resources, and greatly reducing the amount of waste in landfill.

8
APPLIANCES AND HOUSEHOLD GOODS

8 APPLIANCES AND HOUSEHOLD GOODS

When looking at electrical appliances and other household goods with a view to minimising our footprint, there are two objectives. The first is when purchasing a new household item to consider the resources used to create the product and whether the raw materials, as well as the design, have been used with energy efficiency and environmental impact minimisation in mind. We do not change appliances and furniture frequently, but when we do need to purchase a new item, it's a fantastic opportunity to make a choice for an energy-efficient, environmentally friendly design that will last a long time and not ruin the planet.

In running our households every day, we make numerous small decisions without even thinking that significantly impact upon our bills and our greenhouse gas emissions. So the second objective is to utilise the object, once purchased, in the most efficient way and for as long as possible in order to maximise efficiency while saving money and reducing emissions. Whenever possible, a product can then be passed on at the end of its useful life so that someone else can use it, or it can be dismantled for recycling.

Several government-run advisory schemes can help us to make good decisions when choosing new appliances, such as the energy rating label and the Energy Stars label. These are vital in helping us to purchase an appliance that minimises greenhouse gas emissions and that doesn't waste electricity. This chapter will also look at the main appliances in our homes and give a number of tips that will help them to last longer, run better, and save you plenty of money.

The energy rating label

The easiest way to find the most energy-efficient white goods is to look at the energy rating label, which is now required by legislation for refrigerators, freezers, dishwashers, clothes washers, dryers, and single-phase air-conditioners. A product with a high energy rating will save you hundreds of dollars over its lifetime, whereas an inefficient item can actually have higher running costs than the original purchase price. So don't be fooled by a really cheap price. The initial outlay is only one consideration when determining which product to buy, as the costs over the total lifetime of a product are a far better indicator of what you're in for.

Minimum energy performance standards are now required for many products, including air conditioners, fridges and freezers, water heaters, electric motors, ballasts, lamps, transformers, commercial refrigeration, and external power supplies. They are mandated by state government regulation, and any product offered for sale must meet these minimum requirements of efficiency, which is good news for consumers.

> When buying new white goods, always choose one that has an energy rating of at least three and preferably four stars.

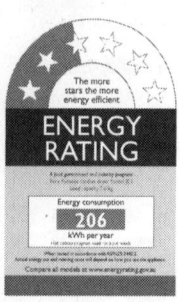

The energy rating website at **www.energyrating.gov.au** provides a handy reference guide, with information on the electricity required to power a product, the running costs over its lifetime, the water consumption if it's relevant, and other features. It ranks different models according to their energy rating and also links you to the manufacturer's website for further information on particular models. You can download and print out a spreadsheet with all this information on the appliance you need, which is handy to take with you when you go shopping. Try to buy the appliance with the highest star rating you can that has the features you need, and as a general rule don't go for any product that is below three stars.

The website also features a Top Energy Saver Award each year to reward the most efficient appliance on the market in each category.

All in all, the energy rating is a helpful government labelling system that minimises the confusion for the consumer and rewards those products that are practising high efficiency, so when you are ready to buy a new appliance check the website before you hit the shops.

Look for the energy rating label.

Energy Allstars

The Energy Allstars label is similar to the energy rating label but promotes only those brands that are in the top

15-25 per cent in their category in regards to energy efficiency. The scheme covers not only products with energy ratings, but also other products that have minimal criteria for efficiency including office equipment, lighting, transformers, and smoke alarms. It provides tips on choosing a product and on operating it efficiently. The website is the main location for information on the Allstars and primarily covers the main white goods, but new products are being added all the time.

The website also provides an Energy Savings Calculator o compare annual energy use of an Allstars product to an average product, and a Lifetime Cost Calculator, which helps you look at running costs over 10 years or more. Overall, this handy website can quickly advise you of the 'best in show' for some products: **www.energyallstars.gov.au**

Choice magazine

An unbiased resource that provides valuable product information for consumers, *Choice* magazine has been around for nearly 50 years. It is produced by the Australian Consumers Association, which buys products and tests them itself, so the results are impartial and focused on consumer needs. It tests a variety of appliances, computers, electronics, baby goods, foods, and financial products. The results of some tests are available free on the website; you can subscribe to the online or the print edition, or both if you prefer. Choice can be helpful when making big purchases, as it considers not only efficiency but also ease of use, noise, and other aspects that we sometimes only remember once we get a product home; see **www.choice.com.au**

Refrigerators and freezers

Refrigeration accounts for 17 per cent of greenhouse gas emissions within the home, and an outdated or inefficient fridge can cost you hundreds of extra dollars in running costs. It could also mean a difference in greenhouse gas emissions of two tonnes over its lifetime between the least efficient and most efficient model.

GREENHOUSE PIE CHART AND WHITE GOODS INFO

You can consult a chart that shows the percentage of greenhouse emissions each aspect of your household produces: **www.greenhouse.gov.au/yourhome/technical/fs41.htm**

The second fridge or freezer that is kept in many garages may be costing you a fortune. First, because it is usually old and inefficient, it soaks up tons of electricity just to run. Second, the garage is usually one of the hottest areas in the home and the fridge needs to work extra hard just to keep its cool. Many people don't think to turn off the second fridge when they go away on holiday, so it continues to churn away, spewing out greenhouse gases, to cool food and drinks that no one is there to consume. Take the time to consider if you really need that second fridge, and if you do, make sure that you are maximising its efficiency.

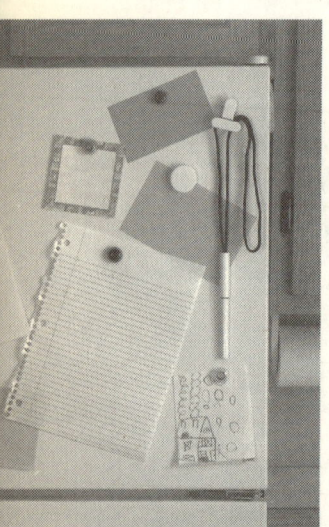

When buying a new fridge, keep size in mind and don't buy one that is too big for your needs: not only will it cost you a lot more to run, but a fridge works most efficiently when it is well-filled. If the fridge is less than two-thirds full most of the time then you probably need a smaller one. If you are looking at a few models with similar features, choose the one that has the most energy rating stars for far more efficient running costs. Many fridges have five-star ratings and some even have six stars. Two-door fridges with a separate freezer door at the top or bottom are generally more efficient than one-door models. Models with special fittings such as automatic ice-makers or ice dispensers on the door use up to 20 per cent more energy and also cost more to purchase than a similar model without this feature.

When buying a new stand-alone freezer, keep in mind that upright freezers with a front-opening door are more convenient to use as you can get the contents out quickly, but they consume more energy than a chest freezer. While the chest freezer holds more cold air in and tends to have thicker insulation, it is less convenient to use: you may need to keep the lid open for a while to find what you are looking for, thereby forcing it to work harder to keep cool.

For your refrigeration needs, keep in mind the following top tips for efficient operation and lower greenhouse gas emissions.

Top Tips for efficient refrigerators and freezers

- If you don't need the second fridge often, keep it turned off with the door open until you actually need it for cooling drinks or food. It should take approximately three hours to get to a good cooling temperature.

- Keep your fridge in a cool position, because heat will force it to work much harder.

- Make sure there is plenty of air flow at the back of the fridge, with an eight-centimetre gap, as well as air flow at the top and sides. Poor ventilation of the fridge can add more than 15 per cent to your energy costs.

- Never place your fridge or freezer in an unventilated cupboard.

- Defrost whenever the frost in your freezer grows to five millimetres thick as ice provides insulation: the more frost there is, the less efficient the model will be.

- Don't open the fridge door for longer than you need to, because it wastes energy.

- Make sure the door seals on the fridge and freezer are tight and clean, so that cold air is not escaping through them. The seal should be able to hold a piece of paper in place when closed. Worn-out seals can be replaced.

- Don't set the internal temperature too low, because a one-degree change in temperature can consume more than five per cent of extra energy. It should be at the middle setting most of the time.

- If you're going away for more than a week or two, consider emptying and turning off the refrigerator to save electricity. Prop the door open so air circulates once you do turn it off.

Dishwashers

A dishwasher has become standard in the modern kitchen and without it many large families just wouldn't cope. Dishwashers are large consumers of both electricity and water, so when buying a new one, it's important to get a model that is really efficient with both.

Keep in mind the size of dishwasher you need, as if it takes a long time to fill, the dishes inside will get smelly. The one-drawer or two-drawer dishwashers are handy, allowing you to wash small amounts when needed. Also, look for a model with both a hot and cold water connection: if there is only a hot water connection the machine will use hot water throughout its cycle, which can be expensive and add to your greenhouse gas emissions unnecessarily.

Top Tips for dishwashing

- Turn the dishwasher on only when fully loaded.
- Don't let it sit in standby mode. Once it has finished its run, turn off the main power switch.
- Use the economy cycle as much as possible.
- Clean the filter between each wash to keep it running efficiently.
- Scrape food off plates but avoid running too much water to rinse them before putting them in the dishwasher.

- Try using white vinegar as a rinse aid in the dishwasher. It does a great job in cleaning glasses, and is cheap and biodegradable.
- If you have off-peak rates for your hot water system, it will be cheaper for you to run the dishwasher at night. Check your electricity bill to determine if you are on off-peak rates.

Clothes washers

The washing machine can be a big consumer of both water and electricity in the average household. The average washing machine emits about 90 kilograms of greenhouse gas to run per year, but if you do a warm water wash it puts out an astonishing 475 kilograms.[57] By purchasing an energy-efficient machine and using it economically, you can significantly reduce your costs and emissions.

When purchasing a new machine, choose one that has a high energy rating, uses the least water, and will spin-dry at a fast pace. Also be aware that some models heat their own washing water internally, which can have a high impact on electricity usage. If you have a solar hot water service it is better to choose a model that has two hoses, so that hot water can be brought in directly from your solar water supply, which is free, rather than using electricity to heat it up.

Purchase the size of machine you need for your family, as a larger machine will cost more and use more energy than a smaller model. Also ensure that it has automatic load

8 APPLIANCES AND HOUSEHOLD GOODS

sensing so it doesn't use more water than necessary for the size of the load.

In general, front-loading washing machines are far more energy efficient and use less water. They also have a superior washing performance, because gravity does some of the work for them washing the detergent through the clothes. A front loader generally has a slower washing time (up to 90 minutes). Some front loaders have limited options for cold water wash, making them more expensive to run, so make sure you look at all the features before making your decision. A good washing machine should last you at least 10 years and maybe even 20, so it's worth making a good choice in your investment.

Top Tips for efficient clothes washing

- Wash your clothes in cold water as much as possible, rather than warm or hot. It doesn't make much of a difference to the wash but will make a huge difference to your energy bill.

- Wash full loads, as a reduced load will take the same amount of electricity.

- Make sure to adjust the water level for small loads if your washer doesn't do it automatically.

- Dissolve powder detergents in the water before you put the clothes in, as this will help performance, particularly in a cold wash.

- Use biodegradable detergents so that chemicals are not being washed into the waterways, particularly if you are recycling your grey water from the rinse cycle.

- If your house has off-peak rates for your hot water system, it will be cheaper for you to run the clothes washer overnight. Check your electricity bill to determine if you are on off-peak rates.

- If your washer has a 'suds saver' option, use it to conserve water and detergent when you are doing several loads in a row.

Clothes dryers

There's no getting around it - clothes dryers consume a lot of greenhouse gases and are a fairly wasteful device when you consider how much sunshine we receive in Australia for most of the year. Drying clothes in a dryer generates more than three kilograms of greenhouse gases each time, whereas on the line or a clothes rack, they generate none.

However, some people can't live without their dryer. If this is you, then pay particular attention to the star rating when purchasing a new dryer, as this will make a big difference to your overall energy use. You may also want to consider purchasing a gas-powered dryer or a heat pump dryer. Both of these are more expensive than electric models and do not have energy-efficiency ratings, but they are much cheaper to run and produce less greenhouse gases over time.

Also make sure to choose a clothes dryer that automatically senses when clothes are dry, rather than working on a timer, as this will save a lot of energy and prevent over-drying of your clothes.

Top Tips for efficient clothes drying

- Dry clothes on the line whenever possible - it's free!

- If it's raining, dry clothes inside in front of the heater and then finish them off in the dryer.

- Make sure the clothes have been spin-dried at top speed in the clothes washer to get all excess water out before putting them in the dryer.

- Try to avoid doing large loads on rainy days and wait for fine weather so you can dry them outdoors.

- Clean the lint filter after each use as it speeds up drying time.

- Dry fabrics of the same weight together, so that they need similar amounts of drying time.

- If you dry a number of loads one after the other, it will make use of the heat already generated in the machine.

- Use the cool-down or permanent press cycle, if there is one, which uses the residual heat in the dryer to finish off the load.

- Externally vent the dryer if possible, or open doors and windows when it's on, so that moist air is removed and isn't recirculated in the dryer. This should make drying time shorter.

8 APPLIANCES AND HOUSEHOLD GOODS

Dry cleaning

As a child, I always loved the fresh smell of dry cleaners. So, I was very disappointed to discover when researching this book that dry cleaning uses a particularly toxic chemical solvent called **perchlorethylene** or **tetrachloroethene** (PERC). Its fumes may be carcinogenic and it has been known to provoke symptoms including depression of the central nervous system, damage to the liver and kidneys, headaches, nausea, dizziness, and nasal irritation. There goes my enjoyment of the dry cleaning smell!

We don't actually need to dry clean items nearly as often as manufacturers recommend, as they are usually just covering themselves in case garments get ruined accidentally. Most items can be hand-washed using pure soap flakes without any damage, which will also save money. For those items you can't resist having dry cleaned, reduce exposure to PERC when you get home by removing the plastic wrap before you enter the house and allowing the clothes to air either outside or in a well-ventilated area for a few hours.

Energy Stars and standby power

The Energy Star label indicates energy efficiency for electronic items including home electronics such as TVs, VCRs and stereos, as well as home office equipment like computers, printers, and photocopiers. This international rating gives a star only to those products that are energy efficient. The rating system particularly focuses on products that automatically switch into sleep mode when not being used or consume a minimal amount of energy in standby mode.

Standby mode allows many of our modern appliances to maintain a convenient, ready for action state so they can be powered up almost immediately at the touch of a fingertip. The amount of power used in standby mode varies widely between brands and products, but it is often excessive for the task at hand.

While most of us don't really consider the many electronic goods in our homes that are left on standby power, they actually contribute up to seven per cent of our electricity usage every year. Energy Star estimates that standby power is costing Australians a total of around $500 million a year, with associated greenhouse gas emissions of five million tonnes, which is a ridiculous amount of

GREENPEACE GREEN ELECTRONICS GUIDE

Greenpeace has produced an international online guide that ranks the leading computer and mobile phone manufacturers on their global policies and actual behaviour with regards to minimising harmful chemicals in their products and recycling the components once consumers have finished with them. This is a great initiative to inform consumers and to place pressure on electronics manufacturers to improve their manufacturing and recycling behaviour. You can download the guide at **www.greenpeace.com.au**

SWITCH OFF STANDBY
Switch off appliances at the power point rather than leaving them on standby wherever possible to save money and prevent a small but constant drain of electricity.

waste for products that are not even being used. The drain on our electricity system caused by standby power has become such as issue that there is an international movement for governments to legislate for a maximum standby level of one watt in all electronic products. In the meantime, the power usage of a product on standby is considered in the Energy Star label.

Products that have been given the Energy Star thumbs up do not cost more than any other, but they will save you plenty of money over the long term. All electronic equipment that has been endorsed by this program will consume up to 75 per cent less energy in standby mode than the average model. Most household electronic equipment must consume less than one watt of energy in standby mode in order to qualify. Office equipment can consume slightly more, depending on the product. Energy Star products also run more efficiently when being used and generate less heat, which helps the product to last longer. For more information on the program go to the website at **www.energystar.gov.au**

RECYCLING OLD APPLIANCES
Don't send your old white goods and computer equipment to landfill. They can be recycled safely and their parts re-used. Check **Chapter 7: Recycling** for further information.

Home entertainment

Home electronics, including TVs, DVDs, stereos, and home theatre systems are present in practically every Australian household. Almost all electronic equipment remains on standby when we switch it off with the remote control, which means it is still using up to 20 watts of electricity per hour and can be producing around 45 kilograms of greenhouse gas every year.[58] Some electronic equipment doesn't even have an off switch any more, which means you cannot control that constant drain of power unless you switch it off at the power point.

We can reduce the electricity drain of our electronics by buying products that have been endorsed by the Energy Star program. Most home electronic products that comply have a sticker on them, but some products aren't labelled, so when shopping it's a good idea to ask to see only the Energy Star products.

> **Look for the Energy Star label on your electronic goods.**

Energy Star products have minimal power wastage in sleep and standby mode. This adds up to a significant saving in money and greenhouse gas emissions over time, because electronics spend the majority of their lives in standby mode. Of course, by switching your electronics off at the power point you can reduce this passive electricity drain to zero.

> **Top Tips** for efficient home entertainment
> - When buying new units, choose those with Energy Stars and save up to 30 per cent on your yearly household energy bills.
> - Most plasma screen TVs are huge greenhouse gas emitters, so if you must have a plasma, choose one that has an Energy Star label.
> - Get into the habit of turning your electronics off at the power point rather than from the remote control to save money and greenhouse gas emissions.

DID YOU KNOW?
A microwav oven can generate more greenhouse gases running the electronic clock than it does over the course of the year.[59]

Home office equipment

Home office equipment – including computers, printers, laptops, and fax machines – is common in most households. Even if we just want to manage and print out our digital photos occasionally, the computer and printer are often left on for days at a time. All electronic equipment consumes a great deal of energy while waiting for you to use it, so its best to turn the item off if you're not going to use it for the next hour at least. And contrary to popular belief, a screensaver does not save energy: it actually uses extra power, and it may stop the main unit from sleeping.

DID YOU KNOW?
An inefficient computer and monitor left on for a year will generate the same amount of carbon dioxide as a car travelling from Sydney to Perth.[60]

It's important to buy Energy Star office equipment, as described above, wherever possible. Office equipment is not always stickered as such, so you need to specifically request Energy Star products when purchasing. In addition, the power-saving features often need to be manually adjusted to get the benefit.

You can program your computer to switch into standby or sleep mode quicker when you haven't been using it for a while by going to the power options menu in the main computer preferences and choosing the Energy Saving option or the option that allows you to adjust sleep or standby mode. An Energy Star product should go into sleep mode after 15 minutes of not being used.

If you reduce that to five minutes, it allows the computer to go into low energy mode more often, but it will still power up as soon as you touch the keyboard or the mouse. Most recently manufactured computers do not lose any Internet connection you may have running when they go into sleep mode. You can also turn the screensaver option off in the same preferences section. By doing this you will save huge amounts of greenhouse gases, keep your equipment much cooler, and often extend its lifetime. If you can't find how to access this mode or need further information, Energy Star provides instructions for manually adjusting all types of computers at **www.energystar.gov.au/consumers/stepbystep.html**

Top Tips for efficient home office equipment

- Adjust the sleep mode on your computer to a minimal amount (I suggest five minutes) of time before it will power down if you don't touch the keyboard or mouse.

- Shut down your computer when not intending to use it again for an hour or more. Your computer and monitor waste a lot of energy waiting for you to return and power them up.

- If you need to leave the computer on but are not actively using it, switch off the monitor. This can reduce power consumption by up to 80 per cent and does not increase the wear and tear on the computer. In fact, it will extend its life.

- Consider buying a laptop computer as it is far more energy efficient and consumes less materials than a desktop computer with monitor.

- An LCD flat screen is more energy efficient than a standard cathode ray tube monitor.

- Reduce paper consumption by using both sides of all paper, using recycled paper, and storing documents electronically where possible, rather than printing them.

- Purchase an Energy Star fax machine and printer that can scan double-sided pages.

- Remember to turn your printer off when not using it or at the end of the working day.

- When printing large documents, reduce the font size and the margins to get more print on the page and minimise the page extent.

Wooden furniture

Wood is a wonderful natural product that is also renewable, recyclable, biodegradable, and non-toxic. Unfortunately, there are many illegally harvested timber products on the market in Australia, most of them coming from China or Indonesia. The Indonesian government admits that over 80 per cent of its wood is illegally logged and the Australian government has reported that $400 million worth of timber products within Australia have come from illegal forests.[61] This is not just an Australian, but a global issue, with our consumption of a variety of woods leading to the destruction of many of the world's rainforests. Less than 10 per cent of the planet is now covered by natural forest and this is decreasing rapidly. Greenpeace estimates that an area of natural forest the size of a soccer pitch is cut down every two seconds somewhere in the world. This is clearly not a sustainable situation.

As an individual consumer it can be hard to know whether the coffee table or dining table you are purchasing has been made from sustainably forested wood, particularly as there is minimal accreditation currently available for timber. The Forest Stewardship Council (FSC) is an international organisation that provides accreditation for sustainable forestry throughout the world; its website is at **www.fsc.org/en** and the Australian office is at **www.fscaustralia.org** It is possible to buy FSC-accredited wood and paper products, but currently very few furniture products are accredited.

When buying wooden furniture ask the sales assistant or the manufacturer where the wood was grown and whether it has come from plantation or intact natural forest. Plantation forestry is better because this means it is from a managed forest and not from old-growth timber. Ask if the item has been produced with FSC-accredited wood. Some manufacturers are concerned about the source of their wood, and the more consumers demand to know the origins of wood, the more they will need to trace its origin. The international furniture chain Ikea sources much, but not all, of its wood from FSC-accredited forests, and it is attempting to move to a completely sustainable forestry system for its wood. If a multinational can manage its business using completely sustainable forestry, it must be possible for many smaller businesses to do so also.

It may be difficult to trace the origin of the wood in your piece of furniture, but be particularly concerned if the furniture or the wood has come from Indonesia, Papua New Guinea, or Brazil. Unless the trader can prove that it came from an FSC-accredited source in those countries, it is likely to be illegally logged.

Also avoid new wooden furniture made from particleboard, plywood, or fibreboard (MDF). All of these composite wood types contain large amounts of formaldehyde and other toxins that are very bad for air quality and have a large ecological footprint.

One way to avoid the possibility that your furniture is the product of illegal logging or made with toxic ingredients is to purchase a second-hand item or one made from recycled wood. Yes, it may still have come from an unsustainable source, albeit some time ago, but at least you are not adding to any land clearing with your purchase. In fact, you are decreasing the amount of timber being logged by choosing products that are made with existing materials.

One further suggestion regarding wooden furniture is to get something made from recycled wood by a local furniture maker. You can get exactly the item you require, with measurements to fit your house, and you can choose the wood and manufacturer yourself. (Check Greenpeace's Good Wood Guide at **www.greenpeace.com.au** for sustainable timber merchants.) Admittedly, it will take a bit more effort and may not be the cheapest option, but it will be a complete original with your own stamp of creativity, and its transport will produce minimal greenhouse gases. Just make sure your manufacturer doesn't use any toxic chemicals such as pentachlorophenol (Penta) to seal or treat the wood. Ask them instead to use a natural, non-toxic product such as linseed oil or beeswax to give a soft finish, or shellac if you are looking for a glossy effect.

8 APPLIANCES AND HOUSEHOLD GOODS

Top Tips for purchasing wooden furniture

- When purchasing a wooden product, ask about the source of the wood and whether it has been sustainably forested.
- Choose products certified by the Forest Stewardship Council wherever they are available.
- If you can't be sure of the source of the wood, buy a product made of recycled wood or buy second-hand.
- Why not design your own piece of furniture and get it made by a local furniture maker with recycled wood? It will be totally unique!
- Look out for toxic chemical finishes on wooden products and always go natural with linseed oil or beeswax where possible.

Rugs

The problem of toxic chemicals emitted from carpets is discussed in **Chapter 9: Building and Renovating**. If you want to install new carpet in your house, the best ones to purchase are those that use minimal toxic chemicals in production.

Handmade rugs are a good alternative to carpets, but they can also raise ethical issues. There are concerns about enforced child labour in many countries, particularly in South Asia, where children sometimes work to pay off debts in conditions similar to slavery. One way to avoid this is to purchase rugs that have the international Rugmark label, which was set up in 1994 by a number of human rights organisations. Rugmark states that nearly 300 000 children are being exploited in the rug-making industry and the organisation works hard to stop this practice, with its label denoting carpets that have been made without the use of child labour. The scheme also guarantees that some money from the sale of each rug goes to educate former child weavers in India, Pakistan, and Nepal. Rugs purchased from fair trade shops such as Oxfam are also made under a scheme where the workers have been paid a fair amount for their labour.

> Look for the international Rugmark label.

Household cleaning

The average modern household contains up to 45 litres of chemicals under the kitchen and bathroom sinks, simply for cleaning with! There are over 70 000 chemicals in cleaning products; many of them have not been fully tested for safety and some of them are known hazardous materials. Most of us don't realise the toxic effect of these chemicals on the air we breathe and the surfaces we put them on, but who hasn't felt dizzy when cleaning the bathroom with ammonia or bleach-based products?

Many natural products on the market are not only highly effective but also biodegradable, low-allergy, not tested on animals, and presented in recyclable packaging. These are far preferable to chemical cleaners as they won't negatively impact on your health and will have a minimal impact on the planet. For an even cheaper cleaning regimen, use simple products that work just as well. Baking soda is fabulous for cleaning most things, as well as clearing drains and deodorising. White vinegar is great on glass, tiles, and mirrors. Essential oils such as tea tree, eucalyptus, and citrus are all excellent disinfectants and add fragrance to other natural cleansers. Pure soap flakes and hot water will perform many cleaning jobs without resorting to chemicals. The expensive but effective Enjo[62] fibre cloths, as well as cheaper microfibre cloths available from supermarkets will not make you wheeze or feel dizzy but will do a great cleaning job with nothing more than a bit of water. So clear the cupboards of the chemicals and go natural. It will minimise your environmental impact, save you money and be much better for your family's health. Don't forget to check with your local council where to take the chemicals for safe recycling, as they shouldn't be tipped down the drain or sent to landfill.

For more information on cleaning the house naturally, there are a number of books available including *Chemical Free Home* by Robin Stewart and *Spotless* by Shannon Lush and Jennifer Fleming.

Fabrics and soft furnishings

The fabrics in our homes include curtains, cushions, furniture coverings, bedding, linen, and towels. Although synthetic fibres are now prevalent in the textiles market, natural fabrics such as linen, wool, hemp and silk, use far less energy-intensive manufacturing processes and are far better for the environment.

In contrast, synthetic fabrics are made from plastics derived from petrochemicals, and may continue to emit toxins long after manufacture. Many soft furnishing fabrics contain PVC and formaldehyde which make them flameproof, shrink-resistant, and wrinkle-proof, but which are not good for the planet or our health. Synthetics also do not absorb moisture and they inhibit evaporation, so they are not ideal close to your skin in bed linen or clothing.

Be cautious about cotton-polyester blend fabrics, especially in bed linen, which all have a formaldehyde finish unless they state otherwise. Cotton also has formaldehyde in it when labelled 'shrink-resistant' or 'non-iron'.

Dyes used in many fabrics can be unstable and may leak from certain fabrics when damp or even if next to damp skin. Some fabric dyes, including dichlorobenzidene, are carcinogenic, and should be avoided where possible. Of course it's hard to know what dyes are used on products; that's why it's best to go organic where possible, which will guarantee that natural dyes are used.

Wool, cotton, and linen are great for mattresses and bedding in general. Wool both insulates and absorbs moisture, and since we sweat up to a litre per night the absorbent qualities of our bed covers are important. Wool is particularly good in winter on the bed, as blankets or woollen doona and as woollen underlay, to retain your body heat and minimise the need for heating in the room.

Cotton allows your skin to breathe and softens over time to become very comfortable. However, cotton is one of the most sprayed crops on the planet, so it comes to us through a process that involves an array of toxic pesticides and herbicides. There is a growing range of cotton and linen products that now promote themselves as being organic and, although they are more expensive, they are far better for your health and will last a lot longer than synthetics. Check **www.greenpagesaustralia.com.au** for organic cotton retailers and choose organic cotton or an alternative natural fibre wherever possible.

> ## Top Tips for healthy fabrics
>
> - Wash everything before you use it to get rid of excess chemicals.
> - Choose natural fabrics over synthetic ones and be wary of special finishes such as 'shrink-resistant' or 'non-iron'.
> - Ask for organic cotton as much as possible. The more we demand it, the more readily available and cheaper it will become.
> - Extend the life of your fabrics by cleaning them carefully, but avoid dry cleaning due to the chemical processes. Use a hand wash or gentle machine wash instead.
> - Insulate your bed with woollen blankets and a woollen underlay in winter to keep you toasty warm and avoid the need for extra heating in the bedroom.

9
BUILDING AND RENOVATING

In many aspects of our lives we can minimise our effect on the planet by simple changes to our behaviour. An even more impressive reduction of our footprint can be achieved over a period of many years when we totally redesign or renovate our home to become more energy efficient and environmentally sustainable.

The average Australian house in the 1950s was about 90 square metres in size; it has now swelled to approximately 260 square metres. Yet the average European house is still only 100 square metres. It is quite extraordinary that the size of our houses has more than doubled in the last 50 years, and this significantly contributes to making the average Australian eco-footprint one of the largest in the world. The larger our houses, the more resources are consumed in making them, and the more resources are likely to be consumed in the running of them.

More than 137 000 new homes are built every year in Australia, and on average we either move house or do a significant renovation every seven years. These times of massive change to our housing situation provide us with a magnificent opportunity to make decisions that will drastically improve energy efficiency, make our homes water-wise, and create spaces that are a delight to live in. If a house is designed well to maximise light and air flow, you may hardly ever need to use an air conditioning

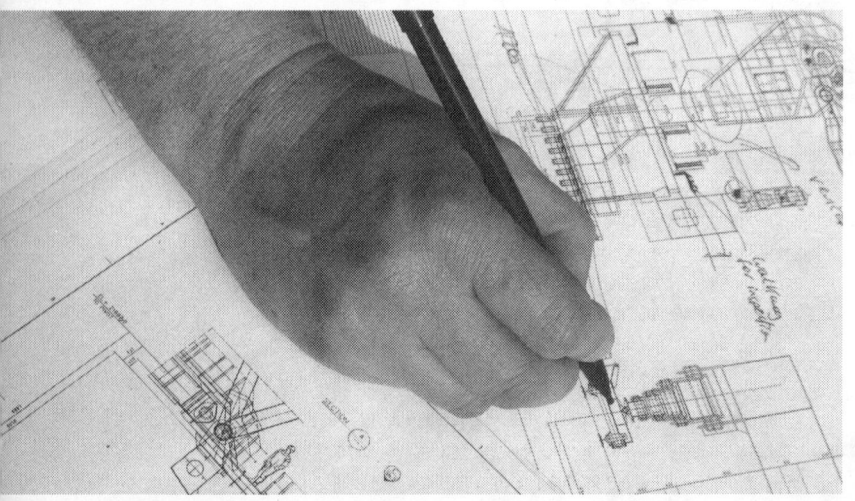

9 BUILDING AND RENOVATING

system. With passive solar techniques, such as maximising the use of sunlight in winter and minimising excess heat in summer, the amount of electricity and gas needed to power your home can become almost insignificant. Many aspects can be incorporated into a house design to make it more sustainable and cheaper to live in, with the benefits accumulating over the years.

Every new building in Australia must now comply with certain energy-efficient requirements, as determined by the Building Code of Australia. These vary depending upon the type of housing and the climate zone. For example, in Victoria new houses must now have either a rainwater tank for toilet flushing or a solar hot water system. Why not have both?

While adding energy-efficient elements will sometimes increase the cost of the house in the first place, they will save you enormous amounts of money in the long term. Also, many sustainable design features cost no more than unsustainable design; it's about putting the house together in an efficient manner with consideration of the elements straight up. Poor design will definitely cost you more in the long run, with greater operating costs and a house that is not as comfortable to live in.

There is no doubt that many of the following suggestions will be required for new houses in the future, so why not get ahead of the curve and add as many efficiencies as possible when building or renovating your home now? You will reap the benefits by living in a pleasant environment that easily maintains a comfortable temperature, increases in value and desirability as time goes by, and can provide a potent example of the benefits of imaginative energy-efficient design. Your sustainable house may look just like everyone else's house on the street, as much sustainable design is now practically invisible, but your bills and your greenhouse gas emissions will be significantly less.

A good architect or builder will consider a number of factors in providing you the most energy-efficient house, including the climatic conditions, the local conditions such as the slope of the property and prevailing breezes, the site orientation, the zoning or location of rooms in your house, as well as the materials and construction techniques. Of course, compromise is sometimes inevitable and we can't always include all the aspects of a sustainable house that we wish for, but incorporating at least some elements will make a difference to your footprint and your ongoing bills. Keep in mind that you don't always have to start from scratch either, as there are a variety of options for adaptation to existing plans. Project homes can also be adapted to add sustainable elements and this is always worth considering if you are more comfortable buying off the plan.

It's important to note that over 40 per cent of the waste accumulating in landfill sites throughout Australia is generated by the building industry. When building your sustainable house, you will want to use as many recycled and recyclable materials as possible and choose a builder who is responsible with waste management. It would be hypocritical to build a fantastic sustainable house that reduces your footprint while making a huge contribution to landfill in the process.

While I do not profess to be a building expert, I am interested in this topic and desperate to design and build my own sustainable house with my partner as soon as possible. So I have compiled a brief overview of the major elements to consider and discuss with your own architect, designer, draftsman, or builder when considering either renovating or building a new home. Read on and start imagining your ideal sustainable home!

Use of the sun

The life-sustaining sun is one of the most powerful elements to consider when building a new home. In Australia, a design needs to maximise use of the sun by facing rooms that are most in use – your family room, kitchen, lounge, and dining room – to the north or northwest. A deciduous tree in front of these windows can provide shade in summer and allow maximum penetration of the winter sun. Rooms that are used less often or primarily at night, such as bedrooms and bathrooms, can be positioned to face south or southeast, which are less light-filled areas of the home. Solar panels should also be directed towards the north in order to maximise solar uptake. If at all possible, it's of great benefit early in the design process to look carefully at where the sun falls on a block of land, as well as any shadows created by trees or nearby buildings, throughout the day during midwinter, as well as the spring and autumn equinoxes. This will give you vital knowledge on how to utilise the sun's rays to best potential.

The sun's path in summer and winter

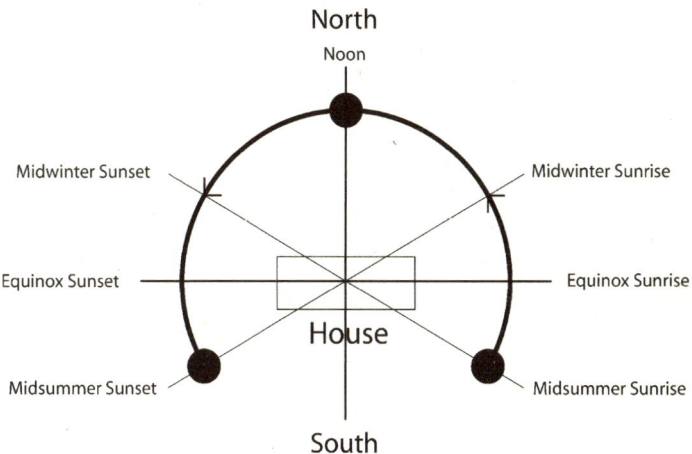

Sun Altitudes Vary Depending on Latitude

Climate

The climate should also be carefully considered, as what is useful in the weather conditions of Victoria or Tasmania may not work or be irrelevant in Queensland. Take into consideration the amount of rainfall in your area, the strength of the light during different times of year, the directional flow of cooling breezes, as well as the quality of the soil in the area.

Choosing a good site

The ideal block of land in many parts of Australia on which to build an energy-efficient house should allow you to design with the main living areas facing north. Ideally,

SUSTAINABLE HOUSE DAY

Every year on Sustainable House Day you can visit some of many hundreds of houses across Australia and New Zealand to see how they have been made more sustainable, and gain ideas and tips for your own renovations or new building. The annual event is held on the **second weekend of September**, and purchase of your ticket at one house allows you to visit all the open houses you can get to with no extra charge. For more information, go to **www.sustainablehouseday.com**

the block should slope down to the north and provide an area to the north of at least 5.5 metres from a single-storey building, or 10 metres from a two-storey building, to allow unimpeded access to the sun. In high-density areas this may not be possible. If your block doesn't allow good access to the northern sunlight because it is overshadowed by other buildings, or because it is small or irregularly shaped or facing east or west, there are ways to overcome this with your design features. In the fierce heat of northern Australia you will want to exclude the sun year-round with small windows and shading devices, and instead focus on making the most of cooling breezes.

Room zoning

To maximise heat distribution and allow you to close off certain areas for heating or cooling, try to zone areas with similar uses together and separate them with doorways so that areas can be shut off from the rest of the house. Large open-plan living areas and really high ceilings, while looking spectacular, can be costly in terms of heating and cooling. It's also a good idea to keep the rooms that require hot water, such as the bathroom, laundry and kitchen, close together to make it cheaper and more efficient to provide their water needs.

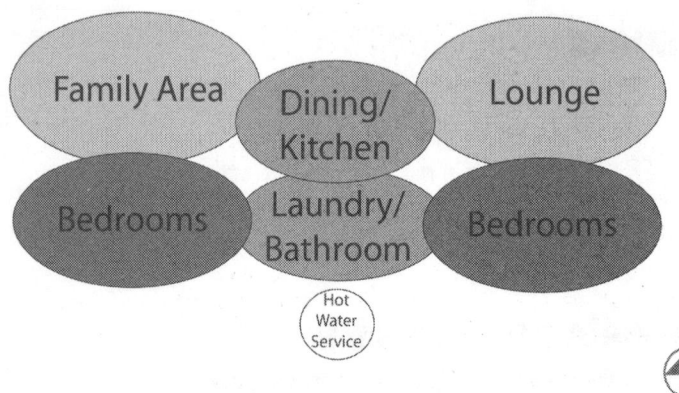

Room zoning contributes to energy efficiency

Flooring and walls

Concrete floors and masonry walls provide thermal mass to absorb heat throughout summer and winter; they then release the heat slowly, helping to maintain the house at an even temperature. Tiles on a concrete slab floor also enable the floor to store heat from windows in the winter. Timber-floored houses need less glass to heat the home in winter, and carpet on the timber floors will also provide extra insulation. Lightweight materials, such as timber or plasterboard, can help internally to allow rooms to heat up or cool down quickly, which can be of benefit in tropical climates where you open doors and windows to cool the house.

If you decide to have timber flooring, ensure that it is recycled or plantation timber and that solvent-based chemical products are not used to seal the floor after sanding. Water-based sealants are a good alternative and won't stink up your house with chemicals.

Windows

As mentioned previously, in most climates it's best to have the largest windows on the north side of the house to maximise sunlight, but they will need some form of external shading during summer or otherwise they will encourage overheating. Trees, pergolas, or eaves over windows are good for external shade, as well as internal curtains or blinds with pelmets. Alternatively, you may reduce the size of these windows if the summer sun will be too intense.

Cross-ventilation is important to allow summer breezes to cool down the house, so try to position windows opposite one another to maximise the use of nature's ventilation.

Windows on the east and west side of the house receive a great deal of sun in summer, but little for the rest of the year, so they are best kept fairly small and should be shaded in summer. South-facing windows should also be kept reasonably small as they receive little winter sun.

Careful consideration should also be given to window frames to maximise your insulation. Window frames that reduce heat loss include timber, vinyl, and aluminium.

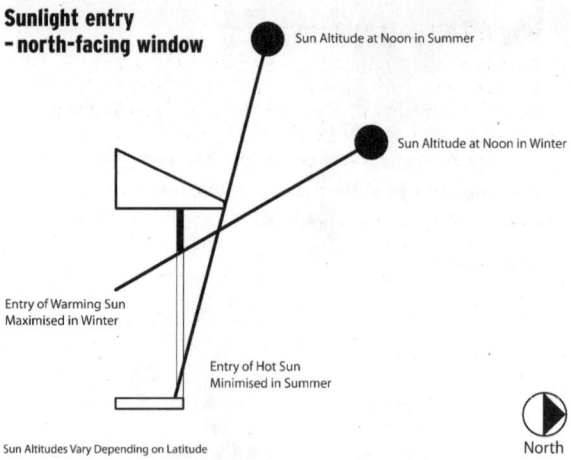

Sunlight entry – north-facing window

Sun Altitudes Vary Depending on Latitude

North

Both vinyl and aluminium need a thermal break that separates the frame into interior and exterior components in order to reduce heat conduction.[63] Pelmets and close-fitting curtains or blinds are also helpful in winter to trap heat inside the house and minimise heating costs.

You can also use specialised glass treatments or double-glazing on your glass to reduce heat transfer, minimise noise from outside, and help to insulate the house. Particularly on a house with large north-facing windows, double-glazing can significantly reduce air conditioning costs in summer and heating costs in winter.

Well-designed eaves keep out the sun in summer and admit it in winter.

Skylights

Skylights can be fitted into both new and existing homes and can let in three times as much light as a vertical window of the same size. They can dramatically increase the available light in a part of the house that has no windows, providing an effective way to admit daylight and save energy. Like windows, skylights need controls such as double-glazing and blinds to maximise insulation. It is beneficial to be able to open or vent your skylight to allow trapped heat to escape in summer, particularly in two-storey houses.

Buying an existing house

You may be considering buying an existing house instead of renovating or building. In this case consider whether the design is energy efficient, and if not, how easily you would be able to renovate with energy-efficient features.

Ask the following questions when inspecting:

- Does the roof have north-facing areas without any impediment from trees or buildings that could be fitted with solar panels?
- Are there north-facing windows in the living areas?
- Does the house have good shade, or allow for the easy addition of such elements as eaves or deciduous trees?
- Does the placement of windows in the house allow good cross ventilation?
- Are the windows double-glazed?
- Is the house easily zoned to block off the bedrooms from living areas?
- Is the house well insulated or is there the potential to add insulation fairly cheaply?
- What are the current heating and air conditioning systems and could they easily be replaced if inadequate?
- Is the house draught-proof or is it losing air through gaps or poor design in walls, floors and around windows?

Insulation

Some people skimp on insulation when building or renovating in order to save a few bucks, but installing insulation is one of the single most effective things you can do in order to improve thermal efficiency. Insulation in the roof, ceiling, walls, and suspended floors can keep you up to seven degrees cooler in summer and 10 degrees warmer in winter. Your climate determines the level of insulation needed, so consult with an expert in your area.

Of course, draughts should be reduced in the house by sealing all gaps in windows and doors, and fitting draught excluders at the base of doors. Any open fireplaces should also have draught excluders so you do not lose valuable warm air up the chimney in winter.

Lighting

If you make the most of the natural light from your windows, you won't need as much internal lighting. Light-coloured walls and ceilings also reflect and maximise light.

Install separate switches for your lights so that you can turn off those that aren't needed, and use fluorescent tubes and compact fluorescent bulbs as much as possible, rather than downlights or low-voltage lamps. These are not energy-efficient, and downlights may require gaps in the ceiling insulation because the transformers get hot and need space around them. These gaps in the insulation cause greater heat loss in winter and more heat penetration in summer. For more information see the section on lighting in **Chapter 4: Energy.**

Water

There are many opportunities for the energy-efficient house to minimise water use and drastically reduce your use of the mains supply, which can be of enormous benefit in many areas. You can cut your current levels of use as much as possible within the house with water-saving techniques (see **Chapter 5: Water**), make better use of rainwater by installing tanks, and recycle your water so that it can be re-used on site. By reducing, re-using, and recycling your water you will maximise what you have and little will need to be thrown away.

Grey water recycling

There are two types of recycled water: grey water, which is the waste water from the shower, bathroom basin and laundry; and black water, which is the waste water from toilet and the kitchen sink after dishwashing. Although it's fine to re-use water from the kitchen that has been used to rinse vegetables or other light rinsing jobs, most dishwater is considered black water because it generally contains chemicals and food scraps, and therefore bacteria. Black water needs biological or chemical treatment before it is suitable for re-using, and can only be used outdoors. Grey water needs much less processing and it can be re-used indoors in the toilet and washing machine, as well as on the garden. The Australian Greenhouse Office estimates that average household produces up to 113 litres of grey water per day[64] that could be recycled and re-used around the home.

To minimise the chemical treatment needed for both types of water, it is imperative to ensure your washing

Top Tips for a grey water recycling system

- Make sure there is no possibility of the grey water being re-used as drinking water.
- Use grey water only from low-contamination sources such as the shower, bathtub, hand basin, and washing machine.
- Dishwashing water should generally not be used in a grey water system because it contains food matter, fat, and grease.
- Don't use grey water on fruit or vegetable patches due to potential contamination of raw fruit and veggies.
- Ideally, to reduce the risk of contamination, grey water should be distributed around the garden by a below-ground system, such as drip irrigation with a thick layer of mulch on the garden.
- Install signs indicating that grey water is being used; the pipes that carry it should be a different colour to the standard plumbing pipes.

detergent, dishwashing liquid, and dishwasher detergents are all biodegradable products that do not put chemicals into the water, as this will increase your treatment costs. This is the case for all water, whether you are recycling it or not: if the chemicals aren't affecting humans they may travel down the drains and affect land animals and marine life.

As a precaution, grey water is also best kept away from fruit and vegetable gardens if you intend to eat the produce raw, just in case any pathogens are still present. It's also important not to use excessive amounts of grey water on the garden, because this can cause problems: excess nutrients and organic material may clog the soil, leach into the waterways, or inhibit plant growth.

There are many different treatment systems for recycling grey water and black water on site, and you need to check with your local council regarding any restrictions on re-using water in your area. In many cases you can divert untreated grey water for re-use directly, but for storage and treatment of water you may need to obtain a permit from your local water authority, and from your local council if you intend to set up a septic system. A licensed plumber must do the work of setting up a grey water or black water treatment system. Check with your state water conservation authority (see **Resources List**) first to determine what level of permit is required, as every state, and sometimes even local council, is different. It is also a good idea to talk to other people in your area who have installed grey water systems, as they will know the local issues that will need to be considered, such as soil type, groundwater, and seasonal rainfall.

Hot water

Water heating in the average Australian home counts for at least 16 per cent of our greenhouse gas emissions and can represent up to 50 per cent of our energy bills. If you are using electricity, heating water will generate about four tonnes of greenhouse gases per year.[65] More than half of hot water use is in the bathroom, one-third in the laundry, and the rest in the kitchen. Installing the most efficient water heater for your household size and water use can save you a lot of money and drastically reduce your emissions.

When designing your home, it's economical to keep the rooms that need hot water, such as the bathroom, laundry, and kitchen, close together, and to install an energy-efficient solar, gas or heat-pump hot water system close to these rooms. You can even create a small drying room or airing cupboard near your hot water service to utilise the heat it gives off to dry your towels and clothes in winter. Insulate or lag hot water pipes, even plastic ones, to prevent loss of heat from the pipes.

Solar hot water

Using solar energy to heat your water produces no greenhouse gas emissions and can provide up to 90 per cent of your requirements, depending on your climate and model of heater. Most solar water heaters need backup for times when there is no sunny weather, and the most efficient backup source is gas rather than electricity. A gas-boosted solar water system is the most energy-efficient form of water heating and will reduce greenhouse gas emissions by over 75 per cent in comparison to a standard electric off-peak system. In most states, this will reduce your greenhouse gas emissions by approximately 3.7 tonnes per year, which is equivalent to taking a small car off the road.

A solar water heater costs more up-front than other types of heaters, but this cost will be offset over a period

---

RENEWABLE ENERGY CERTIFICATES REBATE

In addition to state government rebates for the installation of solar water heaters, the federal government provides rebates in the form of Renewable Energy Certificates (RECs). These are granted when you replace other types of hot water heater with solar, or put one in a new home. The certificates can be sold to renewable energy generators or agents in order to meet their government-required renewable energy targets. You get a certain number of RECs when you purchase a solar water heater, which you can then trade for money or use to reduce the up-front cost of your heater. There is some fine print regarding the details, so check the government website to see if you may be eligible for RECs: **www.orer.gov.au**

of between five and seven years by significantly reduced heating bills. Government rebates are also available in some states for the installation of a solar water heater, so check with your state government sustainability authority (see **Resources List**).

Most solar hot water systems use solar collectors or panels on the roof to absorb the sun's energy and heat water that flows through them. It is then stored in an insulated tank until you need it. In a passive system, which is more energy efficient, water flows unassisted between the collectors and the tank, whereas in an active system the water is pumped between the two, requiring more energy. You can have a split system, where the water tank is on the ground, or a close-coupled system, where the tank is on the roof right next to the panels.

Most, but not all, homes can incorporate a solar hot water system. Ideally, your roof should meet the following requirements in order to maximise the usage of solar hot water:

☐ **a section that faces roughly north (30 degree deviation to the east or west is acceptable) where it can get sunlight in winter from about 9 a.m. to 3 p.m.**
☐ **a slope of between 15 and 30 degrees, although you can use a mounting frame to get the right angle.**
☐ **good weight-bearing capacity if you intend to place the water storage tank on the roof.**

The storage tank is fitted with an electric, gas, or solid-fuel booster that will heat the water when the sun is not enough. Again, gas is preferable, as your emissions will be far lower if you use gas to boost the solar. In hot climates you may be able to turn the booster off over summer to save costs, as well as turning it off when you go away for a length of time. If you live in a cold area you may also need extra insulation or frost protection on the panels, and on the tank if it is housed outside.

Rainwater tanks

With the current drought conditions in Australia and the rapidly decreasing levels of water in our dams and water catchments, it seems ridiculous that the water we use to flush our toilets or water our gardens is top-notch drinking water. The recycling or desalination of water is now a reality in many places, and individuals are also installing rainwater tanks to make the most of what nature provides. Using rainwater in a variety of ways in your household can drastically reduce your water bills and help you become more self-sufficient. A rainwater tank does need regular maintenance, such as checking and cleaning gutters to ensure that the water is healthy and safe to use, particularly if you are intending to drink it. The main contamination risks are from animal droppings and airborne pollutants such as dirt and leaves, but with regular maintenance these should not be a problem. You can also cheaply install a First Flush water filter that will keep the first amount of rainwater out of the tank, as this is more likely to hold contaminants than the rest of the water.

Most people with a rainwater tank are also connected to a mains water system. The size of tank you need will depend on the intended use of the rainwater, your typical water consumption, the area of your roof, whether you are connected to the mains or not, and the amount of rainfall in your area.

If you intend to use rainwater for drinking only, a small tank of 400 to 1000 litres will suffice. It is relatively cheap, and it can be attached to the roof or high up on the side of your house and then gravity-fed to a tap in your kitchen. For garden watering you can fit a tap directly to the tank that can then be used for all your outdoor needs. It depends on how big your garden is, but you would generally need a capacity of between 2000 and 4000 litres for year-round watering.

If you're keen to become entirely self-sufficient with your water, you will need a large tank. The size depends on your daily water usage (you can check a water bill to find this), the size of your roof, and the rainfall in your area throughout the year. Once you know the rainfall, you can calculate the amount of water you will

Composting toilet

The thought of a composting toilet might bring back terrible visions from camping holidays in childhood where the toilet was a terrifying pit covered by a bit of plywood and surrounded by a swarm of blowflies. Composting toilets have come a long way since then; they can now conserve precious water and avoid the disposal of pollutants into waterways without producing any smell. A composting toilet uses no water whatsoever; it decomposes material through a complex bio-chemical process, which produces fertiliser that can be used on the garden. Commercial designs exist or you can build your own with readily available materials. However, the production of compost from your toilet waste can take a while and it can require more maintenance than a standard toilet, so it's certainly not for everyone. For more information and details on contacts for commercially built units in Australia go to **www.compostingtoilet.org**

---

receive, on the basis that one millilitre of rainfall on one square metre of roof will give you one litre of water. You need to be able to store enough water from high-rainfall months to get you through the drier months. So you may need a capacity of up to 30 000 litres to ensure you have water supplies for the entire year.

Most tanks cost well under $8000, including installation and delivery, which is fairly cheap when you consider that a large tank could mean you will never receive water bills again. You can purchase tanks in all sorts of shapes and sizes that can be incorporated as part of the house or garden design, or even buried underground, and thus quite inconspicuous.

Tanks are made from plastic (polyethylene), concrete, or galvanised steel. The steel is cheapest, but it doesn't last as long because it eventually corrodes. Concrete tanks are strong and last a long time. They are usually built on-site so they can be designed to meet your exact needs and they are the best type of tank to bury, although if there is a lot of ground movement they may crack. Plastic tanks are tough, durable, and lighter than other types, as well as readily available through hardware stores and specialist retailers. Most rainwater tanks come with a 20-year warranty. Many states have a rebate scheme for purchasing a new water tank; go to the water conservation authority in your state (see **Resources List**) or your local council for further details.

Energy

The energy source you use for your home can make a huge difference to your greenhouse gas emissions. Most of us are connected to the electricity supply grid and can choose renewable by buying Green Power, but when renovating or building we can make some big decisions that will allow us to generate our own energy, and sell excess electricity back to the grid or even get off the grid completely. While these choices may cost a lot up front, they usually operate at a very low cost and insulate us from future energy price rises. Again, rebates are available for renewable energy power systems.

Options for energy supply include photovoltaic (solar) panels, wind turbines, and micro hydro generators. The most common of these is photovoltaics and that is what I will focus on in this section.

Photovoltaic panels

These panels convert sunlight into electricity and require little maintenance, as they have no moving parts. They last at least 20 years before needing to be replaced, and make no noise. Like a solar hot water system, they need a sloping section of roof that faces north and receives sunlight between 9 a.m. and 3 p.m. in winter. In fact, solar hot water and electricity can often run from the same set of panels.

The module can be fixed onto the roof with a frame mount or integrated into the roof, skylights or awnings. You can buy models with an adjustable frame to tilt manually throughout the year with the changing angle of the sun by season (but you have to remember to tilt them) or have them fixed in their tilt angle. Solar panels are streamlined and an integral part of contemporary architecture and you shouldn't feel you need to hide them away on your roof.

Cash rebates are available from the Australian Greenhouse Office for householders who install photovoltaic systems, and you may also qualify for a state government rebate. For more information go to **www.greenhouse.gov.au** or the energy authority in your

Building materials

The materials we use to build or renovate our homes can have large implications for the environment at different stages of their life cycle. So it's important to consider the impact of a material beyond its use in the home and look at the energy required to extract, process, and transport the material to the site, as well as the waste created from using that material within the building, and what happens to the material at the end of its useful life. By choosing materials that minimise impact on the environment throughout their life cycle, we can make a significant reduction in our ecological footprint.

Every material has its own embodied energy. This is the energy consumed in all the processes involved in taking a material from its natural state, processing it, and getting it to the building site. For example, aluminium has such a high level of embodied energy that it has been called 'congealed electricity', whereas glass has a reasonably low level.

It used to be thought that the embodied energy of a building was relatively small in comparison to the energy consumed during the building's lifetime; however, research has shown that the embodied energy in the building can be significant and equivalent to many years of energy used in operating the building. According to the CSIRO, the average Australian household has embodied energy equal to 15 years of the energy requirements of actually living in and operating the house.[66]

Embodied energy can be justified if it significantly reduces the operating energy of a building: for instance, large amounts of insulation will cut the operational costs of heating and cooling. However, products with high embodied energy are not always used to their maximum potential and can sometimes be wasted. Embodied

EARTH BUILDING

Natural building materials such as mud brick and rammed earth (pisé) have been used for thousands of years worldwide. Even today, up to half of the world's population is housed in earth homes. Mud brick and rammed earth are materials with some of the lowest embodied energy. They need little processing, can often be made on-site by hand, and can be returned to the earth after use. They are also very cheap in comparison to other materials. For more information on earth building, visit the Earth Building Association of Australia website at **www.ebaa.asn.au**

energy is an important consideration in building or renovating an energy-efficient house, and as much as possible you should build with materials that are low in embodied energy. Calculating the exact embodied energy in a product is difficult, particularly when it depends on factors such as the transport of the material. If a material that is innately high in embodied energy, such as aluminium, is used close to where it was manufactured, its total may be lower than timber that has been transported by road from a significant distance. Also, recycled products can greatly reduce the embodied energy in a house. While there can be no hard and fast rules on this topic, the following tips will help you to minimise wastage and reduce embodied energy in your building materials.

Life-cycle assessment

A way to determine the embodied energy of a material, as well as its impact throughout its entire life, is to do a life-cycle assessment (LCA). This examines the total environmental impact of a material or an entire house through every step of its life from extraction – such as logging or mining – through to manufacture, transport, usage, and then disposal or recycling. It is complicated but it can include impacts such as greenhouse gas emissions, energy and water usage, resource depletion, and amount of waste going to landfill. More information is available at the Centre for Design at **buildlca.rmit.edu.au**

Top Tips for reducing embodied energy

- Design a house for long life and the ability to be adapted easily.
- Use an energy-efficient design that maximises passive solar features and minimises material usage.
- Use durable, low maintenance materials.
- Consider using recycled materials where possible.
- Use materials that have been sourced locally to minimise transport emissions.
- Avoid wasting material in the construction.
- Recycle excess material by either re-selling or selling to a recycler.
- Choose materials made with renewable energy where possible.
- Ask suppliers about the embodied energy in their products.

Waste minimisation

When building or renovating it's important to consider what happens to the waste generated, keeping in mind that over 40 per cent of landfill comes from the building industry. To make the most of reducing waste on site there will need to be co-operation between yourself, the builder, and the designer. As you won't be on site all the time, you need to be able to trust your builder to use best practice to minimise waste. It's good to bring up this aspect early in the consultation process to ensure that the builder will participate. Choosing to renovate rather than demolish an existing house can also have a large impact on the amount of waste produced, as will the choice of materials and construction methods.

A waste management plan can be included in the initial tender process and contracts to provide economic incentives for recycling and make clear where responsibilities and benefits lie. You may also include performance clauses regarding recycling and waste minimisation in the contract. Ideally, like-minded professionals who are concerned with sustainability
issues will be most effective at implementing sustainability strategies and minimising waste at
all stages of the project.

Indoor air quality

Another impact of using certain materials in building can be the effect on indoor air quality within the new or renovated home. Exposure to high levels of pollutants from synthetic building materials, paints, carpets, finishes, and even new furnishings can be detrimental to health. Unfortunately, a variety of chemicals used in common materials can place our health at risk, as they have not been objectively tested on their own, let alone on an accumulated basis as they combine with other common chemicals.

New homes or renovations generally emit the most toxins, as the toxic emissions from a product tend to decrease over time. The CSIRO estimates that some new homes generate exposure many times the maximum allowable limits of some indoor air pollutants, and this may continue for many weeks after occupying the home.[67]

When looking at reducing the potential for toxic emissions in your new home, natural materials are generally preferable to synthetic materials, although this is not always the case. Pressed-wood products, including plywood, blockboard, MDF (medium-density fibreboard), and particleboard, are often made with toxic resins and treated with formaldehyde. Avoid these and use untreated products instead.

ECOVILLAGES

There are a number of housing projects popping up around Australia that incorporate sustainable living in their design. One is the **Aldinga Arts Ecovillage** in South Australia, an entire village with communal vegetable gardens and neighbourhood orchards, as well as sustainable houses and townhouses that feature solar water heating, rainwater tanks, and sustainable timbers, and take into account material life cycles during building. Incorporating sustainability practices such as these on a large scale is very exciting and hopefully the way of the future. See **www.aldinga-artsecovillage.com.au**

Carpets are often treated with highly toxic materials in order to repel insects and stains, and these chemicals can make you ill. As many as 120 chemicals may be used in a synthetic carpet, and even wool carpets have toxins added to them to protect them from wear and tear. Keep in mind that children and pets are most likely to suffer the health effects from chemicals in floor coverings as they are close to the floor where most of the toxins are emitted. If possible, minimise the use of carpet in your new home and use rugs on natural flooring surfaces instead.

To avoid high levels of toxicity when buying new products, always check the ingredients or ask to see the product's materials safety data sheet. Make sure that the supplier has satisfied all your concerns regarding toxicity levels before you purchase the product. When renovating a house, be wary of stripping old lead-based paints, which are highly toxic, and call in the experts if you think that asbestos may be present.

It's important to ventilate your house by frequently opening windows and allowing air to flow through, or by installing an air filter. This is particularly important in the first few months of living in a new home. Pot plants can be helpful in improving indoor air quality, and should be used as much as possible. Common plants such as aloe vera, bamboo, peace lilies, and gerberas are effective at reducing vapours released by synthetic chemicals.

Natural building products are far preferable to synthetic products. Ask what finishes are used to treat materials, even natural ones, as a chemical-based finish will counter the positive effect of going natural. The following are all good natural alternatives:

Wood: beeswax polish, linseed oil, or shellac

Brickwork: clay or lime plaster for walls, and lime mortar
Flooring: natural linoleum, cork or bamboo
Countertops, floors, and other surfaces: stone, marble, slate, or granite
Paints and finishes: plant-based rather than petrochemical-based paints, and water-based rather than oil-based finishes.

Timber

Timber house construction has a long history in Australia and is still popular. Timber is a renewable building material that stores carbon during its growing phase, which is very desirable to soak up greenhouse gas emissions. Timber is commonly used as internal and external frames to support construction, as well as in floors and roofs.

Timber can also be re-used or recycled at the end of its working life in a building, and is biodegradable should no further use be found for it. Although it naturally has a low impact, transport and manufacturing processes can add to the greenhouse gas emissions of timber, and toxic treatment processes can also be detrimental to your health.

Another concern when using timber is whether it has come from a sustainable source. Large amounts of timber used throughout the world for building and furniture come from old-growth forests that have been logged, rather than from plantations. In Australia, extensive land clearing and old-growth logging in many states is making a huge contribution to our greenhouse gas emissions.

Softwoods, which come from fast-growing trees, are some of the most sustainable timbers. Willow, bamboo, cane, and coconut are all renewable and fast-growing, although you need to check the origins of the wood. Plantation pine is also a good choice for sustainability.

Recycled timbers are becoming commonly available and are an excellent choice to prevent further tree felling. Timber recyclers available throughout Australia sell a variety of recycled woods, although check that timber has not been chemically treated or impregnated with pesticides before you buy.

When you cannot get what you need from a recycler, try to choose wood that has been sustainably forested; unfortunately, it can sometimes be difficult to verify this. One way to identify timber that is sustainably forested is via the certification of the Forest Stewardship Council (FSC), an international, non-profit organisation that is working towards the sustainable management of the world's forests. Currently few plantation forests in Australia have been certified by the FSC, but it has opened an Australian office so this is set to increase in the near future. You can find it at **www.fscaustralia.org**, or by using the Good Wood Guide developed by Greenpeace, which lists timber merchants and products made from FSC-accredited wood at **www.greenpeace.com.au**

Garden design

When designing a new building for a block of land, it's the ideal time to consider the layout and design of your garden, which can be much more than just decorative. Fruit trees and a vegetable patch are a natural extension of a sustainable home, allowing you freedom from commercially produced foods and the very satisfying ability to grow your own organic food. Gardens also soak

9 BUILDING AND RENOVATING

up carbon dioxide, slow the effect of global warming, provide shade, allow rainwater to seep into the soil, and reduce stormwater run-off.

You will want to carefully consider which trees to plant and where. Native eucalypts and casuarinas are low in water intake, but they are also evergreen and if planted too near the house can provide too much shade over the winter months, causing an increase in your heating bills. In locations where the winters are cold, deciduous trees can play a significant role in allowing the sun access in winter while blocking it in summer.

Permaculture, which was developed by Bill Mollison and David Holmgren in the 1970s, creates sustainable ecosystems that provide biodiversity and give back to the soil what is taken out. Permaculture principles can help you to work out your garden design and consider aspects including the placement of veggie patches, fruit trees and vines, composting areas, ponds, and low-maintenance native plantings. You may even consider having chickens as part of your permaculture garden. Again, its best to think about all this early, so that the design can be incorporated into the site plan and any potential problems can be resolved. There are many books and websites on permaculture, as well as permaculture garden designers, and courses are available on the topic.

Get expert advice

No matter how experienced you are, you will need a great deal of expert advice when it comes to building or renovating a house. The wrong advice can make a huge impact on your ongoing enjoyment, not to mention costs and greenhouse gas emissions, so it's important to get advice that you can trust. There are a number of excellent, impartial resources that provide sound, straightforward advice when going down the exciting path of creating a sustainable home. See the **Resources List** for helpful references.

10
ETHICAL INVESTMENT

Investment is a huge industry that has an enormous impact on the economy, both within Australia and globally. We as investors can have an influence on companies and the share market through our investment decisions. The power of the ordinary investor to choose not to give money to a company that is propping up a corrupt regime, exploiting sweatshop workers, or destroying the environment, is at an all-time high. Likewise, the power of the company shareholder to affect the decisions of management is rapidly growing.

While many of us do not invest directly in the stock market, almost every working person in Australia has superannuation, a passive investment that we often forget about or ignore. Do you know where your super money is invested? Are the companies you are investing in doing anything to reduce their impact on climate change? Are your fund managers thinking about the long-term results of their investment decisions or just the short-term financial return? I certainly didn't pay attention to any of this for many years, but once I did I quickly realised that I didn't like where my super money was going. However, I found it relatively simple to change my investment strategy to something that sat more comfortably with my ethics and concerns for my ecological footprint.

Ethical investing is all about looking at the triple bottom line, not just financial return, and recognising that a number of factors should come into play when considering investment opportunities. It doesn't take much effort to switch to a fund that is better aligned with both socially responsible decisions and your personal philosophy. After all, it would be inconsistent to be minimising your own eco-footprint by using Green Power and reducing other emissions while at the same time your investment money is helping to finance fossil fuel industries.

Note: This chapter does not constitute financial advice. Always consult a financial adviser before making decisions regarding your investments or superannuation.

Triple bottom line

The triple bottom line is an accounting concept that expands the traditional focus of a company from profit to include environmental and social performance. It denotes a greater responsibility that companies have, not only to their shareholders and customers, but also to employees, business partners, governments, local communities, the environment, and society in general. Corporations focused on the triple bottom line recognise they have a social responsibility to achieve sustainable development that minimises harm, rather than just providing a high return to shareholders in the short term that cannot be sustained in the long term.

Ethical investment versus sustainable responsible investment

Often these two terms are used interchangeably, but in fact Sustainable Responsible Investment (SRI) refers to corporate social responsibility; it analyses the environmental, social, labour, and ethical issues that are material to a company's profitability, as well as sustainability. It focuses on the triple bottom line. Ethical investing is a more personal concept, reflecting the values and beliefs of individuals or particular organisations regarding the above issues. What is considered ethical can vary between individuals and is not a fixed ideal, although some areas are generally considered to be unethical, including tobacco, gambling, weapons, and the nuclear industry.

Fund performance

There is a suggestion in the investment community that ethical and SRI funds do not perform as well as mainstream investment strategies, but various market surveys have shown that these funds actually perform better than mainstream investments over the long term. This makes sense when you think about it, because success in the core areas of sustainability – efficiency, looking after workers, minimising impact

GREENWASH

This describes the activity of companies providing information or promoting to the public that they have 'greened' their business activities, when in fact they are still behaving in environmentally unsound ways. It was used during the first wave of environmental awareness in the 1960s, but has since become part of the general lexicon to describe the hypocrisy of pretending to care about the environment while actually destroying it. The most common greenwashers are large **oil** and **motor corporations** that often spend more money promoting their concern for the environment than actually doing anything about it. British journalist and radical thinker **George Monbiot** has started a website to expose greenwashers, including **Richard Branson** and Coldplay's **Chris Martin**: www.turnuptheheat.org

on the environment – not only shows that the company is working efficiently but also implies that it is able to succeed in other areas of its business. Sustainability is about surviving over the long term rather than sacrificing long-term competitiveness for short-term profit.

Sustainable Responsible Investment is currently outgrowing mainstream funds in the financial support these funds are receiving from investors. They are also equivalent to or outperforming mainstream funds in their returns. A survey based on data from Standard & Poors and published by *Ethical Investor* magazine showed that Australian SRI funds performed exceptionally well to June 2006 and, on average, were equivalent to or beat mainstream funds over periods of one, three, and five years.[68]

SHAREHOLDER ACTIVISM

Some investors choose to invest in certain companies so that they can attend shareholder meetings, engage in dialogue with the management, and demand more ethical corporate conduct. Shareholder activists can often have a greater impact on corporate behaviour than outsiders can, helping to make the company more socially responsible.

Screening methods

The established ways of choosing ethical investments are:

Negative screening: Rejects or screens out certain industries, such as tobacco, uranium, and gambling. Investment funds using negative screens are considered to be 'light green'.

Positive screening: Invests in activities or characteristics deemed desirable and with an eye to a sustainable future, such as renewable energy, biotechnology, and water management. Investment funds that apply both negative and positive screens are considered to be 'deep green'.

Best of sector: Selects leading firms in every business sector, based on their financial, environmental and social performance, or triple bottom line.

Social responsibility overlay: Selects investments the usual way, but then looks at issues related to social responsibility and chooses companies that have a good performance record in this area.

Investment options

Several Australian investment houses target ethical investors, and fund managers at various large companies specialise in ethical investments for their clients. If you already have a financial planner, talk to them about your desire to switch to SRI and an ethical investment strategy and ask their advice. Alternately, find an investment manager who specialises in ethical investments. Make sure to quiz them on the screening methods and filters they use in order to choose which companies to invest in. The Ethical Investment Association of Australia has a list of professional financial advisers and managed funds that specialise in Sustainable Responsible Investment at **www.eia.org.au**

Superannuation

You can switch your super to an ethical or SRI fund in one of two ways; choose the one that suits your needs.

Switch to a fund manager that provides ethical super funds, such as Australian Ethical Investments or Hunter Hall (profiled below).

Switch to a SRI fund through your current industry fund or master fund chosen by your employer. The master fund gives you a central account to invest in a diverse range of funds and managers; if you don't make a choice, your money is generally placed in a middle-of-the-range investment fund. However, you usually have the option of choosing which fund within the master fund you want to invest in. Over 100 of the master funds owned by major banks and life insurance companies in Australia now have at least one sustainable option available. So this can be an easy way to stay with your current fund, but still choose a more sustainable investment strategy.

Uranium mining – yes or no?

You may not realise it, but most investment funds in Australia have money invested in uranium mining. This is because one company, BHP Billiton, represents around 45 per cent of our resource sector and because of its dominance in this sector most SRI funds have money in it. In 2005 BHP Billiton bought into the biggest uranium mine in the world, Olympic Dam in South Australia, and is now one of the world's largest producers of uranium. The jury is still out on whether nuclear power plants, fuelled by uranium, are the answer to our current energy problems, but many people have reservations. Some of us are implacably opposed to uranium due to the potential for accidents, fallout, terrorism, and the problems of storing nuclear waste. Others see it as an opportunity to move away from coal-fired power plants. If you are personally opposed to uranium mining and nuclear power, you need to choose a fund that negatively screens uranium to ensure your money does not go to this resource sector. Ask to see the companies your SRI fund invests in; if one of them is BHP Billiton, then you know they have money in uranium.

Ethical fund managers

There are a few fund managers within Australia that focus on the ethical market as opposed to sustainable responsible investment. This means they put an ethical filter on their choices, rather than just looking at sustainability issues. Two of these funds are profiled briefly below.

Australian Ethical Investments

This is a 'deep green' fund manager. All its investments are selected according to criteria it has devised called the Australian Ethical Charter, which has 12 positive and 11 negative investment principles. It focuses on providing investment support to environmental and socially positive activities such as recycling, conservation, energy efficiency, animal welfare, health, education, workplace relations, and protection of the natural environment; see **www.austethical.com.au**

Hunter Hall Group

Advertising itself as Australia's largest dedicated ethical fund manager, it has four ethical investment trusts and a superannuation fund that feeds into its trusts. Its ethical investment policy excludes investments harmful to people, animals, or the environment; it is 'light green' in its investment strategy. In practice, this means it uses a negative screen to restrict investment in companies that derive revenues from the sale of armaments or tobacco, gambling, factory farming, destruction of the environment, and uranium mining. However, it does not

---

PRODUCT DISCLOSURE STATEMENT

Every investment fund is required by law to provide a **Product Disclosure Statement** (PDS) that describes the process it uses to choose companies in its fund, which companies it has invested in, and what the returns from the fund are. By reading the PDS you can learn a great deal about their investment choices and determine if the fund is aligned with your criteria.

restrict investment in mining and it does not consider treatment of employees in its screening process; see **www.hunterhall.com.au**

UN principles for responsible investment

The United Nations launched a voluntary initiative called the Principles for Responsible Investment in April 2006. This is a set of guidelines for businesses that choose stocks for investment portfolios, encouraging them to take into consideration environmental, social, and corporate governance issues when choosing their investments. Signing is voluntary but signatories are asked to consider sustainability issues and ask for disclosure on these issues from the companies in which they invest and to include this information as part of annual financial reports. They do not recommend avoiding certain stocks but instead suggest working with companies and encouraging them to take these factors into account in their reporting. While it is a voluntary set of principles at this stage, it is a framework for the whole investment community to become more aware of sustainability in its practices. For a list of Australian signatories to the principles, see **www.unpri.org**

The Equator principles

These are a voluntary set of investment guidelines undertaken by a number of international banks, including Westpac and ANZ in Australia, which take into account social and environmental issues when considering financing projects. The signatories agree to provide financing to projects above US$10 million only if they are developed in a socially responsible manner. Interestingly, Westpac disclosed that it declined to provide a number of loans in 2006 due to environmental concerns. This is another way in which socially responsible investment is becoming a mainstream concern and paving the way for more environmentally aware business decisions.

QUESTIONS TO ASK BEFORE CHANGING FUNDS

- Is there an exit fee to withdraw my money from my current fund?

- Are there entry fees, management fees, and contribution fees in the new fund? If so, are they reasonable?

- What companies is the new fund investing in and am I comfortable ethically with them?

- Are there performance fees (paid if the fund meets targets) as well as management fees?

- What is the rate of return and how does it compare to the industry average?

- What is the risk level and am I comfortable with it?

11
PERSONAL CARE

11 PERSONAL CARE

You may be surprised to learn that fossil fuel mining is not only powering our electricity and fuelling our cars, but also providing basic ingredients for thousands of personal products. Numerous chemical processes and environmental concerns are involved in the making of common skin and hair products, as well as cosmetics and clothing.

I awoke to the need for reducing my footprint in this area of my life when I read an article in a newsletter sent out by my local health food shop. It described an ingredient found in most commercial hair products called sodium lauryl sulfate (SLS). I'd never heard of this ingredient before because I'd never paid it any attention. Little did I realise, I was literally covered in it.

Extensive academic research has proven SLS causes a dry, itchy scalp, dandruff, and hair loss through destruction of the hair follicles.[69] SLS is not only an irritant on the scalp but is also believed to be potentially carcinogenic (cancer-causing) and a serious concern for those with immune deficiencies and allergies. I had been using the same shampoo for the last few years to tame my frizzy hair, and I had recently experienced a scratchy, flaky scalp and was losing a great deal of extra hair each wash. I wondered if this ingredient could be in my hair products and causing this damage to my scalp.

Checking the ingredients list on the bottles, I was horrified to realise that in both my shampoo and conditioner SLS was right at the top of the list, second only to water. I had been applying a toxic chemical to my hair for years without even realising it!

Next to my hair products was a body wash from the Body Shop – a company I had always believed to be fairly ethical. The Body Shop no longer uses SLS in any of its products, but at that time SLS was the third ingredient in this product, followed by a long list of chemicals and strange names. There didn't seem to be one ingredient in the product that I actually recognised. The alarm bells were ringing as I realised that my own bathroom was awash with toxins. If I was going to minimise my footprint and reduce the chemicals in my life, this was an area I urgently needed to focus on. No longer could I ignore the foreign, fossil-fuel-derived, and certainly unhealthy chemical ingredients that lurked on my bathroom shelves and under the washbasin, causing damage to both the planet and myself. That day, I cleared 15 products out of my bathroom that had the dreaded SLS in them and I really didn't have to try too hard.

Most people believe that if a product is on the shelves at your local chemist or supermarket, it must be okay. But unfortunately, this is not necessarily the case. There is little regulation of hair and skincare products and minimal warnings from official bodies about their side effects. Advertising claims that manufacturers make are only monitored if they claim to be therapeutic (i.e. have some healing effect) or penetrate beneath the top layer of skin, but many products make big claims that have not been verified. The regulatory bodies have little time to check up on cosmetics manufacturers; only when serious health concerns come to light, often

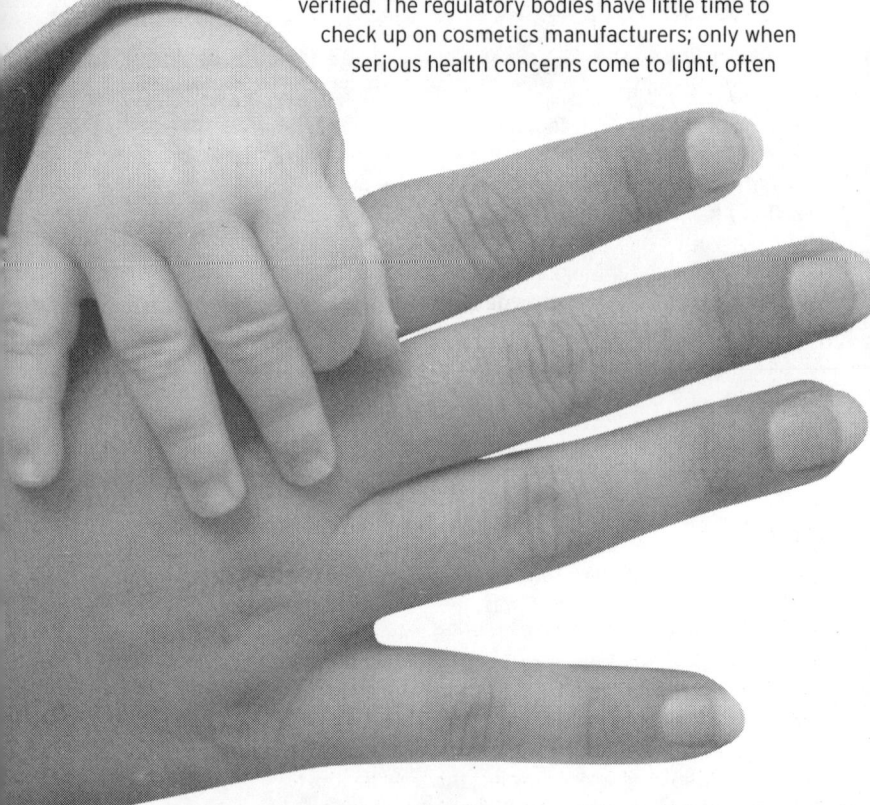

after many years of use, does the regulatory body, the Therapeutic Goods Administration, step in to investigate.[70]

When looking at our ecological footprint and the sustainability of our lifestyles, the build-up of a variety of chemicals within our environment and our bodily systems is of serious concern. If many ingredients are potentially dangerous on their own, it's not hard to imagine that the toxic build-up from the accumulation of skin care products, cosmetics, and household products over the years might be bad for us. And it's not only ourselves we should be worrying about – once we've finished with them, toxic chemicals filter into waterways to do further damage to the ecosystem.

Not only are there concerns regarding the ingredients in many products, but testing on animals is prevalent within the beauty industry. It is often quite unnecessary, not to mention unethical. Therefore, the more we can minimise toxic chemicals and unethical manufacturers in our lives, the less negative impact both on our health and on the health of the planet.

This chapter provides some basic information on toxic chemicals to look out for in everyday skin and hair products, as well as cosmetics and clothing. It names relevant websites where you can check strange chemical names and get information on ethical manufacturers. I will tell you what to look for when checking the ingredients list and also recommend natural alternatives. I also make special mention of nappies as these are often the cause of numerous concerns and confusion about best practice for the environment.

Skin

A 2004 US survey showed that the average person uses nine personal skin care products per day, with a combined total of 126 unique chemical ingredients.[71] According to experts, up to 60 per cent of what we put on our skin is absorbed into the bloodstream, and over a lifetime of 60 years the average woman may absorb over 14 kilograms of moisturising ingredients. Do we want those ingredients coursing through our systems to be natural ones that are predominantly beneficial to our body, or do we want them to be potentially cancer-causing synthetic chemicals? Of course, that question is a no-brainer. However, without the utmost vigilance in scanning individual ingredients in each and every product, and a good working knowledge of the chemical names of some of the worst offenders, we are undoubtedly doing our bodies an injustice.

The commercial definition of 'natural' when it comes to skin care and cosmetics is any ingredient 'derived from' a natural substance. Practically every ingredient has been derived from something that was originally natural, but what is of concern is the chemical processes it may have gone through in order to become what it is. Many ingredients are put through such a chemical transformation that you would be hard-pressed to find any relationship to nature.

BEWARE EMPTY PROMISES

Cosmetic advertising is full of miraculous claims that are nothing but empty promises. Many words used to advertise cosmetics have no standard meaning. So the next time you see such words as **'hypoallergenic'**, **'allergy tested'**, **'dermatologists recommend'**, and particularly **'natural'**, know that these are just slogans to entice you to buy and have no scientific backing or common definition whatsoever.

Some commercial bathroom products, specifically those made in the United States, may contain genetically engineered ingredients derived from maize or soy. Almost all commercial bathroom products use ingredients that come from oil and other petrochemicals, including mineral oil, petrolatum, and methyl paraben, all of which are by-products of fossil fuel mining and are non-renewable. Some products also use small amounts of ingredients that are known to be carcinogenic and highly toxic in large doses.

This sounds ominous, particularly when you realise that some manufacturers of skin care and cosmetic products are more concerned with profits than the health of their customers, and take a cavalier attitude to the toxic chemicals found in small doses in their products. However, there is no need to despair. Nature provides wonderful, healthy ingredients for the skin that can be harvested with minimal environmental impact and are renewable. There are excellent companies who produce natural skincare and makeup products ethically, in recycled and recyclable packing, with an aim to minimise their environmental impact. In general, these companies are small businesses, not multinational corporations. Yet large beauty companies are now being forced to become more eco-aware as consumers voice their concerns about the dangerous ingredients, excessive packaging, and animal testing that are prevalent in the beauty industry.

Hair

The scalp is some of the most absorbent skin on our body. Yet we ask it to endure the drying detergent action of shampooing practically every day, which interferes with its natural barrier and makes it easier for chemicals to penetrate.

Shampoos and conditioners

Many hair products claim to be 'natural' and 'organic' (there is even a range of products called Organics), but when you look at the ingredients you may find the active botanicals are no more than one per cent. Take a look at your shampoo and conditioner sometime and see how many toxic chemicals you can count in the ingredients list.

There are some good ranges of natural hair products on the market, in hair salons, chemists and health food stores, and they work out much better in the long run for your hair. You may also find that you don't need to wash your hair nearly as often without the drying effect of the chemicals on your scalp. It is far better to wash your hair less often and allow the natural oils to develop and look after your hair, as nature intended. Some health food shops also sell products in bulk, which saves the manufacture and disposal of many plastic bottles.

Dyes

Many studies have shown that hairdressers and beauticians are more likely than the average person to get bladder cancer due to their occupational exposure to hair dyes. There is still debate and conflicting studies over the danger for people who dye their hair over a long period of time, but there is certainly cause for concern. So next time you're at the hairdresser ask about natural hair dyes such as henna and vegetable-based dyes that are far better for your scalp. Professional brands that use plant-based dyes include Aveda and Herbatint.

NATURAL HAIR CARE BRANDS
- Alchemy
- Avalon Organics
- Aveda
- Jurlique
- MOP
- Natural Instinct

Cosmetics

Commercial cosmetics have evolved to such a stage of sophistication that they include numerous chemicals, with many petrochemicals as binding ingredients. The dyes are often synthetic; generally, the more colourful an eye shadow or lipstick is, the more chemicals have been used to give it that colour. As much as you can, avoid products that contain petrolatum or mineral oil – not only are they a by-product of fossil fuel mining, but they will block your pores and make your skin more likely to have pimples or other irritations.

The most important cosmetics to buy organic are foundation, mascara, and lipstick. Foundation is one of the most frequently used cosmetics for many women; it is directly in contact with the skin over a long period of time, giving it more opportunity to seep in. Mascaras generally use the highest numbers of toxic chemicals, which may explain why so many people find themselves allergic or sensitive to particular brands. Also note that most mascara, once opened, has a lifespan of only three months; all cosmetics should be thrown out twelve months after opening.

It is often said that most women consume up to four tubes of lipstick in a lifetime. Not a thought to make you lick your lips! Lipstick is brought into our mouths throughout the day, yet most lipsticks contain petroleum, aluminium, and a wide range of synthetic dyes. It's best to buy all-natural wherever possible – it won't dry out your skin and you won't be ingesting toxic chemicals.

The Big Baddie list

The following ingredients are commonly used in commercial skin and hair products and cosmetics. All of these big baddies are known toxins, so look out for them on ingredients lists and boycott products and companies that use them.

Sodium lauryl sulphate (SLS)

As mentioned, sodium lauryl sulphate is a detergent with an effective foaming and degreasing action, which is why it is present in so many products. It dries the skin during the degreasing process, interfering with the skin's natural barrier and making it easier for other chemicals to permeate beneath the surface. It can cause skin rashes, hair loss, and eye damage. So powerful is its effect, SLS is also a common ingredient in engine degreasers and industrial-strength detergents. This big baddie is definitely not subtle. Also watch out for its little cousin, sodium laureth sulphate (SLES); this has undergone a chemical process to make it less of an irritant, but it may still be contaminated with 1.4 dioxane, which has been shown to cause cancer in animals.

Formaldehyde

Present in many cosmetics as a preservative, formaldehyde is a known human carcinogen and skin irritant. It can be hard to recognise as it comes under a variety of jaw-breaking names, including imidazolidinyl urea, diazolidinyl urea, 2-bromo-2-nitropropane-1, 3-diol, DMDM hydantoin, and quarternium 15. It has now been banned completely for cosmetic use in the European Union, but can still be found in American and Australian products.

Petrochemical products

Yes, products that fuel your car are also used extensively in cosmetics and skin care. The reason so many petrochemical products are used is because they are currently up to 20 times cheaper than natural alternatives. However, this is a false economy that does not take into account their many external costs and their greenhouse gas emissions. This cheap availability clearly comes at the expense of the planet. We can look forward to a future where petrochemicals are no longer used in skin care products – not because manufacturers are concerned for our health, but because they will become too expensive – but in the meantime look for products that promote the fact that they have no petrochemical ingredients.

Mineral oil is present in numerous cheap moisturisers and skin care products including baby oil, which is 100 per cent mineral oil. Like petrolatum and paraffin it is a petroleum-originated compound, and so is any ingredient with the prefix propyl-, methyl-, or ethe-. They cannot be absorbed by the skin and actually form a coat over the surface, blocking the skin's natural function and preventing it

from eliminating toxins. The following ingredients are all petroleum-based and should be avoided:

Petrolatum may cause drying and premature ageing of the skin.

Propylene glycol is known to cause cancer in rats and is a possible human carcinogen.

Paraffinum liquidum is the Latin name for paraffin oil.

Mineral oil is manufactured from crude petrol. According to the International Agency for Research into Cancer, mineral oils are probably carcinogenic and are also skin and eye irritants and may be implicated in testicular tumours in the foetus.

> Take stock of your face and hair care products by finding out if they contain Big Baddies.

Methyl paraben and propyl paraben (also ethyl and butyl paraben) are common ingredients found in toiletries, toothpaste, and deodorants because of their preservative and antibacterial qualities. These petrochemical-based preservatives are best avoided for the reasons mentioned above; they also have their own unique problems, including a link to breast and testicular cancer, prostate disorders and sperm dysfunction because they upset the oestrogen balance. They are also a cause of allergic dermatitis.

DEA, TEA, and MEA

These capital letters stand for chemical compounds that are wetting agents in many creams and shampoos. They have been known to cause allergic reactions and irritate eyes and skin, as well as being linked in research with stomach, bladder, and liver cancers.

Artificial colours

Many colouring agents are potential carcinogens, particularly D&C Blue 6, D&C Green 1, D&C Reds 1 & 3, all of which are banned in many parts of the world for use in food and cosmetics. These dyes are derived from coal tar, which comes from bituminous coal; it contains potential carcinogenic substances including benzene, naphthalene, and creosote. In particular, it's best to avoid very brightly coloured eye shadows and lipsticks that have a higher percentage of chemicals to give them their intensity. Keep in mind that many artificial colours and fragrances are there in order to make the product look and smell more desirable and are just another marketing ploy.

Aluminium

Aluminium is prevalent in commercial deodorants and many cosmetics because it's effective at blocking pores and preventing the body from releasing toxins. It may make you smell better but it's really not natural or healthy. Aluminium is also easily absorbed into the bloodstream and has a potential link with Alzheimer's disease and breast cancer. The many aluminium-free deodorants are a much better alternative and just as effective as the commercial varieties. Also watch out for aluminium in many cosmetics and powders, such as pressed powder, where again it is used to block the pores.

Talc

Talc comes from the same mineral group as potentially carcinogenic asbestos. Like aluminium, it blocks perspiration and does not allow the body to release toxins. Many powdered cosmetics and body powders use talc; doctors warn against using it on the genital area, because of an increased risk of ovarian and testicular cancer. Natural alternatives such as cornstarch and arrowroot can be used instead.

Synthetic fragrances

Numerous fragrances are used in commercial cosmetics and they do not have to be labelled separately; they can simply be referred to as 'fragrance'. However, that

---

VASELINE

My mum got me on to Vaseline when I was young, and I used it on my lips copiously as a teenager and in my early twenties because they always seemed to be drying out. However, Vaseline is made from industrial grease and actually blocks the natural flow of the pores, making your lips even dryer than before. I wish I had known that as a teenager!

one word may conceal up to 200 ingredients, many of which are petroleum-based. Synthetic fragrances are often the cause of allergic reactions, skin irritation, and hyperpigmentation from cosmetics. Unfortunately 'fragrance-free' may mean chemicals have been added to mask the smell of all the other chemicals. The best option is to purchase products that are scented with essential oils rather than synthetic fragrances.

Other ingredients

If you are concerned about a particular ingredient in your bathroom product, international lists provide information about various chemicals; they tell you about potential side effects and whether the substance is banned in certain countries. In general, the European Union is far stricter in its cosmetic regulations than either the United States or Australia. Skin Deep **www.cosmeticsdatabase.com** is a good US-based website, run by the non-profit Environmental Working Group, where you can check suspect ingredients. In Australia, the Sustainable Living Directory **www.slf.org.au/directory** allows you to search companies and brands regarding many issues, including their social and environmental impact.

Toothpaste

The gums are a particularly absorbent part of the body. If your gums bleed, it makes it even easier for chemicals from toothpastes to get into the body. Many of the ingredients in commercial toothpaste also do further damage as they wash down the drain. The Big Baddie sodium lauryl sulphate is a common ingredient in most commercial toothpaste, helping it to foam in your mouth.

The use of fluoride, both in the water supply and in toothpaste, is common but has always been hotly debated. Experts claim that it helps prevent tooth decay; however it has also been linked to an increase in bone fractures in eight American studies, and in high doses it is extremely toxic.[72] Concentrations of toxic lead in drinking water have also been traced back to fluoride in water, which strips the protective coating inside lead pipes.

It's probably best to avoid tooth decay by cutting out sugary foods and brushing and flossing regularly, rather than using the standard fluoride and SLS-based toothpastes. If you drink mains water you get plenty of fluoride in any case. The health food section of your supermarket and health food stores have many fluoride-free toothpastes, so that you can choose to avoid this unnecessary extra source of fluoride in your diet.

Natural skin protectors

Environmental pollution, chemicals in the air and on surfaces that we touch, sun damage, smoking, and alcohol all impact on our skin and make it more susceptible to damage and premature ageing. But certain natural products provide a good defence against these pollutants and can help support the skin. Look out for the following ingredients in your natural or organic skin products or include them in products you make yourself.

Borage oil: a good source of essential fatty acids and helps to plump skin cells by improving their ability to absorb moisture.

Calendula: a natural anti-inflammatory that helps skin to heal.

Chamomile: a soothing herb that helps skin heal.

Lecithin: extracted from soy beans, it is a good natural moisturiser. Make sure it is used in an organic product and isn't derived from genetically engineered soy.

Oatmeal: both moisturises and soothes itching.

Vitamin A: helps improve skin elasticity and thickness, and is also helpful for acne-prone skin.

Vitamin C: a good wound healer that stimulates collagen and promotes elastic growth. It also fights free radicals that can damage the skin.

Vitamin E: a fantastic antioxidant that helps fight sun and smog damage. It may also be called d-alpha tocopherol, which is the natural form of Vitamin E.

Make your own

There are many great resources for making your own skin and hair products, which use high-quality botanical ingredients and don't impact on scarce resources. Have a look in your library, bookshop, or the Internet for simple recipes for natural health. Books such as *Feeding Your Skin* by Carla Oates, and *Organic Beauty* by Josephine Fairley are a good place to start.

Cotton balls

Cotton is the most heavily sprayed crop on the planet, consuming over 25 per cent of the world's pesticides, so those cotton wool balls you use to cleanse your skin could be adding traces of pesticides to your face instead, as well as leaving a large footprint on ecosystems through intensive cotton farming. Organic cotton wool is slowly becoming available, and is a much better choice for your face and body. Look out for it at health food stores and online organic stores.

Sanitary products

The average woman uses more than 11 000 tampons in her lifetime, but the majority of women's sanitary products are not free of the high levels of toxicity found in the personal care industry in general. Most production of tampons and pads involves chlorine bleaching to whiten and clean the fibres. This process produces dioxins, which are carcinogenic and extremely polluting to the environment. Some tampons are imbued with artificial fragrances to make them smell better, and with parabens, which are chemical preservatives. Most of them are made from synthetic fibres, such as rayon. Some women are allergic to the chemicals in these products and don't realise, thinking instead they have persistent thrush. Occasionally women still flush tampons down the toilet, which leads to further toxification and damage to our waterways.

Some brands promote themselves as 100 per cent cotton, but unfortunately they are not made from organic cotton. However, there are natural organic alternatives on the marketplace (Natracare and Mooncup).[73] I strongly recommend seeking them out, to prevent both pollution of the environment and contact of toxic chemicals with intimate parts of our body.

Animal testing

Practically every ingredient in cosmetics has been tested on animals at some stage. Many may not have been tested for a long while, but any revolutionary new ingredient that claims to go beneath the top layer of skin (which seems to appear with monotonous regularity) will have been extensively tested in the lab prior to being approved for safety on the marketplace.

One of the most notorious tests, the LD50, involves force-feeding animals or forcing them to inhale the product until at least 50 per cent of the animals have died. Hair dye, cosmetics, and even household cleansers are commonly tested using the LD50. The Draize Eye Test involves extensive application of shampoos and skin care products to the eyes of animals, often rabbits, to see how irritating they are. The animals, which are not anaesthetised, are held in restraints for the duration of the test. These tests are either acute, using one large dose, or chronic, where repeated doses are applied over a period of 28 days. The result is always the same – extreme suffering and often death on the part of the animal. Animals commonly used are rabbits, rats, mice and guinea pigs, but beagles are also used due to their docile temperament and short fur.

It can be difficult to avoid products tested on animals because the labels many companies use on their products, such as 'cruelty-free' or 'not tested on animals', do not have one standard meaning. They may suggest that the finished product has not been tested on animals

DID YOU KNOW?
One animal dies in a laboratory in the United States every second, in Japan every two seconds, and in the United Kingdom every twelve seconds.[74]

> **Tallow** is not toxic, but vegans and vegetarians may want to avoid this commonly used fat. It is a by-product of abattoirs, obtained by boiling the organs and tissues of sheep and cattle. It is present in many soaps, lipsticks, shampoos, and shaving creams.

even though the individual ingredients have been; or the cosmetics company did not test on animals but its suppliers did; or the ingredients were tested on animals by another company and given approval for other manufacturers to use.

There are plenty of alternatives to these tests, including human volunteers (which makes a lot more sense since humans will actually be using the products), natural products that have a history of safe use, or laboratory tests that replicate the common tests but use synthetic skin. There is no real need for animal testing and yet it continues to occur in many countries, particularly in the United States, where many of our cosmetics and skin care products originate.

SKIN CARE AND COSMETIC BRANDS THAT DON'T TEST ON ANIMALS AND DON'T USE BIG BADDIES
- Aesop
- Al'chemy
- A'kin
- Aveda
- Jurlique
- Living Nature
- Mi'essence
- Natural Instincts
- Organic Care
- Sanctum

Choose cruelty-free

The only way to know that you are not inadvertently consuming products that have been tested on animals is to seek out suppliers that endorse cruelty-free manufacture. A non-profit Australian group that is associated with Animal Liberation, called Choose Cruelty Free, has surveyed all the main brands and provides a list of those that they have verified do not test on animals, do not use cruelly derived ingredients, and maintain the same stance with their suppliers. The list, which is regularly updated, can be downloaded from **www.choosecrueltyfree.org.au**

Some companies, including Natio, Australis, and the Body Shop, do not condone animal testing but still use petrochemical-based toxins and many other Big Baddies in their products. The Body Shop (which is now owned by L'Oréal, which does do animal testing) has publicly committed to phasing out some of the worst offenders, which is a good sign. However, it can be a real challenge to find companies that both use completely natural ingredients and do not harm animals in their testing processes. I have emailed some of the companies above to praise their stance on animal testing and to encourage them to go completely natural. Why not do so too? The more we demand natural skin care from manufacturers, the more likely they are to see the commercial benefit in it.

Nappies

A baby will use over 5000 nappies in the first few years of life, and for the majority of babies the nappies will be disposable. Worldwide millions of disposables are used each day, making a significant contribution to rubbish in landfill sites where they will take up to 500 years to decompose. There is a great deal of debate and misinformation – often provided by disposable nappy companies themselves – about whether to use disposables or cloth nappies for a newborn baby, and the impact on both the baby and the environment. There is no significant difference in the rate of nappy rash between babies wearing cloth nappies and those wearing disposables, but the cost and environmental impact of disposables is much greater.

According to research done by Victoria's Royal Women's Hospital, in every aspect of their life cycle – from raw materials, energy, and water used in manufacture through to the amount of landfill needed at the end of their life cycle – disposables have between two times and 90 times the environmental impact of cloth. Disposables also require over 26 times the land area for growing raw materials compared to home-washed cloth nappies.[75]

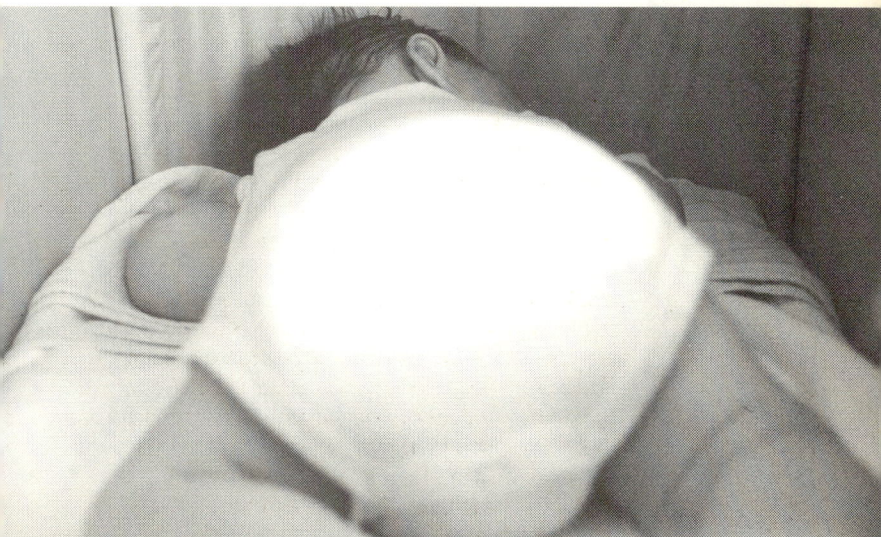

The argument against cloth nappies is often based upon the need for large amounts of water to wash them. However, this argument does not consider the amount of water needed to manufacture disposable nappies. When manufacture is taken into account, disposables actually have 2.3 times the water usage of cloth nappies.[76] It is true that in an ordinary household, water used to wash nappies can represent up to five per cent of water consumption, but in a water-wise household with a highly efficient front-loading washing machine, water consumption can still be less than in a regular household using disposables. Keeping nappies in a dry pail prior to washing is now common, which again cuts down on water, and you don't need to use highly toxic chemicals in the machine – a warm water wash and biodegradable detergent or bicarb of soda will do the trick.

Commercial wash services for cloth nappies are now readily available, but ask about their methods before signing up as they sometimes use more than twice as much water as home-washed nappies, as well as chemicals such as chlorine which leaves dioxin residues in the nappies. Cloth nappies can be used many hundreds of times before they need to be recycled as rags or discarded. You can reduce your impact even further by drying cloth nappies on the line rather than in the clothes dryer and not ironing them.

Disposable nappies are convenient but they do have a high environmental impact. The financial cost of disposables is also more than double the cost of cloth nappies. Even if you don't use them all the time, cloth nappies reduce greenhouse gas emissions and waste. There is also an award-winning brand of compostable nappies in Australia called Weenee that has a microfibre cloth insert; once soiled, the insert can be either composted or flushed down the toilet. However, if you can't give up the convenience of disposables, there are now better nappies on the market which break down up to 70 per cent of their weight in 90–150 days and are a far better option for the environment than the standard non-biodegradable type. But be sure to use a nappy liner and flush faeces down the toilet; don't wrap the nappy in a plastic bag when disposing of it, as this makes it

> **TOXIC RUNOFF**
> Not only are chemicals toxic for our bodies, but studies are proving that the toxic runoff in our waterways is having a dramatic effect on plant and animal life. A 2006 study in the United Kingdom found that one-third of male fish in English rivers are changing sex due to 'gender-bending' pollution.[77] Researchers tested 51 rivers and streams throughout the country and concluded that female hormones from the contraceptive pill and hormone replacement therapy are being washed into rivers and causing male fish to produce eggs. In one waterway, near a heavy discharge of treated sewage, more than 80 per cent of the male fish had female characteristics.

harder to break down. Remember that, despite what the packaging says, no nappy is 100 per cent biodegradable. Online shops that sell cloth nappies as well as Weenee nappy inserts and biodegradable disposables are **www.natureschild.com.au** and **www.neco.com.au**

Clothes and shoes

There are many ethical issues in the clothing that we wear, ranging from pesticide use on cotton plantations through to sweatshops and child labour in developing countries. Of particular concern regarding our ecological footprint are the huge tracts of land devoted to commercial crops of cotton, which consume 10 per cent of all herbicides and 25 per cent of all pesticides used in the world today. Cotton is also subjected to an intense manufacturing process that includes chlorine bleaches, heavy-metal dyes, and formaldehyde finishes to make clothing shrink-resistant, many of which are highly toxic.

One way to avoid the toxic processes of conventional cotton is to buy organic cotton products. While organic cotton is not yet widely available, it is on the increase; a few big companies, including Levis and Nike, use organic cotton in at least part of their range. Hemp is also making a comeback in popularity; the crop has a minimal need for chemicals, it grows fast, and makes a durable cloth, so its environmental impact is much lower than cotton.

Another issue in the manufacture of clothes and shoes is the domination of sweatshops in the developing world, where the majority of our clothes are made. Factories far away from our laws and regulations offer less than ideal conditions to their workers and they may receive less than one-fiftieth the amount that a garment worker in a Western country would earn for the same work. Children working in sweatshops are commonly paid even less than the adults and are sometimes in conditions of 'bonded labour', essentially slaves paying off a family debt.

China now makes over 50 per cent of the world's clothing and shoes, and yet its government does not recognise independent trade unions. China has a reputation for using sweatshop labour and a poor human rights record.

Workers in China have no right to protest or demand better conditions, and many work long days, seven days a week for minimal pay. A boycott of Chinese products may be unrealistic, and probably would not help the country to become more democratic, but it is worth considering how and by whom those ubiquitous and outrageously cheap products are manufactured. Of course, there are undoubtedly many well-managed and ethical factories in China, but from this distance it can be very difficult to determine exactly what type of factory made a particular product.

If you are shopping in a branded clothing store, ask the sales staff where the clothing is made and under what conditions. They may not know the answers but this simple question highlights to the manufacturers and retailers that these issues are important to consumers and should be taken into account when running their business.

You can avoid goods made in sweatshops by purchasing Fairtrade clothing and shoes, which are available from a limited number of suppliers at this stage. Buying Australian-made clothing and shoes is also a good idea; although the garment worker may have been paid a low piece rate compared to the average wage, they have a right to join a union, their working conditions will be regulated, and the transport emissions of getting the clothing to you will be minimal in comparison to products coming from overseas. Nevertheless, some Australian manufacturers have been found to have sourced garments from poorly paid outworkers who are denied proper health and safety conditions.

Many young fashion designers are re-using and re-inventing old textiles and fabrics to create their products, which requires much less energy than that needed to create new products. Buying second-hand from opportunity shops or second-hand boutiques also saves resources and often the money goes back to charity, which is a win-win situation.

We all want and need new clothes and shoes from time to time, and in some cases we can't consider where something was made as the final arbiter of our purchasing

FAIRWEAR

The Fairwear campaign is focusing attention on helping Australian workers in the textile, clothing, and footwear industries to secure better wages. It asks Australian clothing manufacturers to sign a voluntary Homeworkers Code of Practice, which aims to provide basic standards of pay and working conditions for their outworkers both here and overseas. Accredited signatories can attach a 'No Sweatshop' label to their garments, and designers including Collette Dinnigan, Teena Varigos, Jets, Puma, and Bardot have all signed. For more information see **www.fairwear.org.au**

decision. But it's good to be aware of the issues and to take them into account at least some of the time when shopping, and also to make retailers and manufacturers aware of your interest in these issues.

Fairtrade clothing is available at **www.nosweatstuff.com.au** and Oxfam shops. Check **www.greenpagesaustralia.com.au** for suppliers of organic and hemp clothing.

Top Tips for sustainable clothing shopping

- Consider if you really need, or just desire, that new piece of clothing.
- Look for the 'Made in Australia' label on clothing.
- For products that are made overseas, choose Fairtrade when you can.
- Choose organic cotton, hemp, or wool when you can.
- Buy guilt-free at opportunity shops, recycle shops and garage sales.
- Mend tears or alter clothes to fit, rather than throwing them out and buying new ones.
- Question sales people and companies regarding where and under what conditions their products are made.
- Avoid the ubiquitous 'Made in China' label at least some of the time.

12
AT THE OFFICE

12 AT THE OFFICE

It's great to incorporate all these cost-cutting, emissions reducing strategies into our home lives, but what happens when we go into the office five days a week? Does it all get thrown out the window or can we incorporate these new ways of thinking into the way we do business?

For those of us who don't work in corporate offices some of these suggestions may not be entirely relevant, but many of them can be applied to industries such as hospitality, manufacturing, and retail, where the reduction of waste, recycling, and efficient energy use are still important issues.

There's no doubt it's a lot easier to implement changes to your footprint at work if you happen to work for yourself or own the company. You can create overall directives to make the business more environmentally friendly. But if you're just a lowly employee at the bottom of the pecking order, sticking your neck out and requesting changes to the way your company does business can be confronting and sometimes job-threatening. I certainly don't want to give advice that will lose you your job, although any company that is too resistant to change in its business practices in response to sustainability issues probably doesn't have a rosy future ahead of it anyway.

Some of these suggestions reflect changes in overall company policy that will need to come from the top down, but many can be implemented at your own desk, at the printer and photocopier in your department, and by sharing ideas with your fellow staff members. Most people have some thoughts about how things could be run more efficiently in their workplace, but they often don't get the opportunity to discuss them or to become a part of implementing change. With a little bit of encouragement and support, many people are happy to put simple changes in place to minimise wastage and improve efficiency.

Companies all over the world, from the corner store to multinational corporations like BP and Xerox, understand that unless they change the way they do business and consider the triple bottom line their profitability will be seriously impeded. Most of them are not waiting

DID YOU KNOW?
For every tonne of paper that is recycled you save 13 trees, 2.5 barrels of oil, 4100 kilowatt-hours of electricity, four cubic metres of landfill and 31 780 litres of water.[78] Now that's worth doing!

for government legislation to force them to clean up their act, but are actively cutting their environmental impacts as a response to consumer demand and market competitiveness. So don't be scared about bringing these issues up. As in every other aspect of your life, minimising your eco-footprint at the office will not only feel good, it will save money – often large amounts of money. You may even be in line for a promotion, because saving money is a concept that every business appreciates!

> If you're concerned about broaching this topic at the office, make a copy of this chapter (on double-sided paper of course!) and anonymously put it in the in-tray of the person who makes the purchasing decisions.

Individual changes

Many little things can have a big positive effect at the office; simply changing the way you work will not cost anything to implement. Reducing the mountain of paper used at the office comes at the top of the list.

HOW TO HALVE YOUR PAPER COSTS
Simply use both sides of the paper every time. Easy! Every 100 reams of recycled office paper that is printed double-sided saves two trees, more than a tonne of greenhouse gas and almost a cubic metre of landfill space.[79]

Paper usage

Does your office go through a lot of paper every day? Unfortunately, most offices consume tonnes of paper and a lot of it is unnecessary. The paper-free office was a beautiful dream of the 1990s that never eventuated. Most of us are still printing emails, tediously filing in huge cabinets that will never see the light of day, and throwing away thousands of pages of paper, most of which is printed on only one side. Paper reduction and recycling at the office can reduce the cost and environmental impact of paper use by up to 95 per cent, so it's definitely worth doing.

Top Tips for minimising paper use

- Always consider beforehand whether you really need to print out a document, and try to file as much as possible electronically or on disk.

- Do a spell-check and read through again before you press Print. It's amazing how many mistakes can be missed on the first reading.

- Print drafts or office copies double-sided.

- Keep a stack of paper near your desk that has been used on one side, for scrap, draft printing, and note taking.

- Reduce the margins and font size on the standard page format. Common default settings for computers are 12-point type and 3.2 cm left and right margins. By using 11-point type and 2.5 cm left margins and 1.3 cm right margins, you can increase the amount of information on a single page by up to 27 per cent while still allowing margins for binding and hardcopy filing.

- Ask the boss to buy recycled, unbleached paper for all your everyday office printing and stationery needs. Recycled paper cuts energy consumption and reduces air and water pollution.

- Place trays of paper that has been printed on one side near the printer and photocopier and encourage people to use it for their in-house printing needs.

- Re-use everything as much as possible, including packages and envelopes that the company receives. These can be sent out again with an address label to cover the original information.

- Keep used files and binders in the stationery cupboard so that staff can re-use them.

- Use inter-office envelopes that can be re-used many times.

- Don't use a cover sheet when sending faxes. It's unnecessary.

- Send memos and reports electronically rather than faxing or mailing.

- Cancel the fax confirmation sheet on the fax machine.

- Avoid coloured papers as they consume more energy in the manufacturing process.

- Set up an electronic archiving system on your computer rather than printing materials that you need archived.

Top Tips for personal computer use

- If everyone in the office changes the settings on their computer so that it goes into sleep mode within five minutes of not being used, you can save hundreds of dollars per year.

- Don't use screensavers. They don't save energy or money and consume the same amount of power as active use of the computer. Turn your screensaver into 'none' or 'blank' and let your computer go into sleep mode instead.

- Turn off the computer when you go home at night. Leaving it on wastes power, costs money, and does nothing to extend the life of the computer.

- Ideally, switch off your computer at the power point to reduce its power usage to zero; when switched off at the terminal, it will still draw a small amount of power.

- If you're leaving your desk for a short time but don't want to switch off your computer, just turn off the monitor to save some energy.

Courier bags

Reconsider before sending something via courier bag. It's expensive; it may go by air freight, producing large amounts of greenhouse gases; and it's often unnecessary. Express Post bags in many cases are also sent by air freight. If we are organised, we can send materials a day or two earlier via standard post, which travels by road transport, and they will still arrive at the same time. Or they can be faxed or scanned and emailed or put on an intranet site for viewing, rather than being couriered. Couriers and Express Post are very handy but have now become a standard practice that results in large amounts of greenhouse gases, rather than a solution to an occasional tight deadline.

DID YOU KNOW?
Most equipment, such as computers and monitors, still draws approximately two watts of power when switched off. You have to turn it off at the power point in order to reduce the power consumption to zero.

Other top tips at the office

- **Bring your own mug to work and take it with you if you grab a takeaway coffee. You are saving a paper or polystyrene cup.**

- **Avoid using too many paper towels in the kitchen and bathroom. They use up trees and add to landfill.**

- **Bring your lunch to work in re-usable containers. Not only will you save money, you'll save on the plastic containers takeaway lunches come in.**

- **Talk to other people about what you're doing at the office to minimise emissions, and see what ideas they have that can be incorporated too.**

Overall changes to company policy

As well as small changes that we can all make at the office, overall changes in purchasing decisions and equipment management can reduce the environmental impact of the company over a period of time. You may need to establish a staff committee to oversee sustainable purchasing decisions and they may take a while to fully implement, but it's well worth it. You could also make an initial audit of paper and power usage, as well as current levels of recycling, so that when you do implement eco-friendly solutions you can accurately quantify the savings made.

Know your paper

It takes significantly less energy to manufacture recycled paper than it does to create a new piece of paper: up to 90 per cent less water and 50 per cent less energy.[80] So to reduce the impact of paper usage at your company and reduce the possibility that you are helping to destroy old-growth forests – a lot of the world's paper comes from old-growth forests, even in Australia – it's important to choose recycled paper for the office. Buy it in bulk so that you don't need to purchase non-recycled if you run out unexpectedly. However, not all recycled papers are equal and you need to understand the various symbols used.

▢ **Recyclable:** Don't be fooled! This is a very misleading symbol that simply means the product can be recycled – and of course almost all paper can be recycled.

▢ **Recycled:** Made from paper material used before. You can assume it is made from 100 per cent recycled material unless it states otherwise, although many products state they contain a much lower proportion. Look for paper that is at least 50 per cent recycled, with 100 per cent the ideal.

▢ **Recycled content:** Made from reprocessed waste materials; the amount of recycled content is usually measured as a percentage of total weight.

▢ **Pre-consumer content:** Made from material that is left over from manufacturing processes, which means it may well be offcuts of virgin paper rather than legitimately recycled paper.

▢ **Post-consumer content:** Made from material that has been returned for recycling by consumers. The more post-consumer content, the better.

▢ **FSC-accredited:** Contains wood from forests that have been accredited by the Forest Stewardship Council and are deemed sustainable. It may have only a percentage of FSC paper in it, but the more the better. (For information about the FSC, see 'Wooden furniture' in **Chapter 8: Appliances and Household Goods**.)

CHLORINE IN PAPER

Chlorine is often used to bleach paper pulp to give it the brilliant white look, but chlorine dioxins produced from this process are carcinogenic and considered to be some of the most toxic chemicals around. They also remain in trace levels in the products created using chlorine. To avoid adding more dioxins to the atmosphere – especially inside your office – choose paper that is either Totally Chlorine Free (TCF) or Process Chlorine Free (PCF).

☐ **Non-tree paper:** Sourced from agricultural waste, hemp, flax, sugar cane, or even banana trees. While some of this paper may come from industries that use a lot of water and chemicals, at least it is not causing the destruction of native forests.

Communal facilities

☐ Purchase recycled toilet paper for staff and customers, rather than the white, fluffy stuff.

☐ Take away paper towels for drying hands and ask staff to use the air dryer or hand towels instead, to save significant amounts of paper. If you are using Green Energy the greenhouse gas emissions from the air dryer will be zero, whereas most used paper towels are sent to landfill.

☐ In the kitchen, use tea towels and cloth napkins instead of paper wherever possible. You will need a roster to determine who washes the tea towels.

☐ Have real plates, glasses, and mugs for staff and guests to use rather than paper or polystyrene cups and plates.

☐ Keep a recycling bin in the kitchen for recycling glass, cans, and plastics, and set up a roster for people to empty it in the company's recycling bins every few days.

☐ Use biodegradable, environmentally friendly cleaning products in the bathroom and kitchen.

DID YOU KNOW?
Empty printer cartridges and photocopier toner bottles are a valuable resource that can be used over and over again, and can be recycled at the end of their useful life.

Purchase Energy Star office equipment

Purchasing energy-efficient office equipment that has been endorsed by Energy Star and maximises time in low-energy modes can save a business up to $180 per 1000 kilowatt-hours of energy and reduce the electricity bill by nearly 80 per cent.[81] It can also slash air conditioning costs because the equipment emits less heat and so the air conditioning system doesn't need to work as hard.

Energy Star has standards for personal computers and monitors as well as photocopiers, printers, fax machines, scanners, and multifunction devices that can print, fax, scan, and photocopy. All Energy Star equipment powers down when not in use and powers up again when needed. However, it does sometimes need to be enabled before working; ask the installer or the IT staff to ensure that the energy-saving function is enabled. For more information on Energy Star office equipment and the most efficient models go to **www.energystar.gov.au**

Top Tips for purchasing office equipment

- Ensure that all equipment purchased is Energy Star compliant by including this specification in purchasing policies and procurement contracts.

- Purchase the most energy-efficient models that meet your requirements and enable them to switch to low power or sleep modes within five minutes of not being used.

- Keep in mind that flat-screen LCD computer monitors are far more energy efficient than standard monitors. Laptops are more efficient than desktop computers.

- Buy printers and photocopiers that can use recycled paper and can print double-sided. Make sure to explain that function to all employees, and set double-side printing and copying as the default option.

- Before purchasing, ensure that your printer and photocopier can take refillable toner cartridges and that this will not void their warranties. There are many commercial refillers and do-it-yourself kits that can save money and minimise costly cartridge manufacture.

- Consider how much print cartridges cost and how long they last before purchasing a particular printer or photocopier, as a cheap purchase price does not mean cheap running costs.

- Keep in mind that inkjet printers use 90 per cent less energy than laser printers do.

- When purchasing a fax machine, choose a plain paper machine that can take recycled paper.

- Thermal fax paper is expensive, often fades, and cannot be recycled.

- As a fax machine is often left on all the time, it's important to choose one that uses minimal energy in sleep or standby mode. Choose an Energy Star model and check energy usage on standby.

- After office hours turn off all fax machines except one and divert calls to it to save on energy costs.

- Install timers on all your equipment so that you can specify times when it will automatically switch off. Let staff know how to override the timer on their machine if they need to work after hours.

- Buy office equipment from a company that recycles and refurbishes its products after use, and make sure to return it to that company at the end of its useful life.

- Choose office furniture that is made from sustainable or recycled materials wherever possible.

- Choose office stationery items made from recycled material. For example, Pilot now has a range of writing instruments made from recycled materials called Begreen.

- Buy in bulk whenever possible. It's cheaper and cuts down on transportation costs.

Green Power the office

Another huge contribution the office can make to reducing greenhouse gas emissions is very simple: it can be achieved with just one phone call. By switching your electricity supply to accredited Green Power sources such as wind and solar, you can reduce emissions from power sources to zero. Green Powering the office also shows that your company is serious about minimising its impact on the environment and offers public relations opportunities, including the usage of the Green Power logo for marketing purposes. The electricity bill will be slightly higher, but the extra cost can be more than offset by adopting electricity-saving practices throughout the office. There is more information about Green Power in **Chapter 4: Energy** and on the government website at **www.greenpower.gov.au**

DID YOU KNOW?
Lights account for up to 60 per cent of energy use in an office tenancy[82] and many are left on unnecessarily. Turn the lights off whenever possible!

Top Tips for efficient energy use at the office

- Encourage all staff to turn off their computers, printers and lights at lunchtime and at night when they leave. While integrating the policy, elect a monitor to go around at the end of the day turning off equipment that hasn't been turned off and reminding staff still there to do so.
- If people ignore the policy, you can install Energy Management Option (EMO) software that switches computers off automatically when they're not being used.
- Replace all your light bulbs at the office with energy-efficient compact fluorescent lamps and standard fluorescent tubes.
- Make the most of natural light and turn off lights that are not performing a necessary function.
- Install motion sensors that switch off the office lights whenever there is no movement for 15 minutes.
- Have an override switch that turns off all lights at a certain time at night and tell staff what time this occurs.
- Ensure that the air conditioning runs only when necessary to heat or cool the building for staff.
- Activate sleep mode on all computers to kick in after five minutes of no keyboard movement.

Recycling at the office

Managing recycling in large offices can sometimes be difficult because they generate so much material. It's often good to get the professionals in to help with provision of recycling containers, information about recycling, and collection of recyclables. Companies such as Visy Recycling offer site inspections and waste audits for your business to help you identify opportunities for improvement. They then recommend a strategy for dealing with recyclables and non-recyclables at the office and can arrange regular collections to pick up the recycling. Planet Ark collects used toner cartridges for recycling free at 1600 boxes at Australia Post and Harvey Norman stores across Australia. If your company consumes more than three cartridges per month you are eligible for a free in-house collection box. Go to **www.closetheloop.com.au** for more information.

Keep staff involved

People at the office can become resentful if things are changed around them without consulting or even telling them beforehand. Most people, if given a choice, want to do things to help the environment, so educating them

DID YOU KNOW?
It is a myth that turning a computer on and off uses more energy and reduces its life. That was the case for many early model computers, but they are now designed to be turned on and off regularly and it is far better to do so than to leave a computer on standby. Leaving your computer and monitor on all the time can create as much greenhouse pollution annually as driving your car from Melbourne to Perth![83]

and making them part of the process can improve the likelihood of successful change as well as increasing everyone's job satisfaction. Once policies have been drafted, or even at the consultation phase, send a group email to the staff explaining the concept of lightening the footprint of the business and the many ways in which they can become involved. Ask for ideas and input, as no one knows the company better than the people working in it. By becoming involved, people will take the mission of reducing the office footprint on themselves and will be motivated to help and encourage others.

Encourage sustainable transport to the office

One of our biggest energy uses as individuals is driving to and from work every day. Proactive companies can take responsibility for staff travel to the workplace and encourage better forms of transportation than the seriously inefficient solo driver in the company car. How can you do that? By giving incentives to choose alternative modes of transport. Not only will it reduce transport emissions but it may also reduce stress and improve productivity, both in the office and while commuting. While travelling to work on a train you can read through paperwork, think about priorities for the day, and prepare yourself for work in a way that isn't possible when agitated by peak-hour traffic.

Here are some suggestions among a myriad of possibilities that might suit your workplace.

Top Tips for encouraging sustainable transport to and from work

- Encourage car pooling by providing free parking spaces near the front of the office for cars that bring two or more employees to work.

- Set up a bulletin board or an intranet for employees interested in car pooling so that they can contact staff members who live in their area.

- Offer free emergency transport if the car pool driver unexpectedly cannot drive home.

- Provide bike racks in the car park and showers for people who ride their bikes to work. Offer emergency transport if sudden inclement weather makes the homeward journey difficult.

- Provide a free breakfast once a month for bike riders to the office and promote the yearly event, Ride to Work Day, to the entire office to encourage others to start riding to work.

- When a new employee starts, provide a free weekly public transport ticket to encourage them to adopt public transport rather than drive to work.

- Provide local transport maps and timetables on a bulletin board to encourage use of public transport.

- Offer payroll deductions for annual public transport tickets.

- Hold offsite company events at places that are accessible by public transport and encourage staff going to the events to use public transport or car pool.

- Don't offer a company car to staff unless they really need it for their job. Too many people rack up miles and emissions on the company car in order to keep up the mileage and avoid Fringe Benefits Tax.

- When choosing new fleet cars, check the Green Vehicle Guide **www.greenvehicleguide.gov.au** and choose fleet cars that are highly fuel-efficient. Better yet, make it company policy to use hybrids as fleet cars.

- Consider whether some company cars can be replaced by shared vehicles; where a car is needed only occasionally, it may make sense to join a car sharing scheme (see **Chapter 3: Transport**).

- Make it a standard policy to buy carbon offsets for the mileage of company cars (see **Chapter 2: Carbon Offset Schemes**). Encourage staff to minimise their mileage by informing them of this policy.

- Consider having a pool of company vehicles that staff can book for off-site business meetings, rather than providing cars for all people at a certain level.

Case study: a sustainable office

The 60L Building in Carlton, Melbourne is one of the most sustainable office spaces in Australia. It houses the head office of the Australian Conservation Foundation, as well as other businesses that have agreed to incorporate green practices into the running of their offices. The building itself has been constructed with a majority of recycled materials. It has a natural passive ventilation system that allows individuals to control their own climate with windows they can open, automated louvre control, light shafts and skylights, as well as night purging of air in summer. This drastically cuts the need for artificial heating and cooling. The building uses only 10 per cent as much mains water as a conventionally built counterpart and obtains the rest of its water from tanks and 100 per cent on-site treatment of grey water and sewage. It utilises 100 per cent Green Power, with extra rooftop solar panels, and has close to zero greenhouse gas emissions. It also practises a high level of recycling and waste management. All companies that lease space in the building must sign a lease that enforces the Environmental Management Plan and employ energy-saving techniques. All new staff receive an orientation kit advising them of the environmental practices they should follow on site. In all ways this building is striving for distinction in environmental efficiency and waste minimisation. What a great place to work!

For more information go to **www.60lgreenbuilding.com**

GREENHOUSE CHALLENGE PLUS

Part of the government's climate change strategy, Greenhouse Challenge Plus enables Australian companies to form partnerships with the government to improve energy efficiency and reduce their emissions. It provides information on monitoring emissions and opportunities for reducing waste and saving energy as well as industry advisers, workshops and online tools such as fact sheets and newsletters. Participating companies obtain marketing benefits by promoting themselves as Greenhouse Friendly. For more information on the program go to **www.greenhouse.gov.au/challenge**

Is that business trip really necessary?

Many businesspeople undertake a lot of travel. Particularly at the executive level, people go here, there, and everywhere to keep the business running smoothly. But are all these trips really necessary?

In our high-tech world there are ample opportunities for the safe electronic transfer of many documents, as well as teleconferencing and video conferencing. So it seems surprising there is still so much business travel with all the associated expenses and greenhouse gas emissions. If travel is vital for the business, make a commitment as a company to offset the emissions from plane travel and incorporate it into the expense of the trip for a full picture of the cost of the trip.

Assess your building's greenhouse performance

The Australian Building Greenhouse Rating gives a star rating to buildings depending on their environmental efficiency and performance. For a building to obtain an accredited rating it needs to be assessed by a third party, but you can also self-assess the rating of the building you own or lease with a Performance Rating Calculator online at **www.abgr.com.au**

13
TRAVEL AND EVENTS

You may be able to get into a carbon-saving routine at home and at work, but what happens when you're out and about? Holidays and celebrations offer many opportunities for lightening your footprint on the earth. This chapter looks at tourism and managing events.

Responsible travel

As mentioned earlier, air travel has a larger impact than any other form of transport on greenhouse gas emissions. Although total worldwide air travel currently produces only two per cent of global greenhouse gas emissions, this is set to rise drastically over the next 50 years as flights become cheaper and international mobility escalates. As more people choose to fly to their holiday destinations every year, the air mileage they accumulate is not the only unwanted impact on the environment; often a great deal of unwitting damage to the local community and landscape can be a by-product of tourism. Some of the first places affected by global warming will be small islands and developing communities that Australians traditionally love to visit for holidays. In some ways, we are hastening their demise when we travel there.

While it is unrealistic to suggest that we give up overseas holidays, each of should be aware of our impact on the local community and environment to ensure that we are responsible tourists when we travel. Responsible travel is about treading lightly on the planet, immersing yourself in the local culture as much as possible, and having a positive benefit on the community as a whole, rather than allowing it to be exploited by your visit.

Ecotourism

Ecotourism is a buzz word these days and many tourist operators are trying to get in on the act. Sometimes ecotourism means no more than that you will be outdoors during your trip. Ideally, it means a great deal more. Ecotourism Australia defines it as 'ecologically sustainable tourism with a primary focus on experiencing natural areas that fosters environmental and cultural understanding, appreciation and conservation'.

SOUVENIRS

We all love to take home souvenirs from our trip to remind us of our experiences, and often you can help the local community by buying their handmade goods. Just make sure the product is really made locally and not in China, and that it is not made of wild animal skins, ivory, bone, or wood from old-growth forests. Be sure to buy from local merchants, not large corporations. Enjoy – your holiday may be short but your souvenir can last a lifetime!

It has developed an Eco Certification program to assure travellers when an operator is truly following best practice for ecological sustainability. For a list of certified operators go to
www.ecotourism.org.au

Before you sign up for an eco-tour, make sure you ask your tour operator some tough questions to determine how 'eco' they really are, including:

☐ **Do they have a written policy regarding their environmental impact?**

☐ **How are they dealing with the main environmental issues of their operation?**

☐ **Do they employ local guides and local staff and provide training and opportunities for them?**

☐ **Do they bring business to the local community or is it going to overseas multinationals?**

☐ **Do they limit the size of their groups to minimise their environmental impact?**

☐ **Do they have a 'green' purchasing policy?**

☐ **How do they minimise the waste generated by the tour groups?**

If it all checks out, go for it. And while you are there, remember to minimise the impact of your own footprints by sticking to the trail, not picking native flora, and not getting too close to native animals.

Coral bleaching on the reef

Climate change is predicted to have an enormous impact on the world's largest coral reef system and one of our most popular tourist sites – the Great Barrier Reef. By 2050, it is predicted that approximately 95 per cent of the reef will suffer from coral bleaching every year. Rising sea temperatures and sea levels threaten the wildlife and fish species that depend on the reef to survive. CoralWatch is a non-profit organisation that is helping to save the reef. Their Coral Health Chart uses simple colour matching to determine the level of damage on a section of reef. They are asking everyone to help by using the Coral Health Chart when on the reef. You match the colour of the coral with the colours in the chart and record your findings on the website data sheet at **www.coralwatch.org** Providing this information is one way each of us can significantly help scientists in their understanding of the impact of climate change on our beloved reef.

Voluntourism

There are many opportunities for travellers who want to make a positive contribution to a place by volunteering their skills when they visit, rather than just having a holiday. Before you sign up you need to ask questions similar to those listed above for ecotourism to ensure that the money you pay and the work you do will directly help the local community, rather than a tourism operator, and that the locals really do want you to help them. There's nothing worse than help that is not wanted nor needed. See the **Resources List** for some books and websites that provide information on ecotourism and voluntourism holidays.

Top Tips for responsible travel

Travel less often and spend more time on the ground when you get there to minimise your emissions and maximise your enjoyment.

Try to get the most direct flight to your destination available.

Offset the carbon emissions from your flights once you have booked.

Minimise your emissions within a country by travelling by train, bus, and local transport rather than flying.

Learn as much as possible about the country you are visiting before you get there, including religion and culture, a few words of the language, and the local etiquette.

Support locally owned businesses, restaurants, and products so that your money goes into the local community.

Buy souvenirs that are locally made; when bargaining, remember that a small amount to you may represent a huge amount to the seller, so don't quibble over the small stuff.

Don't take shells, stones, or other native objects from the ecosystem.

Always ask first before photographing or videoing people.

Take care of the local environment. Don't litter, use alternatives to plastic bags where possible, and don't drop cigarette butts.

Water bottles are a huge problem, particularly in Asia, as they are often not recycled. Instead of constantly purchasing water bottles, bring a solid water bottle from home and boil your water or use purification tablets.

Holding an event

So you want to hold an event and make it carbon neutral? Fantastic. Maybe it's a work function, a birthday party, a family picnic, or a wedding. Without too much stress you can minimise the impact from your event and offset anything that can't be controlled, and this section shows you the basics as well as providing resources for further information.

An event impacts on a lot of people, so it's a good opportunity to get them talking about the issues and thinking about how they can minimise their own eco-footprint. Show them how easy it is and expand the influence that you are having on those around you – in a positive way.

Waste management

A big aspect of running a successful event is waste management because events seem to produce more than their fair share of the stuff. To significantly reduce the amount of waste going to landfill, you can compost organic waste and recycle all glass, aluminium, plastic, and paper that is used. The most efficient way is if your participants are able to easily sort the waste at the bin into recyclables and non-recyclables so that they can be taken for recycling.

Ideally, you want four bins for best recycling practice – one for paper and cardboard, one for all other recycling (glass, plastic, aluminium, etc.), one for compostable vegetable matter, and one for landfill waste. Colourful bin tops and good labelling, with pictures or actual sample products, are vital to help people determine which bin to use.

For a large event, you may need to organise a waste removalist or recycler such as Visy Recycling to provide bins and pick up recyclable material. You may even make money from aluminium can recycling. Your local council's Waste Management office may provide bin tops and signage for your event free of charge.

Compostables need to be added to a compost heap for further breakdown before being used as mulch or garden fertiliser. If you don't have facilities, consider if there is a school or community garden nearby that may be able to take your compost. They may in fact be grateful for it.

If your event is small and it's not possible to work on such a large scale, just have two bins – one for recyclables and one for non-recyclables. The recyclables can go in your standard recycling bins; you can sort the paper and other recyclables yourself if pick-up in your area demands it. For a really small event, ask everyone to take their rubbish with them and recycle in their bins at home.

For waste management to work effectively, it's important to get people on board by explaining that waste management is an aim in any prior promotion, having clear signs on bins, and getting your MC to mention it during the event to keep people aware of the need to recycle. In Victoria and New South Wales you can also make your event 'Waste Wise' and utilise their logo to help promotion. Further details are in the **Resources List**.

Container deposit

If your event is big enough you may be able to set up a deposit system, where patrons pay an extra 50 cents or dollar when they purchase a can or bottle. They then need to return the container, ideally to a volunteer so there are no staff costs, who gives them a refund and puts the can or bottle in a bin for recycling. This is an effective method of ensuring recycling, as the deposit really motivates people.

Cutlery and plates

Plastic plates and cutlery are generally not recyclable; nor are the ubiquitous polystyrene cups. Avoid them if possible, as well as cling wrap, aluminium foil wrap, and paper serviettes, which are usually compromised by food scraps and cannot be recycled.

There are two ways to reduce waste going to landfill from your plates and cutlery. For a small event, it's probably best to use standard kitchenware including glasses, ceramic plates, and stainless steel cutlery or re-usable plastics that can be washed after the event. For a really big event, or one held outdoors without easy access to a kitchen, it may be better to use compostable cutlery and crockery made from sugar cane pulp and cornstarch, or from the bark of trees. These fantastic environmentally friendly alternatives to plastic and polystyrene can be placed in the organic waste bin and composted. However, you will need to have at least three bins (recyclables, compost, and general waste) in order to maximise the composting benefits and ensure that they do get composted. Label the bins clearly and perhaps stick a sample plate and cutlery onto the compost bin so people understand where it goes. The costs for compostable plates and cutlery are comparable to plastic and will significantly reduce the environmental impact of your event. You can find some at **www.ebabioproducts.com.au**

Powering the event

To make your event sustainable, provide renewable energy to power it as much as possible. A large event may need solar generators or even biodiesel generators onsite. If it's indoors then the best way is to use Green Power: either purchase renewable energy through the energy retailer who supplies power to the venue, which only takes a phone call, or else purchase an offset for the amount of electricity used (see **Chapter 2: Carbon Offset Schemes for details**).

If your event is held in someone else's venue and they don't have Green Power, offsetting the electricity is probably the best option. There are numerous offsetting companies that can help you with this, and they have calculators to help you figure out how much electricity you used to power your event if the venue provider is not able to give you a daily estimate of electricity usage to make the calculations. Two Australian offset companies, Easy Being Green and Carbon Planet, specialise in offsetting emissions from events. If you want to promote that you are using Green Power for your event, apply to use the Green Power logo from the government website at **www.greenpower.gov.au/events/**

Food and drink

Sustainability in agriculture is an important issue, and the food and drink you choose will have a large impact on the footprint of your event. Wouldn't it be great to have an event that supplied only organic food and drink? This might seem a tough task, but it is possible.

If you employ a caterer, try to choose a company that supplies organic food. If you can't find any or you must use the food provided by the venue, then go vegetarian. Almost all companies have vegetarian options; if they don't, ask them to provide them. By choosing vegetarian, you minimise the impact of the event because livestock has a much greater eco-footprint than plant crops.

Organic wines, beers and soft drinks can be sourced fairly easily these days, either from a large bottle shop, a health food store, or an organic winery. The many cleanskin wine shops that have sprung up around the country sometimes sell organic wines and will add your own unique label to commemorate the event.

Provide free drinking water so that people can fill glasses, recyclable cups, or their own water bottles and do not have to buy plastic bottles of water. This minimises the need for recycling and the possibility that water bottles will end up in landfill.

If you serve tea and coffee, make sure it's organic or Fairtrade. Provide organic milk and put sugar in a bowl, not individual sachets. Use ceramic mugs for tea and coffee, rather than paper; if it's an outdoor event where you are worried about mugs disappearing, ask for a 50-cent deposit to encourage returns.

Printed material

There is always printed matter associated with an event, whether it is an invitation circulated beforehand, further details once patrons arrive, or promotional material for them to take away. The key is to think carefully about what is really necessary, as opposed to what will just be thrown out. Provide invitations and information electronically wherever possible, and recycle what printed material is used.

Most people are used to being sent information electronically and it's becoming rare to receive a paper invitation in the mail. Email is acceptable for almost all events, except perhaps weddings and other major celebrations. A website can even be set up to handle RSVPs, provide further details, and to post speeches or thanks after the event.

However, there's usually something that needs to be printed – if not an invitation it's a special offer, a menu, or background information. When getting a quote, look for a printer who can produce your material with recycled paper, vegetable-based inks, and no alcohol-based solvents. Vegetable-based inks are an alternative to petroleum-based inks and significantly reduce emissions. The printed product is also easier to de-ink when being recycled. Solvents used in the inks, in film and plate processing, and to clean the printing press between jobs are a major source of emissions from printers. Instead of recycled paper, you could ask for non-tree paper made from sugar cane waste, hemp or bamboo.

Also ensure that you maximise paper usage by printing on both sides, having small margins, and keeping the page extent as low as possible. If you distribute any paper material make sure it will be recycled after use, so put recycling bins near the exit and print a reminder on the material itself.

Water usage

Minimising water usage, particularly at outdoor festivals in Australia, is an important consideration. Remind patrons and stall holders of the importance of being frugal with water in their activities. Use only biodegradable eco-friendly dishwashing and hand-washing products so that grey water can be recycled on site or nearby.

Transport

A big part of the emissions generated by your event come from travel to and from the event. As with travel to and from work, you want to encourage people to use public transport, car pool, or ride their bikes. A venue in a central location that is easily accessible by public transport is a good way of ensuring that transport emissions are minimised. Explain the transport options on the invitation to reinforce the need for people to consider their means

SUSTAINABLE EVENTS AROUND AUSTRALIA

Womadelaide
- South Australia

Peat's Ridge Festival
- New South Wales

Sustainable Living Festival
- Victoria

Perth Sun Fair
- Western Australia

World Solar Challenge
- Northern Territory

---

of attendance. Perhaps even advise that minimal parking is available and that it will be prioritised for car pooling.

If the organisers of the event need to travel by car or plane in preparing for and holding the event, or an important speaker or performer needs to fly in, offset their transport emissions with a carbon offsetting company (see **Chapter 2**). Note how much travel occurs in the lead-up and the staging of the event, jotting down the mileage for car and plane trips. Tally it up after the event is over and offset it all in one go.

Name tags

Name tags in plastic sleeves are a ubiquitous symbol of an event, particularly of the corporate kind. They consume plastic and metal, and are rarely, if ever, recycled. Sticky-backed paper labels have less of an impact on the environment and can be recycled. If the professionalism of name tags is important, remind people when you hand out plastic-sleeved tags that you would like them back after the event, provide a bin, and place a couple of volunteers at the door as people leave to remind them to give back the tags.

Stall holders

Stall holders need to understand your commitment to a waste-minimised event and you should inform them of the requirements before they sign on. Make a bond part of their contract and explain clearly that it will not be refunded unless they comply with the conditions of the event. Ask them not to use plastic bags or excess promotional material, and to ensure that all the products given away to customers from their stall are either recyclable or compostable. Help them to source organic foods by choosing a favoured supplier, circulating an orders list, and co-ordinating all the orders for one bulk delivery to the site. Bulk food deliveries are another way of keeping down transport emissions and can make a big difference in your event's overall footprint.

Toilets

If you need to provide your own toilets for the event,

use recycled toilet paper and chemical-free disinfectant. Consider composting toilets, which are waterless, odour-free, and provide fantastic compost down the track. There are companies that specialise in supplying composting toilets for events.

Evaluating your event

After your event, measure how much waste was recycled and prevented from going to landfill, as well as transport and electricity emissions that were saved by using Green Power and offsetting. Send out a media release and circulate the information among staff and patrons of the event. Pat yourself on the back for the good work done.

You can then look at areas that need more work and consider how these can be improved next time. It's an ongoing process, so don't be too tough on yourself. Every little bit that you do is having an impact, not only on minimising your direct emissions but also in generating public awareness on climate change and the solutions.

See the **Resources List** for further information to help in planning an event.

14
BE AN ACTIVIST

14 BE AN ACTIVIST

Never doubt that a small group of thoughtful, committed citizens can change the world. Indeed, it's the only thing that ever has. – **Margaret Mead**

Did you know that politicians assume that for every one person that writes to them, there are 200 who feel the same way but haven't written? Politicians pay attention to every letter or email they receive, because if they get it wrong about how their voters feel, their jobs are on the line.

It's not only politicians that think that way. Large companies have to listen to the voices of shareholders, consumers, and the media. They pay attention to what people are telling them, and sometimes they even change their policies as a result. But if all we ever do is mutter about the issue from the safety of our lounge room, they will never know how we feel and they won't be compelled to act.

Our world is at the brink of a serious environmental crisis and yet there are still deniers and apologists out there who are trying to plant doubt in people's minds and keep them from acting. If we don't unite to fight this global problem and make significant changes, then the world in 25 or 50 years will be a very scary place indeed. Every one of us needs to become an activist for global change.

Educate yourself

Knowledge is power. The more you understand about climate change, the more you can be part of the process of change. There are many excellent books and websites out there to stimulate your mind on this topic. It's a bit like Alice in Wonderland going down the rabbit-hole; the further you go, the more complexities and wonders you discover. Some of my favourites are in the Resources List but I also recommend you discover your own. I learn something new every day about this topic, and sometimes it requires totally fresh ways of thinking. Educating yourself is both terrifying and inspiring, but it is vital.

Use the media

It's the media's job to report on what is happening out there, so if you know some important information that hasn't been reported, let them know and ask them to report on it. If they don't, then why not write an article yourself? Send it to relevant organisations, politicians, and media outlets. That way the issue can be given broader attention and it's more likely that change will happen.

Look at how the media and the public have finally paid attention to climate change. Awareness about this issue has been there for over 20 years, but only in the last few years has it reached critical mass. Now everyone is interested in the topic and wants to know what should be done. Families are debating global warming around the dinner table, teenagers are discussing Al Gore as they would a movie star, and movie stars are embracing the joys of sustainable living and the Toyota Prius. The world is definitely changing and we are all part of that change.

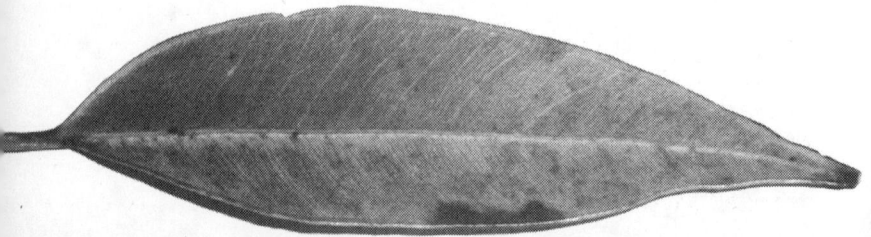

Write to politicians

One letter and they assume 200 people feel the same way – that's pretty good odds for making a difference. Politicians' email and work addresses are readily available. Part of their job description is to listen to their constituency – that's us. So when an issue comes up regarding our future and you know they will be voting on it soon, get in touch and let them know how you feel. You can contact your local member or the appropriate minister, or both. Don't forget to write letters of support to politicians who do the right thing. By emailing or writing to politicians you can have a direct impact on their votes in parliament and potentially make a huge difference to the future of the country.

Volunteer

A great way to improve the situation from your own backyard is to volunteer some of your time to help out. Over 30 per cent of adult Australians give approximately 700 million hours every year to non-profit organisations. It's an impressive amount of time that represents everything from caring to the elderly, teaching new immigrants English, protecting the natural environment, and much more. Volunteering provides numerous valuable opportunities to provide support for tackling climate change on a broader canvas and help our community at the same time.

Plant trees

This book is about the numerous ways we can reduce greenhouse gases. Well, here's one simple way to do your own carbon offsetting: plant trees. Every tree you plant has the potential to soak up many tonnes of greenhouse gases during its lifetime and turn it into oxygen for people to breathe. Trees provide shade and habitat for native animals, reduce erosion, and improve the water table. They're also great to hug when you're stressed out! Planet Ark organises a national day to plant trees each July if you want to do it in company. So don't delay. Planting trees is a powerful way of acting against global warming.

Go in peace

I hope that this book has given you the tools and the inspiration to make big changes in your own life. Now it's time to go out and spread the word to as many people as possible, not just your family and friends. Let businesses know that you want to eat local organic food and buy products that aren't derived from fossil fuels. Let politicians know that you want them to take direct action on climate change. Let the media know you want them to take a more active role informing people of the solutions.

Climate change is the most significant issue that humanity has ever had to face. How we deal with it now will have an impact for centuries to come. Go in peace but know that we need to transform our society and it begins with each and every one of us. If we don't adapt and learn new skills to deal with this crisis, we will be jeopardising the lives of the 6.6 billion humans who call this planet home, as well as countless future generations. So don't be shy – speak up and show your passion for the planet. It truly can help to change the world.

Top tips to shrink your footprint

These little nuggets are distilled wisdom from the book, attacking the activities that send the greatest amount of greenhouse gases floating out into the atmosphere, or cause the most overall destruction to the environment.

If you follow these you will reduce your greenhouse gas emissions by more than 70 per cent and will make a significant contribution to reducing climate change.

Tackle one area for a few weeks at a time, or try a number of easy ones together, or go for gold and do them all at once!

Transport
- Walk or ride a bike more.
- Drive efficiently and offset your car emissions.
- Fly a lot less, and purchase carbon offsets when you do.
- Buy a hybrid car or use biofuels.

Energy
- Buy accredited Green Power.
- Replace all your light bulbs with energy-efficient CFLs.
- Turn appliances and electronics off at the wall.

Water
- Have five-minute showers.
- Buy a water-saving showerhead.
- Install a rainwater tank.

Food
- Buy local.
- Buy organic.
- Eat less meat and dairy products.

Recycling
- Refuse plastic bags and excess packaging.
- Reduce, re-use, recycle.
- Compost all your vegetable matter.

Appliances
- Purchase Energy Star appliances.
- Use your appliances as efficiently as possible.

Building
- Insulate your house to maximise heating and cooling.
- Get off the grid – go for solar energy and hot water.
- Make your house energy-efficient.

Investment
- Switch your superannuation and investments to an ethical or SRI fund.

Personal
- Choose natural skin care and clothing.
- Use cloth nappies for your baby.
- Buy sustainably forested wood products.

Office
- Use less paper.
- Recycle at the office.
- Turn your computer off every night.
- Get public transport to work.

- **Be an activist**
- **Learn more about climate change.**
- **Write to politicians.**
- **Volunteer to help others.**
- **Plant trees.**

If you do all this, you will
- **Save money**
- **Reduce your greenhouse gas emissions more than 70 per cent**
- **Change your life**
- **Maybe even change the world**

Resource List

Books

THE WEATHERMAKERS by Tim Flannery (Text Publishing, 2005).
This accessible, extensively researched book by esteemed scientist and Australian of the Year, Tim Flannery, gives you the basic evidence on climate change and looks at the solutions that need to be adopted as soon as possible on a national and international level.

THE ROUGH GUIDE TO CLIMATE CHANGE by Robert Henson (Rough Guides, 2006). An excellent introduction to the science of climate change, looking at the symptoms, debates and solutions in readable, succinct prose; it includes diagrams and photographs to illustrate the issues.

THE REVENGE OF GAIA by James Lovelock (Penguin 2005). Originator of the Gaia theory, influential scientist James Lovelock has written a fascinating and terrifying book about the way our planet is rapidly changing in response to excessive greenhouse gases in the atmosphere. Lovelock then offers some radical solutions to safeguard the future of human life.

HEAT: HOW TO STOP THE PLANET BURNING by George Monbiot (Penguin, 2006). Influential thinker and journalist George Monbiot takes a careful look at government policies needed to cut carbon emissions by 90 per cent before 2030. He supports his proposals with extensive research and examples of what works and what doesn't. The book concentrates on the British situation but has worldwide relevance.

THE ETHICS OF WHAT WE EAT by Peter Singer and Jim Mason (Text Publishing, 2006). Internationally renowned philosopher and ethicist Peter Singer and his colleague Jim Mason have produced a very readable account of factory farming and the difficult decisions we face when making food choices. They look at the eating habits of three different American families, the first eating the standard American diet, the second conscientious omnivores, and the third vegans. This Australian edition has been updated with information on Australian farms and suppliers. This is fascinating reading on the topic of ethical eating.

Websites

AUSTRALIAN GREENHOUSE OFFICE: Extensive information on the greenhouse gas emissions from transport, house building, appliances and much more, and how to reduce them. It also provides links to a number of sustainability programs and tips for reducing emissions in the home
www.greenhouse.gov.au

THE GREEN DIRECTORY: A helpful resource to direct you to businesses selling products and services focusing on sustainability and reducing emissions. Topics include building, body and skin care, finance, health care, and transport.
www.thegreendirectory.com.au

TREEHUGGER: This US-based website is friendly and accessible, listing plenty of environmentally sound products, practical information on what you can do, the latest news on environmental issues, celebrity environmentalists, and blogs on hot topics.
www.treehugger.com

ENVIRONMENTAL HEALTH NEWS: Summaries and quick links to the latest articles around the world on issues such as chemical contamination, water quality, genetic engineering, and the latest scientific findings on the health aspects of climate change and biodiversity.
www.environmentalhealthnews.org

AUSTRALIAN CONSERVATION FOUNDATION: Among a number of non-profit organisations working on the issue of climate change, the Australian Conservation Foundation has been very active with its Green Home sustainability project, as well as working with Al Gore to train many Australians to become educators on the issues. This is an excellent website with many useful resources on going carbon neutral, ethical investing, the latest climate change news, and more.
www.acfonline.org.au

State sustainability authorities

AUSTRALIAN CAPITAL TERRITORY:
Territory and Municipal Services - Sustainability
www.tams.act.gov.au/live/sustainability

NEW SOUTH WALES:
Dept of Environment and Climate Change
www.deus.nsw.gov.au

NORTHERN TERRITORY:
Natural Resources, Environment and the Arts
www.nt.gov.au/nreta/environment

QUEENSLAND:
Environmental Protection Agency - Sustainability
www.epa.qld.gov.au/environmental_management/sustainability

TASMANIA:
Department of Tourism, Arts and the Environment
www.environment.tas.gov.au

VICTORIA:
Sustainability Victoria
www.sustainability.vic.gov.au

WESTERN AUSTRALIA:
Sustainable Energy Development Office
www1.sedo.energy.wa.gov.au

Water

SAVEWATER! ALLIANCE: A not-for-profit website that has fantastic tips for saving water throughout the house and in the garden. It also provides

information on water usage at a national, regional and local level as well as directing you to the water authority in your area.
www.savewater.com.au

AUSTRALIAN WATER ASSOCIATION: An independent association committed to promoting sustainable water management within Australia.
www.awa.asn.au

State water conservation authorities

AUSTRALIAN CAPITAL TERRITORY:
Think Water, Act Water
www.thinkwater.act.gov.au

NEW SOUTH WALES:
Water For Life
www.waterforlife.nsw.gov.au

NORTHERN TERRITORY:
Waterwise Alice Springs
www.nt.gov.au/nreta/naturalresources/water/waterwise

QUEENSLAND:
Queensland Water Commission
www.qwc.qld.gov.au

SOUTH AUSTRALIA:
Watercare
www.watercare.sa.gov.au

TASMANIA:
Waterwatch Tasmania
www.taswaterwatch.org.au

VICTORIA:
Our Water, Our Future
www.ourwater.vic.gov.au

WESTERN AUSTRALIA:
Water Corporation
www.watercorporation.com.au

Building and renovating

GREENHOUSE OFFICE: The Australian Greenhouse Office provides a great deal of information on sustainable renovating and building a new home in its guide *Your Home*. Compiled by scientists, researchers, and the design and construction industries, this website covers in exhaustive detail many aspects of building including the principles of good design, the impact on the environment and the impact on your wallet.
www.greenhouse.gov.au/yourhome

ARCHICENTRE AUSTRALIA: Archicentre is the building advisory service of the Royal Australian Institute of Architects. It provides a great deal of information for those wanting to build, renovate or buy, including free

technical advice, pre-purchase home inspections, many downloadable fact sheets, ongoing seminars throughout Australia, and a database of accredited architects available to work with you throughout the country.
www.archicentre.com.au

ALTERNATIVE TECHNOLOGY ASSOCIATION: This non-profit organisation promotes sustainable technologies and practical solutions for sustainability. They have branches throughout Australia which provide expertise and they also publish two print magazines: *Renew*, which features the latest in sustainable building practices and renewable energy products, and *Sanctuary*, which focuses on stylish, sustainable home design.
www.ata.org.au

ECOSPECIFIER: Ecospecifier aims to help building professionals as well as keen homeowners find the latest, best-practice, ecological materials to build with. You can search the database for specific materials and specify which state you live in as well as other requirements, such as being a good environmental choice or a particular energy rating. Much of the material is available free but you can also subscribe fairly cheaply for a six-week period when building a home to give you access to a broader range of suppliers
www.ecospecifier.org

GOOD ENVIRONMENTAL CHOICE LOGO: This environmental labelling program looks at the environmental performance of a product throughout its life cycle and awards the label to those products that meet voluntary performance standards. The program is internationally recognised and products that are registered include paper, furniture, linoleum, printers, and even cements. Although they have a wide range, most of the products are relevant in a commercial building or home building environment. You can search their products at the Australian Green Procurement Database at
www.greenprocurement.org

Ethical investing

ETHICAL INVESTMENT ASSOCIATION: Its website contains research on ethical investment options and links to ethical investment advisers and funds. www.eia.org.au

ETHICAL INVESTOR: This magazine and website provide numerous articles and advice on ethical investing as well as regular listings of investment holdings and performance of various SRI funds for subscribers.
www.ethicalinvestor.com.au

CORP RATE: Compiled by the Australian Consumer Association, Australian Conservation Foundation and Oxfam, this report ranked the top 50 companies in Australia in 2003 on criteria including corporate governance, environmental performance and social behaviour. The ACF also has other articles on ethical investment at:
www.acfonline.org.au

In the office

OFFICEMAX: This online office supply company has a recycled product range and focuses on making environmental management easier for companies.
www.officemax.com.au

SCHIAVELLO: This Australian company focuses on environmentally sustainable workplace environments, furniture made with recycled content, and office fit-outs.
www.schiavello.com

CARTRIDGE WORLD: Refills and remanufactures printer cartridges, with over 220 stores throughout Australia.
www.cartridgeworld.com.au

DALTON PAPER: It offers a wide range of Australian-made recycled papers and sells FSC-accredited papers, and provides technical and environmental fact sheets on all their papers on its website.
www.dalton.com.au

Travel

CODE GREEN: Experiences of a Lifetime by Kerry Lorimer et al. (Lonely Planet, 2006). This book profiles 82 responsible travel experiences around the world that will have a positive impact on the environment, culture, and economy of the regions visited.

ECOTOURISM AUSTRALIA: This organisation provides information on ecotourism and lists tourism operators in Australia who have been accredited under its Eco Certification Program.
www.ecotourism.org.au

INTREPID TRAVEL: This tour company provides volunteer and ecotourism tours throughout the world. In 2007 it introduced a mandatory carbon offset payment with all flights booked from Australia.
www.intrepidtravel.com

RESPONSIBLE TRAVEL: Based in the UK, it offers more than 2000 holidays all over the world that follow the principles of responsible travel.
www.responsibletravel.com

BIOSPHERE EXPEDITIONS: This UK-based site offers volunteering holidays focusing on sustainable conservation of wildlife in many parts of the world. It guarantees that two-thirds of your money will go to the local community.
www.biosphere-expeditions.org

Events

WASTE WISE: In Victoria and New South Wales you can run a Waste Wise event and receive accreditation and help with minimising waste.
Victoria: www.sustainability.vic.gov.au/www/html/1507-waste-wise.asp
NSW: www.environment.nsw.gov.au/education/WWE_Home.htm

Organisations to contact for waste removal and recycling are:

SITA: Provides commercial recycling **www.sita.com.au**

VISY: Provide commercial recycling **www.visy.com.au**

SULO: Provides wheelie bins and colour-coded bin tops **www.sulo.com.au**

BIOPLATES made from the Areca palm tree can be purchased from the manufacturers **www.ebabioproducts.com.au** or **www.bioplates.com.au**, or from the online shop **www.neco.com.au**

COMPOSTING TOILETS can be obtained from Natural Event **www.naturalevent.com.au**

TO SEE HOW OTHERS DO IT, have a look at Peat's Ridge Festival **www.peatsridgefestival.com.au** or A Greener Festival, a UK non-profit that has great case studies from events including Glastonbury **www.agreenerfestival.com**

Notes

1 Introduction

1. Michael Brissenden, 'Climate change report paints grim picture for Australia', The 7.30 Report, transcript at www.abc.net.au/7.30/content/2007/s1885192.htm
2. James Lovelock, *The Revenge of Gaia*, Penguin, 2005, p. 7.
3. Lovelock, *The Revenge of Gaia*, p. 13.

2 Carbon Offset Schemes

4. www.greenvehicleguide.gov.au

3 Transport

5. Australian Greenhouse Office, 'Global Warming: Cool It', www.greenhouse.gov.au/gwci/index.html
6. Federal Chamber of Automotive Industries, 'Motor vehicle sales second highest on record', 4 January 2007, www.autoindustries.com.au
7. Australian Greenhouse Office, 'Global Warming: Cool It', www.greenhouse.gov.au/gwci/index.html
8. Rebecca Blackburn, 'Train vs bus', *G Magazine*, Jan.-Feb 2007.
9. Transport and Population Data Centre, 'Household Travel Survey', Sydney, NSW, 2002, www.planning.nsw.gov.au
10. Australian Greenhouse Office, 'Global Warming: Cool It', www.greenhouse.gov.au/gwci/index.html
11. World Tourism Organization, 'Tourism Highlights, 2006', www.world-tourism.org/facts/menu.html
12. World Tourism Organization, 'Tourism Highlights 2006', www.world-tourism.org/facts/menu.html

4 Energy

13. Australian Greenhouse Office, 'Global Warming: Cool It', www.greenhouse.gov.au/gwci/index.html
14. Nigel Wilson, 'Industry taps into $12b seam', *Weekend Australian*, 9-10 September 2006.
15. Tim Flannery, 'Saving precious water at the flick of a switch', *Age*, 12 February 2007.
16. Based on Australian Greenhouse Office calculation of 15 tonnes total and energy use of 60% of total (excluding transport and waste).
17. Sustainability Victoria, 'Wind energy: the myths and the facts', www.sustainability.vic.gov.au/www/html/2148-wind-energy-myths-and-facts.asp
18. Sustainability Victoria, 'Wind energy: the myths and the facts', www.sustainability.vic.gov.au/www/html/2148-wind-energy-myths-and-facts.asp
19. Tim Flannery, *The Weathermakers*, Text Publishing, Melbourne, 2005, pp. 276-7.
20. Australian Greenhouse Office, 'Global Warming: Cool It', www.greenhouse.gov.au/gwci/index.html
21. Sustainability Victoria, 'Choosing a heating system', www.sustainability.vic.gov.au/resources/documents/choosing_a_heating_system.pdf
22. www.sustainability.vic.gov.au/resources/documents/choosing_a_heating_system.pdf
23. www.sustainability.vic.gov.au/resources/documents/choosing_a_heating_system.pdf
24. www.choice.com.au/viewArticle.aspx?id=100340&catId=100519&tid=100008&p=9&title=Your+heating+options
25. Sustainability Victoria, 'Types of heating systems', www.sustainability.vic.gov.au/www/html/1991-types-of-heating-systems.asp
26. Sustainability Victoria, 'Fans', www.sustainability.vic.gov.au/www/html/1995-fans.asp
27. Sustainability Victoria, 'Air conditioning: sizes and features', www.sustainability.vic.gov.au/www/html/1998-air-conditioning---size-and-features.asp

5 Water

28. This and other figures on water usage are from Savewater! Alliance, www.savewater.com.au
29. www.waterfootprint.org

6 Food

30. Rachel Gibson, 'Kinder staff struggle with allergies burden', *Age*, 13 May 2006.
31. Peter Weekes, 'This meal has travelled all over the world', *Sunday Age*, 7 May 2006.
32. T. Lang, 'Towards a sustainable food policy' in G. Tansey and J. D'Silva (eds), *The Meat Business*, Earthscan Publications, London, 1999.
33. James Randerson, 'Organic farming boosts biodiversity', *New Scientist*, 11 October 2004.
34. Peter Singer and Jim Mason, *The Ethics of What We Eat*, Text Publishing, Melbourne, 2006, pp. 4, 34.
35. Coles-Myer, 'RSPCA and Coles launch barn-laid eggs', 23 January 2001, www.coles.com.au
36. Australian Lot Feeding Industry Overview, September 2002, www.feedlots.com.au
37. Meat and Livestock Association, 'Industry Overview, Feedlot Industry', www.mla.com.au
38. Singer and Mason, *The Ethics of What We Eat*, p. 62
39. Singer and Mason, *The Ethics of What We Eat*, p. 249.
40. Lara Zamiatin, 'The ethics of eating', *Age*, 13 May, 2006, quoting Seafood Importers Association of Australia.
41. Australian Conservation Foundation, www.acfonline.org.au
42. Marine Stewardship Council, www.msc.org
43. Oxfam, www.oxfam.org.au/fairtrade
44. Greenpeace, 'Australian GE canola contamination found in Japan', 14 July 2005, www.greenpeace.com.au

45. In fact, the reverse can happen. In Canada, a farmer whose crops were contaminated by GE canola was taken to court by multinational company Monsanto, who claimed that he infringed upon its copyright because of the seeds that had blown into his field. Read about the ongoing court battle and more details about Monsanto's litigation against farmers at www.percyschmeiser.com
46. 'It's better to green your diet than your car', *New Scientist*, 17 December 2005.

7 Recycling
47. Australian Bureau of Statistics, waste generation 2002-03, www.abs.gov.au
48. Nolan-ITU Pty Ltd and Sinclair Knight, Independent Assessment of Kerbside Recycling in Australia, volume 1, Merz REF: 4046-01, January 2001, at www.packcoun.com.au
50. Port Phillip Council, *Sustainable Living at Home*.
51. Victorian Litter Action Alliance, 'Littering Statistics Fact Sheet', www.litter.vic.gov.au
52. Victorian Litter Action Alliance, www.litter.vic.gov.au
53. Victorian Litter Action Alliance, www.litter.vic.gov.au
54. Recycling Expanded Polystyrene Australia, www.repsa.org.au
55. Auto Parts Recyclers Association of Australia, www.apraa.com
56. Department of the Environment and Water Resources, 'Recycling used oil – why?', www.oilrecycling.gov.au

8 Appliances and Household Goods
57. Australian Greenhouse Office, www.greenhouse.gov.au/gwci/clothes.html
58. www.greenhouse.gov.au/gwci/standby.html
59. Australian Greenhouse Office, www.greenhouse.gov.au/gwci/standby.html
60. www.energystar.gov.au/about/index.html
61. Jaako Pöyry Consulting,'Overview of Illegal Logging', Prepared for the Department of Agriculture, Fisheries and Forestry, September 2005.
62. For more information on Enjo products, go to www.enjo.com.au

9. Building and Renovating
63. For further information on this topic, visit www.greenhouse.gov.au/yourhome/technical
64. Included in table at www.greenhouse.gov.au/yourhome/technical/fs23.htm
65. www.greenhouse.gov.au/gwci/households.html and www.greenhouse.gov.au/gwci/water.html
66. Australian Greenhouse Office, 'Embodied Energy' www.greenhouse.gov.au/yourhome/technical/fs31.htm
67. www.greenhouse.gov.au/yourhome/technical/fs33.htm

10 Ethical Investment
68. www.ethicalinvestments.com.au/Tech%20Talk/ethicalvsmainstream.htm
Ethical Investment Association of Australia has a full report on SRI at www.eia.org.au

11 Personal Care
69. See P. Dingle and T. Brown, *Dangerous Beauty*, Healthy Home Solutions, 1999 and www.healthy-communications.com/ journal_of_the_american_college_.html for further details on SLS.
70. Such as the recent case of the supposedly natural hormone replacement therapy treatment administered by doctors, which was blamed for two cases of uterine cancer. The manufacturers have been sued for misleading advertising in their claims that the product was natural: 'Fears over hand-made hormones' and 'ACCC: Natural therapy a sham', Sunday Age, 12 August 2006.
71. 'Exposures add up - Survey results', June 2004, Skin Deep, www.cosmeticsdatabase.com
72. Timothy Gower, 'The danger in our water' *Prevention Magazine*, gives a good overview of the latest research www.prevention.com
73. For further information and stockists, go to www.natracare.co.uk and www.mooncup.co.uk
74. From the British Union for the Abolition of Vivisection, www.buav.org
75. Well Women, 'Disposable vs. cloth nappies – making an informed decision', Royal Women's Hospital, www.rwh.org.au/wellwomens
76. Well Women, 'Disposable vs. cloth nappies – making an informed decision', Royal Women's Hospital, www.rwh.org.au/wellwomens
77. Fiona Macrae, 'Third of male fish in rivers are changing sex', *Daily Mail*, 19 July 2006.

12 At the Office
78. Sustainability Victoria, 'Paper use and printing', www.sustainability.vic.gov.au/www/html/1414-paper-use-and-printing.asp
79. Australian Greenhouse Office, 'Green Office Guide', p. 5.
80. Australian Greenhouse Office, 'Green Office Guide', p. 8.
81. Australian Greenhouse Office, 'Green Office Guide', p. 4.
82. Sustainability Victoria, www.energy-toolbox.vic.gov.au
83. www.energystar.gov.au/about/index.html

Acknowledgments

I am grateful to many people who have been of assistance to me during the writing and publishing of this book. Although one person's name is on the cover, every book published is a collaborative process involving many people with widely differing but very important skills.

The first person I need to thank is my partner, Tim Blyth, who brainstormed with me on the original concept, gave advice throughout the process, and drew the diagrams in the Building and Renovating chapter. When I made challenging adjustments to our lives to make them more sustainable, he never complained, and he was particularly supportive in the frantic final weeks prior to my deadline.

I must thank Andrea McNamara and my classmates at RMIT who assisted me in shaping the early manuscript by providing extensive feedback and critique.

I am very appreciative of all the hardworking publishing professionals at Scribe, including Henry Rosenbloom, Russ Radcliffe, Nicola Shafer, Tamsyn Hutchinson, Susan Hornbeck, Tamsin Wagner, and John Hunter. Thanks to my editor, Janet Mackenzie, who did a great job on tidying up the manuscript and my designer, Josh Durham, who made the book look so beautiful. You have all made the process an extremely enjoyable one. Thanks also to Caroline Trainor for her work on developing the website and to my colleagues at Penguin for selling in and distributing the book.

I admire many inspiring individuals who are helping us to find our way towards a more sustainable future for humanity – in particular, Tim Flannery, Peter Singer, Ian Lowe, George Monbiot, James Lovelock, and Al Gore. Without these writers and environmentalists leading by example, I could never have gone so far down my own path to walk with a lighter footprint.

Thanks to Australian organizations, including the Australian Greenhouse Office, Sustainability Victoria, savewater!® Alliance, Australian Marine Conservation

Society and Ecotourism Australia for permission to reproduce information found on their websites. Thanks to the Marine Stewardship Council International for allowing me to use their logo (MSC20377), to the various organic food accreditation bodies for allowing me to display their marks, to the Rugmark Foundation, and to Penguin UK, Earthscan, and *New Scientist*.

Despite everybody involved giving their utmost attention to detail, there will always be some errors that have slipped through or information that has suddenly become outdated, but I take all responsibility for any mistakes.

Finally, I would like to thank my family and the many friends who have provided support, enthusiasm, and feedback for this project along the way. I am fortunate to have such a vital peer group of amazing people to turn to when I need help and to debate the problems of the world with. I won't name you individually for fear of leaving someone out, but you know who you are. Thank you.